M000306218

MURTY CLASSICAL
LIBRARY OF INDIA

Sheldon Pollock, General Editor

TULSIDAS
THE EPIC OF RAM
VOLUME 6

MCLI 31

TULSIDAS

तुलसीदास

THE EPIC OF RAM

VOLUME 6

Translated by
PHILIP LUTGENDORF

MURTY CLASSICAL LIBRARY OF INDIA

HARVARD UNIVERSITY PRESS

Cambridge, Massachusetts

London, England

2022

SERIES DESIGN BY M9DESIGN

Library of Congress Cataloging-in-Publication Data
Tulasidasa, 1532–1623.
The epic of Ram / Tulsidas ; translated by Philip Lutgendorf.
volume cm. — (Murty Classical Library of India ; 31)
In English and Awadhi on facing pages.
Includes bibliographical references and index.
ISBN 978-0-674-42501-9 (cloth : alk. paper) (vol. 1)
ISBN 978-0-674-08861-0 (cloth: alk. paper) (vol. 2)
ISBN 978-0-674-97501-9 (cloth: alk. paper) (vol. 3)
ISBN 978-0-674-97502-6 (cloth: alk. paper) (vol. 4)
ISBN 978-0-674-98614-5 (cloth: alk. paper) (vol. 5)
ISBN 978-0-674-25821-1 (cloth: alk. paper) (vol. 6)

I. Lutgendorf, Philip, translator.
II. Tulasidasa, 1532–1623. Ramacaritamanasa. English.
III. Tulasidasa, 1532–1623. Ramacaritamanasa. IV. Title.
PK1947.9.T83R313 2016
891.4'312—dc23   2015016322

CONTENTS

INTRODUCTION

The Rāmcaritmānas *and Tulsidas*

The *Rāmcaritmānas* (Divine lake of Ram's deeds) by Tulsidas is among the most beloved and revered works of Indian literature.[1] An epic poem composed in Hindi in the late sixteenth century, the *Mānas* rapidly acquired the renown and sanctity usually reserved for compositions in Sanskrit, the ancient and elite "language of the gods." Over the next three centuries its fame grew steadily, spread by oral expounders, itinerant singers, and scholarly exegetes, some of whom were patronized by the princely rulers of the Indo-Gangetic Plain. In the colonial era, British scholars and administrators recognized it as "the Bible of Northern India" and "the best and most trustworthy guide to the popular living faith of its people."[2] In the twentieth century it assumed an important place in the emerging Hindi literary canon, inspired major works by modernist poets, and was regularly quoted during India's freedom struggle by Mohandas Gandhi, who wrote that he considered it "the greatest book of all devotional literature."[3] Later its impact was enhanced by the release of millions of inexpensive printed copies, by performances available on records, audiocassettes, and compact discs, and by a television serialization partially based on it that held much of India spellbound in 1987–1989. A comprehensive early twenty-first-century study of the development of Hindi literature assesses the *Mānas* as "a defining work of Indian culture" and concludes that it "remains the leading vernacular scripture of north India today."[4]

A retelling of the ancient and popular tale of Ram and Sita, which first appeared in literary form in Valmiki's Sanskrit epic *Rāmāyaṇa* (last centuries B.C.E.), the *Mānas* belongs to a long tradition of works that recast the narrative in distinctive ways. Despite the prestige accorded the Sanskrit archetype, subsequent retellings never favored literal translation. Instead, poets and storytellers working in Sanskrit, various Prakrits, and later regional literary vernaculars of southern and northern India exercised great freedom in crafting original versions that, while preserving the basic characters and outline of the narrative, introduced significant innovations. The result was a multiform oral and literary tradition that, although sometimes encompassed by the generic label "Ramayana," may better be termed *Rāmakathā,* or "Rama storytelling." Tulsidas's own version emerges from an influential current in this vast river of story, imbued with the ideology of "sharing" in or devotion to—*bhakti* is the Indic term—a personal god or goddess and the emotional, public worship of that deity.

A poet of extraordinary versatility and vision, Tulsidas is celebrated as the author of a dozen works, most of which are dedicated to Ram, and which collectively advance a theology in which Ram is adored as the supreme, transcendent God to whom other revered Hindu deities are ultimately subordinate. Through his writings and his legendary biography, Tulsidas has come to exert a profound and perhaps unsurpassed influence on the ideology and practice of popular Hinduism throughout much of northern and central India and beyond, including several communities of the Indian diaspora. Not surprisingly, a figure of such stature is also, in certain contexts, controversial; his works have been subject to vastly differing interpretations, and there are few details of his biography that have not been contested, beginning with his date of birth (variously posited as 1497, 1526, and 1543—the last being favored by the majority of modern scholars); a death date of 1623 is widely accepted. He was evidently literate—a few manuscripts survive that may be in his own hand—and seems to have received a classical Sanskrit education that was, in his day, generally the prerogative of the Brahman caste. Some of his works hint at autobiographical details, and three include dates of composition, indicating that he was active during the reigns of the Mughal emperors Akbar and Jahangir. There is evidence that he spent a good part of his life in Banaras, regularly participated in the public performance of devotional texts, including his own, and was supported in part by the offerings of appreciative listeners. His name means "servant of tulsi," referring to the "holy basil" plant considered especially pleasing to Vishnu, and thus signals the poet's likely initiation into a Vaishnava religious order or guru-lineage, -*dās* being a common suffix for initiatory names in several orders. The poet himself often shortens this name to "Tulsi" in his poetic "signature" (*chāp* or *bhaṇitā*). Yet although he has been proudly claimed by a number of branches of one ascetic order (the Ramanandis), Tulsi's formal affiliation has never been proven to the satisfaction of nonsectarian scholars. He does not seem to have established a sect, yet he came to be revered in his own lifetime as a *gosāī,* or "master"; today "Goswami" (in its standard Anglicized spelling) is typically prefixed to his name to indicate his status as preceptor and exemplar to millions.

Tulsi's most celebrated work, the *Rāmcaritmānas,* bears a date of composition corresponding to 1574. It comprises roughly 12,800 lines, divided into 1,073 "stanzas" set within seven sections, which early manuscripts simply denote as numbered "stairs" or "stairways" (*sopāna*)—"first stair," "second stair," and so on—descending into the allegorical Manas Lake to which the title alludes (1.36–43). Later tradition has given them additional names as *kāṇḍs,* or sub-books, that reflect the architecture of the *Vālmīki Rāmāyaṇa.* But apart from its basic storyline, the *Mānas* bears only an occasional direct resemblance to Valmiki's poem. Instead, drawing creatively on many sources, Tulsi retells the story of Ram, as he says, "for his own inner joy" (1.0.7), through a set of four interlocking dialogues that ingeniously frame the epic tale. The conversations between the gods Shiva and Parvati, the Vedic sages Yajnavalkya and Bharadvaj, the immortal crow Bhushundi and the divine eagle Garuda, and finally the discourse of Tulsidas to his presumed audience, interwoven throughout much of the text, are announced in the allegory of Lake Manas as its framing banks, or ghats. To traditional commentators, they suggest four distinct "points of view" from which the epic tale may be interpreted, even as they invoke a lineage of transmission that encourages future interpretive performances. A vibrant tradition of such performances—by storytellers and singers, and by amateur and professional actors who mount annual drama cycles collectively known as *Rāmlīlā* ("Ram's play")—has existed for centuries and remains influential in many parts of India today.

The Laṅkā Kāṇḍ

The "sixth stair" of the *Rāmcaritmānas,* like the comparable sub-book of the *Vālmīki Rāmāyaṇa,* primarily describes the climactic battle that pits Ram and his devoted allies against the demonic forces of Ravan, culminating in the latter's defeat. *Mānas* editions traditionally call it *Laṅkākāṇḍ,* the "Lanka sub-book," invoking its principal setting and following a precedent found in some manuscripts of the classical Sanskrit epic, though the name more commonly used therein is *Yuddhakāṇḍa,* or the "battle sub-book."[5] In Tulsi's version, it opens with the spectacle of Ram's army of monkeys and bears bridging and then crossing the ocean that separates Lanka from the mainland, after Ram has consecrated and worshiped a lingam embodying Shiva on its shore, promising blessings to future pilgrims to the site. The news of the army's crossing shocks Ravan but is dismissed by his sycophantic counselors; however, his chief queen, Mandodari, and several courtiers warn him of Ram's divinity and urge him to surrender the kidnaped Sita, Ram's wife, and make peace. Camped with his army on Mount Subel, Ram contemplates the rising moon behind the citadel of Lanka and then follows the aged bear Jambavan's advice to dispatch the monkey prince Angad, heir apparent to the throne of Kishkindha, as an emissary, offering Ravan a last chance to avert conflict. But Angad, despite his eloquence and heroism, fails to sway the arrogant *rākṣasa,* and war becomes inevitable.

During the first day of battle, the four divisions of the monkey army lay siege to Lanka's principal gates; in spite of some setbacks, they succeed in decimating a large number of the Lankan forces. Ravan is dismayed and is again urged (this time by an elder in his own clan) to surrender to Ram. However, he rejects this good advice when his firstborn son, Meghnad, promises to perform heroic feats the following day. The crown prince delivers on his pledge, slaughtering great numbers of Ram's soldiers, conjuring dreadful illusions, and engaging in single combat with both Hanuman and Ram's brother Lakshman; at day's end he succeeds in mortally wounding Lakshman with his formidable *śakti* weapon, but he is unable to lift and carry off the fallen prince, who (as Shiva reminds his wife) is actually Shesh ("the residual")—the cosmic serpent who bears on his many heads both Lord Vishnu and the cosmos. As Ram laments his brother's unconscious state, Hanuman fetches from Lanka a physician who reveals that a miraculous herb growing in the Himalayas can save the stricken hero, provided it is administered to him before dawn. When Hanuman undertakes to find and bring back the herb, Ravan, warned by spies, sends the demon Kalnemi, disguised as a holy man, to waylay him. Although briefly deceived, Hanuman quickly divines the ruse, slays the demon, and reaches the mountains. Unable to recognize the medicinal herb, he uproots an entire summit and begins to fly back with it, carrying it on his palm. His journey is again interrupted—this time by Bharat, who mistakes his enormous form for a flying demon and shoots him down with a blunt arrow, occasioning a poignant meeting between these two devotees of Ram during which Bharat learns of his brother's adventures—yet Hanuman succeeds in returning before sunrise, saving Lakshman's life and banishing Ram's despair.

Frustrated again, Ravan now awakens his gargantuan brother Kumbhakaran from his half year of slumber and enlists his aid. Though he, too, lectures Ravan on Ram's divinity and praises the decision of their younger brother, Vibhishan, to ally with their foe, Kumbhakaran dutifully joins the fight and, with his monstrous size and strength, wreaks havoc on Ram's army before ultimately being dismembered and slain by Ram himself. As the gods exult and Ravan mourns, Meghnad vows to avenge his uncle's death, and the next day he succeeds in binding both Ram and Lakshman with serpent-snares. The illusory reptiles are soon dispatched by Garuda, Vishnu's divine eagle (an intervention that will cause Garuda to doubt Ram's divinity and hence, in sub-book seven, to ask the immortal crow Bhushundi for a narration of the *Mānas-kathā*), and the frustrated Meghnad retreats to a cave to undertake a Tantric rite that will render him invincible. Learning of this, Ram sends Lakshman and several monkey champions to disrupt the ritual; they succeed, and Lakshman finally slays the Lankan heir apparent, devastating his parents.

Now deprived of all his stalwarts, Ravan rides out with the remnants of his army, determined to fight to the death. Ram's lack of a chariot dismays Vibhishan, a reaction that occasions a famous lecture by Ram concerning the metaphorical "chariot of dharma" (6.80); it also, eventually, causes Indra, king of the celestial gods, to place his own vehicle and driver at Ram's service. After Ravan deploys many illusions and engages in fierce single combat with both Lakshman and Hanuman, he too undertakes a dark ritual to turn the tide of battle; again the monkeys disrupt it, this time humiliating Ravan's wives, and the demon is forced to abort the rite and return to the field. In the final confrontation, amid vast slaughter that creates a macabre river of blood, Ravan seemingly remains a challenging foe; each time the Raghu prince's arrows sever his many heads and arms, new ones grow in their place. This regenerative ability, as well as Ravan's multiple feats of demonic illusion, frustrate Ram's forces, until Vibhishan reveals the secret to slaying his elder brother. Ram duly delivers the fatal blow and Ravan falls, bellowing Ram's name and thus winning spiritual liberation.

Amid mourning royal women, Vibhishan performs his brother's funeral rites at Ram's request and then ascends the throne of Lanka. Humbly crediting his victory to his feral allies, Ram sends Hanuman to bring Sita, bathed and freshly adorned, from the Ashoka Garden. Their reunion, briefly described, only hints at displeasure on Ram's part; inspired by him, Sita orders Lakshman to build a pyre onto which she willingly steps, soon to reemerge escorted by the god of fire, who attests to her inviolable purity. Now fully reunited in a tableau of immense beauty, Ram and Sita are worshiped by the celestial gods, by Brahma the creator, by Indra (who, at Ram's request, uses divine nectar to revive all the slain monkeys and bears), and by Shiva, as well as by the spirit-form of Ram's father, whom they venerate.

Vibhishan invites Ram to rest and refresh himself in Lanka, but Ram can think only of his brother Bharat, anxiously awaiting him in Avadh as the stipulated period of Ram's exile nears its end, and expresses his wish to return there as quickly as possible. Vibhishan then offers Ram the flying palace called Pushpak ("flower") that Ravan had stolen from their divine half-brother Kuber. After dismissing most of his troops but permitting his close companions to accompany him, Ram and his entourage board the Pushpak and it ascends into the sky. As it flies north, Ram points out to Sita the sites of many of his wanderings and adventures, and they stop to pay homage to the sages of the Dandak Forest and Mount Chitrakut. When the marvelous craft nears Avadh, Ram sends Hanuman ahead, disguised as a Brahman student, to inform Bharat of his imminent return, while he himself, at the confluence of the Rivers Ganga, Yamuna, and Sarasvati, greets the Brahman sage Bharadvaj and then the tribal chieftain Guha; the *kāṇḍ* ends with Ram's fervent embrace of his low-born devotee and friend.

Themes and Variations

Though warfare looms large in the sixth sub-book in both the classical Sanskrit and Avadhi epics, there are notable differences in how the two revered poets approached it. *Yuddhakāṇḍa* is the biggest sub-book in Valmiki's masterpiece—nearly twice the length of the next-longest segment, *Ayodhyākāṇḍa*—and as recent English translators have observed, "Its grand narrative of heroism and violence... is in many ways the core and culmination of the epic."[6]

In comparison, Tulsi's *Laṅkākāṇḍ* is the shortest of his four longer sub-books, and although it contains masterful passages on the themes of statecraft and violence that are said to dominate Valmiki's text, they are often greatly condensed.[7] Instead, the poet and his several narrators regularly pause, even in the midst of battle, to meditate on Ram's beauty and graciousness—the latter is notably extended to Ram's demonic foes, to whom he invariably grants an exalted spiritual state after slaying them. Indeed Ram's divinity is always foregrounded, and as usual, whenever Tulsi is about to describe a display of human "weakness"—for example, in Ram's lament over the wounded Lakshman that occupies the whole of the unusually long stanza 6.61—he begins by reminding his audience that his protagonist is actually "all-pervading God, unassailable lord of the worlds," and is merely acting out grief "like an ordinary man" (6.55.3; 6.61.1). That such "ordinary" emotion includes a negative comparative valuation of Sita (6.61.6) reminds us that, in the Ramayana's idealized world of patrilineal kinship bonds, fraternal love necessarily trumps conjugal ties.

Despite its relative brevity, the sub-book offers plenty of martial action and carnage, including Tulsi's own version of the conventional simile-laden description of a "river of blood" coursing through the battlefield (6.87.5–88.3). The frenzy of battle is signaled by increased use of the more ornamental *harigītikā chand* meter, which Tulsi also used, in a very different emotional register, to express the joy of Ram and Sita's marriage festivities in the first sub-book. Beginning at 6.78 and continuing for more than thirty stanzas to 6.109, after Ravan's death, nearly every set of *caupāīs* is followed by one or more lyrical quatrains (appearing, in my translation, as eight lines), inserted before the stanza's concluding *dohā*. As usual, these begin by recapitulating, refrain-like, the final part of the preceding *caupāī* and then expand on it, creating crowded canvases of word-images conveyed through dense patterns of internal rhyme and alliteration.

But before the gory feast of battle begins, Tulsi serves up an unexpected appetizer in his account of crown prince Angad's mission to Lanka. Though present in the *Vālmīki Rāmāyaṇa*, the incident receives only brief treatment there; Angad simply repeats, with little modification, a warning message that Ram has instructed him to give, and Ravan says nothing apart from angrily calling on his guards to slay the messenger (6.31.49–79). Tulsi, however, extends this scene into an eighteen-stanza dialogue in which the monkey and the demon exchange deliciously barbed insults, recalling Lakshman's encounter with Parashuram in *Bālkāṇḍ*.[8] Although Ram's emissary always manages to get the better of Ravan, the latter has ample opportunity to display wit and sarcasm. It seems clear that, as in the *Bālkāṇḍ* exchange, Tulsi is having fun here, and this scene is also a favorite of audiences at the famous *Rāmlīlā* pageant of Ramnagar. When I had an opportunity to witness it in 1982, the actor who had played Ravan for many years (and who was respectfully and affectionately referred to as "King Ravan" in his nearby village) was known not only for his skill in delivering the scripted prose dialogue that followed the chanting of each *Mānas* speech but also for his witty ad-libs, sometimes including references to current events or politics, which would elicit delighted laughter from spectators.

Hanuman's two aerial journeys to the Himalayas, in the *Vālmīki Rāmāyaṇa,* to obtain herbs to heal wounded warriors in Ram's army (6.61.26-68, 6.89.13-21) are combined by Tulsi into a single mission to save the critically wounded Lakshman. But the story is charmingly expanded, following the *Adhyātmarāmāyaṇa* account (6.6.36-7.33), by the monkey hero's encounter with and subsequent slaying of the demon Kalnemi, whom Ravan had sent to stop him (6.56-58). Tulsi then adds the apparent innovation of the second interruption in Hanuman's journey—this time for an emotional meeting with Ram's devoted brother Bharat—on the return trip (6.58-60b).

When Ravan's death finally comes in stanza 103—preceded by omens that, despite the poet's regular derision of him, portend the fall of a great if tragically flawed monarch—it seems almost an anticlimax, for as Shiva, narrating the tale, has several times reminded Parvati, the Lord is omnipotent and could slay his adversary at any time. The many twists and turns of battle that precede the final showdown, including moments when the demons seem to gain the upper hand and cause panic in the bear and monkey ranks, are expressions of both Ram's "play" and also of his compassion, for they allow his friends and allies to display their heroism in his service— as when Vibhishan, Ravan's circumspect and generally timid junior brother, becomes enraged by a frontal assault on Ram and boldly attacks his senior with a mace (6.94).

The scene of Ram and Sita's reunion after the battle stands in particularly stark contrast to its classical Sanskrit prototype (*Vālmīki Rāmāyaṇa* 6.101–106). Here, no tension is evident when Ram calls for Sita to be brought from Lanka; she does not demur at Vibhishan's instruction that she be bathed and adorned, and she climbs happily into her palanquin, nor does she show dismay or embarrassment when Ram orders her out of it, to approach him on foot in full view of his monkey troops. Then Tulsi returns to a motif that he briefly introduced in *Araṇyakāṇḍ* but has not referred to since.[9] With a single *caupāī* (6.108.7) he reminds his audience that the Sita who experienced abduction, imprisonment, and anguish was not the real princess but an illusory substitute for Ram's supremely inviolate feminine counterpart, who took shelter in the sacred fire of their hermitage. This gives an entirely different slant to the scene that follows in the Sanskrit epic, in which Ram repeatedly assails Sita's virtue while she despairingly yet spiritedly defends herself. The long, painful exchange between Ram and Sita, which occupies two *sargas* in Valmiki (6.103–104), is reduced in the *Mānas* to a single *dohā* (6.108). Its opening phrase, "For this reason alone," invokes the illusory-Sita motif and dismisses the need for further explanation of Ram's "harsh words," which are mentioned but not repeated. The princess herself says nothing. Hence what is conventionally termed Sita's "fire ordeal" (*agniparīkṣā*) becomes, in the *Mānas*, merely a pretext for burning away the simulacrum of Sita and restoring her real, divine form—a revelation accompanied, as was her departure from Lanka and entry onto the battlefield, by pure happiness and copious showers of celestial blossoms (6.109a, b). Yet although this is what the *Mānas* text says, it is not necessarily what its audience understands, for the more agonistic and pained interpretation of Sita's self-immolation has never disappeared from the popular imagination. Not even Tulsi, with his tactful recourse to the "shadow Sita" of the *Adhyāt-marāmāyaṇa,* could definitively disperse the long shadow of one of Valmiki's most troubling episodes.

Acknowledgments

I am grateful to Rohan Murty for his generosity and to the production staff of Harvard University Press for the extraordinary care and diligence they have brought to the production of this translation series. I thank general editor Sheldon Pollock and coeditor Francesca Orsini for offering me the opportunity to undertake this translation and for their subsequent guidance. I also thank the late Shrinath Mishra, a revered *rāmāyaṇī* (traditional *Mānas* scholar) of Banaras, for his generous help and encouragement, and Pranav Prakash for his careful editing and proofreading of the Devanagari text. Among early mentors who guided me toward this work, I gratefully cite Professors Emeritus Colin P. Masica and the late Kali Charan Bahl of the University of Chicago.

I dedicate this translation to Meher Baba, who inspires me; to the many *Mānas* scholars and devotees who have instructed and encouraged me; and to the memory of three dear mentors and friends—Ramji Pande, A. K. Ramanujan, and Chandradharprasad Narayan Singh ("Bhanuji").

NOTES

1 For a more detailed general introduction to the *Mānas* and its author, see volume 1 of this translation (Lutgendorf 2016: vol. 1, vii–xxii).

2 Macfie 1930; Growse 1978: xxxviii.

3 Gandhi 1968: 47; on the role of the *Mānas* in the emerging Hindi literary canon, see Orsini 1998.

4 McGregor 2003: 917–939.

5 See Goldman, Goldman, and van Nooten 2009: 5 n.9.

6 Goldman, Goldman, and van Nooten 2009: 3, 5, 17–42.

7 It is only about half the length of *Bālkāṇḍ* and *Ayodhyākāṇḍ*, and is slightly shorter than the concluding *Uttarkāṇḍ*.

8 See 6.17.2–35.7; compare to 1.270–284 in volume 2 of this translation (Lutgendorf 2016: 177–199).

9 See 3.23.4–24.3 in volume 5 of this translation (Lutgendorf 2020: 69–71).

NOTE ON THE TEXT
AND TRANSLATION

Despite its prestige and popularity, the *Rāmcaritmānas* has not been accorded a truly critical edition, which might yet be assembled from careful comparative study of (reportedly) surviving manuscripts dating to the first hundred years after its composition. Copies of some of these were in the possession of celebrated *Mānas* expounders of the nineteenth century and became the basis for published versions, edited by them and issued by the new vernacular presses of the period. Differences among them were (by the standards of premodern Hindi literature) comparatively minor but of course much debated, and in the twentieth century, three more authoritative and scholarly editions attempted to resolve them—though none could claim to have adhered to the standards followed, for example, in the long-term projects to reconstruct the early texts of the Sanskrit *Rāmāyaṇa* and *Mahābhārata*.[1] The first of these, issued by the industrious Gita Press of Gorakhpur and accompanied by a readable gloss in Hindi, has become, by default, the standard edition of the epic, and has been used by every translator since Growse, including me. However, I also constantly consult the most elaborate and celebrated of published commentaries, *Mānaspīyūṣ* (Nectar of the *Mānas*), which incorporates the insights of many traditional scholars of the nineteenth and twentieth centuries. It, too, uses the Gita Press edition as basic text, but it periodically offers variant readings from manuscripts and older published editions. When such variations seem significant, I explain this in an endnote, as I do in the (very rare) instances in which I adopt a variant reading in preference to that found in the Gita Press version.

Readers may note occasional discrepancies between the Avadhi of Tulsidas's Devanagari text and the transliteration scheme adopted for characters' names in the translation, notes, and glossary. Thus, "Shankar," one of the common names of the god Shiva, appears as *saṅkara* (in its Devanagari equivalent) in the original text and in any notes that quote it directly, but as "Shankar" (the common, modern Hindi pronunciation) in the translation. Standard Sanskritic transliteration (e.g., *śaṅkara*), used in much scholarly writing, is additionally offered in the glossary.

The *Rāmcaritmānas* had already seen nine complete English translations before I undertook this one—and a tenth was added in 2019.[2] Although this is not surprising for such an influential scripture—the *Bhagavadgītā* can boast of more than two hundred—it is more than have been accorded any other long premodern vernacular work in the Indian tradition. Why, then, yet another? The obvious reason, of course, is to try to improve on them. Seven of the translations are into prose, and although two of them have considerable merit (Growse's is spirited and Hill's is admirably accurate), they all produce an effect that is on the whole turgid and "prosaic"—a sad fate for a poem that regularly urges the "singing" of its lines, and whose rhythmic recitation has been moving audiences for more than four centuries. On the other hand, two complete rhyming-verse renditions (by Atkins and Satya Dev), though certainly labors of love and tours de force in their way, take unfortunate liberties with the meaning of the verses in order to produce a metrical effect that often sounds jangling and trite, like a Victorian greeting card.[3]

The challenges inherent in rendering the *Mānas* in English have been noted before.[4] As a devotional work intended for episodic oral performance, the text seems repetitious when set in a linguistic medium that is normally experienced through individual, silent communion with the printed page, and its frequent use of formulaic phrases (though common in epic poetry worldwide) may appear redundant and saccharine—for example, "eyes filling with tears" and "limbs thrilling with love" (the latter, one choice for the nearly untranslatable *pulak*—in plain English, "goosebumps" or the dismally medical "horripilation"; besides "thrilling," I sometimes use "trembling," "quivering," "flushed," or "shivering"), and the poet's often-repeated assertion that some person, place, event, or emotion "cannot be described," which he usually follows with its very apt description. Some of Tulsi's apparent "repetitiveness," however, actually reflects the great asymmetry in lexicons between the two languages. English has more than one verb for "seeing"— the most important and recurrent act in which *Mānas* characters engage, especially "seeing" the unworldly beauty of Ram and Sita—but it does not have (as I have counted in *Bālkāṇḍ* alone) fourteen. Similarly, one can think of several synonyms for the adjective "beautiful"—but not the twenty-two, each slightly different, that Tulsi deploys to convey the overwhelming visual attraction of his divine characters and their world. And, like "camel" in the Arabic lexicon, "lotus" in the *Mānas* is not a single word—rather, it is, by my count, twenty-nine, each nuanced and suited to different contexts of meaning, meter, rhyme, and alliteration. Tulsi's vocabulary is indeed immense, and he is often credited with having expanded the lexicon of what would become modern Hindi through his revival and adaptation of Sanskrit loanwords; no Sanskrit chauvinist, he also used, according to a recent count, more than ninety Arabic and Persian ones.[5] In English, much of this verbal richness (to echo the poet) simply "cannot be expressed."

My own engagement with the epic began more than three decades ago, after several periods of travel in north India made me realize the extent to which the *Mānas* was ingrained in its living culture. In my initial study of the text as a graduate student, I was fortunate to have a teacher who insisted that I learn to chant its verses aloud to simple melodies— a skill that I have since shared with many students, since I know that it enhances both enjoyment and understanding of the work.[6] My first book grew out of that in-class "performance" and examined the many ways in which the *Mānas* "lives" in its cultural context. My initial effort at translating a section of the epic—its beloved "Fifth Stair," *Sundarkāṇḍ*—came much later.[7] Although I was not altogether happy with it, I loved the opportunity it gave me to engage deeply with the poem and (imaginatively) with its author. It was also my first sustained attempt at what, following the commission and editorial guidelines of the Murty Classical Library of India, I am now attempting to do for the complete epic: produce a straightforward, readable, free-verse rendering in contemporary language. I readily concede that most of the enchanting music of Tulsidas—his rhyme, alliteration, and almost hypnotic rhythm—is lost in my version. What I seek to preserve, as much as possible, is clarity, compactness of expression, and a certain momentum. I am especially happy to be contributing to a dual-language version, and I hope that serious readers, even if they do not know Hindi, might at least acquire facility with its easy, phonetic script so that they can begin to sound out the lines of the original—for truly, there is verbal magic in every stanza of the *Mānas*.

NOTES

1   The three scholarly editions are Poddar 1938, Mishra 1962, and Shukla et al. 1973.

2   A list appears in the bibliography.

3   The most recent, by Chowdhury (2019), is, like mine, in free verse.

4   Growse 1978: lvii–lviii; Hill 1952: xx; Lutgendorf 1991: 29–33.

5   McGregor 2003: 938; Stasik 2009.

6   I would like to pay tribute to my University of Chicago mentors, Kali Charan Bahl, who taught me to chant the *Mānas,* and Colin P. Masica, who helped me understand its cultural impact. A. K. Ramanujan and Wendy Doniger were also inspirations, both as scholars and translators.

7   See Lutgendorf 1994, 1995, 2001.

The Epic of Ram

Prelude to War

१	रामं कामारिसेव्यं भवभयहरणं कालमत्तेभसिंहं
योगीन्द्रं ज्ञानगम्यं गुणनिधिमजितं निर्गुणं निर्विकारम् ।
मायातीतं सुरेशं खलवधनिरतं ब्रह्मवृन्दैकदेवं
वन्दे कन्दावदातं सरसिजनयनं देवमुर्वीशरूपम् ॥

२	शङ्खेन्द्वाभमतीवसुन्दरतनुं शार्दूलचर्माम्बरं
कालव्यालकरालभूषणधरं गङ्गाशशाङ्कप्रियम् ।
काशीशं कलिकल्मषौघशमनं कल्याणकल्पद्रुमं
नौमीड्यं गिरिजापतिं गुणनिधिं कन्दर्पहं शङ्करम् ॥

३	यो ददाति सतां शम्भुः कैवल्यमपि दुर्लभम् ।
खलानां दण्डकृद्योऽसौ शङ्करः शं तनोतु मे ॥

To Ram—worthy of worship by Kama's foe,* who removes   1
    the dread
of rebirth and is a lion to stalk death's deranged elephant,
who is master of yogis, approachable through knowledge,
a treasury of merits, unconquerable, without attributes,
    flawless,
and beyond illusion, the Lord of gods, ever intent
on annihilating evildoers, and the one God of Brahmans,
who is lovely as a dark rain-bearing cloud, the lotus-eyed
God embodied in an earthly king—I give homage.[1]

To him—whose most beautiful form is lustrous as a conch   2
or the moon, who is garbed in a tiger skin,
wears deadly, venomous serpents as ornaments,
and to whom Ganga and the moon are dear,
lord of Kashi† and cleanser of Kaliyug's amassed filth,
who is the wishing tree of benevolence,
spouse of the mountain's daughter,‡ and sea of virtues,
annihilator of Kama—to most worshipful Shankar, I bow.

May Shambhu,§ who assuredly bestows   3
the rare state of enlightenment on holy ones,
and wields the rod of punishment against the wicked,
may he, Shankar, advance my well-being.

―――

* Shiva.
†   Banaras, or Varanasi.
‡ Parvati.
§ Shiva.

०क लव निमेष परमानु जुग बरष कलप सर चंड ।
भजसि न मन तेहि राम को कालु जासु कोदंड ॥

०ख सिंधु बचन सुनि राम सचिव बोलि प्रभु अस कहेउ ।
अब बिलंबु केहि काम करहु सेतु उतरै कटकु ॥

०ग सुनहु भानुकुल केतु जामवंत कर जोरि कह ।
नाथ नाम तव सेतु नर चढ़ि भव सागर तरहिं ॥

१ यह लघु जलधि तरत कति बारा ।
अस सुनि पुनि कह पवनकुमारा ॥
प्रभु प्रताप बड़वानल भारी ।
सोषेउ प्रथम पयोनिधि बारी ॥

२ तव रिपु नारि रुदन जल धारा ।
भरेउ बहोरि भयउ तेहिं खारा ॥
सुनि अति उकुति पवनसुत केरी ।
हरषे कपि रघुपति तन हेरी ॥

३ जामवंत बोले दोउ भाई ।
नल नीलहि सब कथा सुनाई ॥
राम प्रताप सुमिरि मन माहीं ।
करहु सेतु प्रयास कछु नाहीं ॥

He whose fierce arrows are fleeting instants,   0a
seconds, moments, epochs, years, and aeons—
why, mind, do you not adore that Ram,
whose great bow is deadly time?[2]

When Lord Ram heard the ocean's words,   0b
he summoned his counselors and said,
"Now why delay any longer?
Build a causeway so our army may cross."

"Splendor of the solar line,"   0c
said Jambavan, palms joined in reverence,
"your name alone, master, is the causeway
 mounting which men cross rebirth's ocean,

so how long will crossing this little sea take?"   1
At this, the son of the wind* then spoke:
"Your radiance, lord, is the great submarine fire[3]
that has already dried up the ocean's water.
But the torrential tears of your enemies' wives   2
have refilled it and made it salty."
Hearing the son of the wind's eloquence,
the monkeys gazed happily at the Raghu lord.
Then Jambavan summoned those two brothers,   3
Nal and Nil, and explained the matter fully,
adding, "Recalling Ram's glory in your hearts,
build a causeway, and it will be no effort at all."

———

* Hanuman.

5

४ बोलि लिए कपि निकर बहोरी ।
सकल सुनहु बिनती कछु मोरी ॥
राम चरन पंकज उर धरहू ।
कौतुक एक भालु कपि करहू ॥

५ धावहु मर्कट बिकट बरूथा ।
आनहु बिटप गिरिन्ह के जूथा ॥
सुनि कपि भालु चले करि हूहा ।
जय रघुबीर प्रताप समूहा ॥

१ अति उतंग गिरि पादप लीलहिं लेहिं उठाइ ।
आनि देहिं नल नीलहि रचहिं ते सेतु बनाइ ॥

१ सैल बिसाल आनि कपि देहीं ।
कंदुक इव नल नील ते लेहीं ॥
देखि सेतु अति सुंदर रचना ।
बिहसि कृपानिधि बोले बचना ॥

२ परम रम्य उत्तम यह धरनी ।
महिमा अमित जाइ नहिं बरनी ॥
करिहउँ इहाँ संभु थापना ।
मोरे हृदयँ परम कलपना ॥

३ सुनि कपीस बहु दूत पठाए ।
मुनिबर सकल बोलि लै आए ॥
लिंग थापि बिधिवत करि पूजा ।
सिव समान प्रिय मोहि न दूजा ॥

6

Then he summoned the monkey legions and said,   4
"Listen, all of you, to my requests:
place Ram's pure feet in your hearts
and perform a wonder, bears and monkeys—
go forth quickly, formidable simian horde,   5
and bring back heaps of trees and mountain peaks."
At this, the monkeys and bears departed, roaring,
"Victory to the Raghu hero, treasury of glory!"

Lofty mountains and huge trees   1
they playfully uprooted and hefted
and brought to Nal and Nil,
who arranged them to form a bridge.

Those monkeys brought great boulders   1
to Nal and Nil, who caught them like balls.
Seeing the splendid design of that bridge,
Ram, ocean of grace, smiled and said,
"This place is utterly charming and exalted,   2
of a limitless glory beyond description.
Here I will install and worship Lord Shambhu,
for this is my heart's dearest resolve."
At this, the monkey king sent many messengers   3
to summon and bring all eminent sages.
Installing a lingam and performing its ritual worship,
Ram said, "None is as dear to me as Shiva.

४ सिव द्रोही मम भगत कहावा ।
सो नर सपनेहुँ मोहि न पावा ॥
संकर बिमुख भगति चह मोरी ।
सो नारकी मूढ़ मति थोरी ॥

२ संकरप्रिय मम द्रोही सिव द्रोही मम दास ।
ते नर करहिं कलप भरि घोर नरक महुँ बास ॥

१ जे रामेस्वर दरसनु करिहहिं ।
ते तनु तजि मम लोक सिधरिहहिं ॥
जो गंगाजलु आनि चढ़ाइहि ।
सो साजुज्य मुक्ति नर पाइहि ॥

२ होइ अकाम जो छल तजि सेइहि ।
भगति मोरि तेहि संकर देइहि ॥
मम कृत सेतु जो दरसनु करिही ।
सो बिनु श्रम भवसागर तरिही ॥

३ राम बचन सब के जिय भाए ।
मुनिबर निज निज आश्रम आए ॥
गिरिजा रघुपति कै यह रीती ।
संतत करहिं प्रनत पर प्रीती ॥

४ बाँधा सेतु नील नल नागर ।
राम कृपाँ जसु भयउ उजागर ॥
बूड़हिं आनहि बोरहिं जेई ।
भए उपल बोहित सम तेई ॥

Hating Shiva but calling oneself my devotee,   4
one cannot even dream of attaining me.
Hostile to Shankar, yet craving devotion to me—
that one is a witless fool, fit for perdition!

Loving Shiva but hating me,   2
or serving me while hating Shiva—
such a one, for a full aeon,
will dwell in the foulest of hells.

Those who behold 'Ram's lord,' Rameshvar,   1
on leaving the body, go to my world,
and one who brings Ganga water to offer here
gains the release of union with me.[4]
To one who worships here, without desire or guile,   2
Lord Shankar will give devotion to me,
and one who beholds this bridge of mine
will effortlessly cross the sea of rebirth."
Ram's declaration pleased all their hearts,   3
and the great sages returned to their ashrams.
Shiva observed: "This is the way of the Raghu lord,
Girija—to always cherish humble suppliants."[5]
The skillful Nil and Nal constructed the causeway   4
by Ram's grace, acquiring radiant renown.
Stones, that would of themselves sink
and make others drown, became like boats.

9

५ महिमा यह न जलधि कइ बरनी ।
पाहन गुन न कपिन्ह कइ करनी ॥

३ श्री रघुबीर प्रताप ते सिंधु तरे पाषान ।
ते मतिमंद जे राम तजि भजहिं जाइ प्रभु आन ॥

१ बाँधि सेतु अति सुदृढ़ बनावा ।
देखि कृपानिधि के मन भावा ॥
चली सेन कछु बरनि न जाई ।
गर्जहिं मर्कट भट समुदाई ॥

२ सेतुबंध ढिग चढ़ि रघुराई ।
चितव कृपाल सिंधु बहुताई ॥
देखन कहुँ प्रभु करुना कंदा ।
प्रगट भए सब जलचर बृंदा ॥

३ मकर नक्र नाना झष ब्याला ।
सत जोजन तन परम बिसाला ॥
अइसेउ एक तिन्हहि जे खाहीं ।
एकन्ह कें डर तेपि डेराहीं ॥

४ प्रभुहि बिलोकहिं टरहिं न टारे ।
मन हरषित सब भए सुखारे ॥
तिन्ह की ओट न देखिअ बारी ।
मगन भए हरि रूप निहारी ॥

But the glory of this cannot be ascribed to the sea, 5
nor to the nature of the rocks or feats of the monkeys—

it was by the power of the great Raghu hero 3
that boulders floated on the deep.
How foolish is one who, forsaking Ram,
goes off to worship any other lord.

The causeway was crafted most sturdily, 1
and when he saw it, the merciful one was pleased.
The army, indescribably vast, advanced,
with its hordes of monkey warriors roaring.
Lord Raghu ascended the end of the bridge 2
and the gracious one gazed at the ocean's expanse.
In order to behold him—compassion's very essence—
vast numbers of marine creatures appeared:
dolphins, crocodiles, all kinds of fish and serpents,[6] 3
with immense bodies a hundred leagues long,
and some who could devour even these,
and yet others of whom these latter, too, were afraid.
But seeing the Lord, they remained still, 4
their hearts delighted, and all became happy.
Packed so densely that no water could be seen,
they were absorbed in gazing at Hari's form.

५ चला कटकु प्रभु आयसु पाई ।
   को कहि सक कपि दल बिपुलाई ॥

४ सेतुबंध भइ भीर अति कपि नभ पंथ उड़ाहिं ।
   अपर जलचरन्हि ऊपर चढ़ि चढ़ि पारहि जाहिं ॥

१ अस कौतुक बिलोकि द्रौ भाई ।
   बिहँसि चले कृपाल रघुराई ॥
   सेन सहित उतरे रघुबीरा ।
   कहि न जाइ कपि जूथप भीरा ॥

२ सिंधु पार प्रभु डेरा कीन्हा ।
   सकल कपिन्ह कहुँ आयसु दीन्हा ॥
   खाहु जाइ फल मूल सुहाए ।
   सुनत भालु कपि जहँ तहँ धाए ॥

३ सब तरु फरे राम हित लागी ।
   रितु अरु कुरितु काल गति त्यागी ॥
   खाहिं मधुर फल बिटप हलावहिं ।
   लंका सन्मुख सिखर चलावहिं ॥

४ जहँ कहुँ फिरत निसाचर पावहिं ।
   घेरि सकल बहु नाच नचावहिं ॥
   दसनन्हि काटि नासिका काना ।
   कहि प्रभु सुजसु देहिं तब जाना ॥

With the Lord's permission, the army went forth—   5
who can describe the vastness of that monkey horde?

The bridge became so densely crowded   4
that some monkeys flew into the sky
while others clambered onto sea creatures
and so made their way across.[7]

The two brothers beheld this spectacle   1
with amusement; then the gracious Raghu king set forth.
That hero reached the far shore with his army—
an indescribable multitude of monkeys and their chiefs.
The Lord made camp on the edge of the sea,   2
and gave orders to all the monkeys:
"Go and find good fruits and tubers to eat."
At once, bears and monkeys ran off here and there.
All the trees fruited for Ram's sake,   3
whether in season or not, forsaking time's regimen.
The troops feasted on sweet fruits, shook the trees,
and hurled hilltops in the direction of Lanka.[8]
Wherever they caught a demon roaming about,   4
they all cornered him and forced him to dance,
bit off his nose and ears with their teeth,
and only let him go when he glorified the Lord.

५ जिन्ह कर नासा कान निपाता ।
तिन्ह रावनहि कही सब बाता ॥
सुनत श्रवन बारिधि बंधाना ।
दस मुख बोलि उठा अकुलाना ॥

५ बाँध्यो बननिधि नीरनिधि जलधि सिंधु बारीस ।
सत्य तोयनिधि कंपति उदधि पयोधि नदीस ॥

१ निज बिकलता बिचारि बहोरी ।
बिहँसि गयउ गृह करि भय भोरी ॥
मंदोदरीं सुन्यो प्रभु आयो ।
कौतुकहीं पाथोधि बँधायो ॥

२ कर गहि पतिहि भवन निज आनी ।
बोली परम मनोहर बानी ॥
चरन नाइ सिरु अंचलु रोपा ।
सुनहु बचन पिय परिहरि कोपा ॥

३ नाथ बयरु कीजे ताही सों ।
बुधि बल सकिअ जीति जाही सों ॥
तुम्हहि रघुपतिहि अंतर कैसा ।
खलु खद्योत दिनकरहि जैसा ॥

४ अतिबल मधु कैटभ जेहिं मारे ।
महाबीर दितिसुत संघारे ॥
जेहिं बलि बाँधि सहसभुज मारा ।
सोइ अवतरेउ हरन महि भारा ॥

Those whose noses and ears were severed   5
went and reported all this to Ravan.
Hearing with his own ears of the sea being bridged,
he anxiously blurted out of his ten mouths:

"What? Did they really bridge the sea, the ocean,   5
abode of waters, the deep, the sovereign of streams,
the watery abyss, restless waves, milky expanse,
the supreme reservoir, and lord of rivers?"[9]

But then, nervously marking his own distress,   1
he suppressed his fear, laughed, and entered his abode.
When Mandodari heard of the Lord's coming
and how he had playfully bridged the great ocean,
she took her husband's hands, led him to her chamber,   2
and spoke in a most persuasive voice.
She bowed at his feet and held out her sari border,[10]
saying, "Dearest, abandon your anger and heed my words.
One should take on only that adversary, husband,   3
who can be defeated by cunning and strength.
The difference between you and the Raghu lord
is truly like that between a firefly and the sun.[11]
He who slew almighty Madhu and Kaitabh   4
and slaughtered Diti's most valorous sons,
who bound Bali and killed the thousand-armed king—
that very one has descended to relieve earth's burden.[12]

15

५ तासु बिरोध न कीजिअ नाथा ।
काल करम जिव जाकें हाथा ॥

६ रामहि सौंपि जानकी नाइ कमल पद माथ ।
सुत कहुँ राज समर्पि बन जाइ भजिअ रघुनाथ ॥

१ नाथ दीनदयाल रघुराई ।
बाघउ सनमुख गएँ न खाई ॥
चाहिअ करन सो सब करि बीते ।
तुम्ह सुर असुर चराचर जीते ॥

२ संत कहहिं असि नीति दसानन ।
चौथेंपन जाइहि नृप कानन ॥
तासु भजनु कीजिअ तहँ भर्ता ।
जो कर्ता पालक संहर्ता ॥

३ सोइ रघुबीर प्रनत अनुरागी ।
भजहु नाथ ममता सब त्यागी ॥
मुनिबर जतनु करहिं जेहि लागी ।
भूप राजु तजि होहिं बिरागी ॥

४ सोइ कोसलाधीस रघुराया ।
आयउ करन तोहि पर दाया ॥
जौं पिय मानहु मोर सिखावन ।
सुजसु होइ तिहुँ पुर अति पावन ॥

Do not antagonize him, husband,   5
whose hands hold time, karma, and every soul.

Surrender Janak's daughter to Ram,   6
bowing your head at his pure and lovely feet,
bestow the kingdom on your son, and go
to the forest to worship the Raghu lord!

Husband, the Raghu king is merciful to the meek—   1
a tiger won't devour one who submits before him.
You have already done everything you needed to do,
triumphing over gods, demons, and all creatures,
and it is the counsel of holy ones, ten-headed lord,   2
that a king, in old age, should repair to the woods.[13]
There, dear husband, engage in worship of him
who is creator, sustainer, and destroyer—
this very Raghu hero, who adores the humble.   3
Worship him, lord, abandoning all egoism.
He, toward whom the greatest sages strive,
for whom kings renounce realms and become ascetics—
this very one, the Raghu king and lord of Kosala   4
has come here out of compassion for you.
Dear one, if you heed my admonition,
you will win purest fame in all three worlds."

७ अस कहि नयन नीर भरि गहि पद कंपित गात ।
नाथ भजहु रघुनाथहि अचल होइ अहिवात ॥

१ तब रावन मयसुता उठाई ।
कहै लाग खल निज प्रभुताई ॥
सुनु तैं प्रिया बृथा भय माना ।
जग जोधा को मोहि समाना ॥

२ बरुन कुबेर पवन जम काला ।
भुजबल जितेउँ सकल दिगपाला ॥
देव दनुज नर सब बस मोरें ।
कवन हेतु उपजा भय तोरें ॥

३ नाना बिधि तेहि कहेसि बुझाई ।
सभाँ बहोरि बैठ सो जाई ॥
मंदोदरीं हृदयँ अस जाना ।
काल बस्य उपजा अभिमाना ॥

४ सभाँ आइ मंत्रिन्ह तेहिं बूझा ।
करब कवन बिधि रिपु सैं जूझा ॥
कहहिं सचिव सुनु निसिचर नाहा ।
बार बार प्रभु पूछहु काहा ॥

५ कहहु कवन भय करिअ बिचारा ।
नर कपि भालु अहार हमारा ॥

८ सब के बचन श्रवन सुनि कह प्रहस्त कर जोरि ।
नीति बिरोध न करिअ प्रभु मंत्रिन्ह मति अति थोरि ॥

18

Thus she spoke, her eyes filled with tears   7
and her body trembling, clinging to his feet.
"Worship the Raghu lord, my lord,
that I may remain unwidowed!"

Then Ravan lifted up Maya's daughter,*   1
and the villain began to boast of his valor.
"Listen to me, dear. Your fears are baseless,
for what warrior in the world is my equal?
Varun, Kuber, Pavan, Yama, and Kala—   2
my arms' might has bested all the guardians of space.[14]
Gods, demons, and men—all are in my power,
so why has this fear arisen in you?"
After many such admonitions to her,[15]   3
he went and sat once again in his court,
while in her heart Mandodari understood
that his resurgent pride foretold his doom.
In the assembly hall he asked his ministers,   4
"How then shall we confront the enemy?"
His counselors replied, "King of night-stalkers,
what is this that you keep asking, lord?
What danger, do tell, merits our concern?   5
Men, monkeys, and bears are mere food for us."

Having fully listened to all their boasts,   8
Ravan's son Prahast joined his palms and spoke:
"Lord, do not violate prudent policy.
These ministers have but little wisdom.

---

* Mandodari, daughter of the demon architect, Maya.

19

१   कहहिं सचिव सठ ठकुरसोहाती ।
      नाथ न पूर आव एहि भाँती ॥
      बारिधि नाघि एक कपि आवा ।
      तासु चरित मन महुँ सबु गावा ॥

२   छुधा न रही तुम्हहि तब काहू ।
      जारत नगरु कस न धरि खाहू ॥
      सुनत नीक आगें दुख पावा ।
      सचिवन अस मत प्रभुहि सुनावा ॥

३   जेहिं बारीस बँधायउ हेला ।
      उतरेउ सेन समेत सुबेला ॥
      सो भनु मनुज खाब हम भाई ।
      बचन कहहिं सब गाल फुलाई ॥

४   तात बचन मम सुनु अति आदर ।
      जनि मन गुनहु मोहि करि कादर ॥
      प्रिय बानी जे सुनहिं जे कहहीं ।
      ऐसे नर निकाय जग अहहीं ॥

५   बचन परम हित सुनत कठोरे ।
      सुनहिं जे कहहिं ते नर प्रभु थोरे ॥
      प्रथम बसीठ पठउ सुनु नीती ।
      सीता देइ करहु पुनि प्रीती ॥

९   नारि पाइ फिरि जाहिं जौं तौ न बढ़ाइअ रारि ।
      नाहिं त सन्मुख समर महि तात करिअ हठि मारि ॥

These foolish counselors mouth only flattery,[16]   1
and you will not succeed, master, in this way.
A single monkey leaped the sea and came here,
and everyone is still stunned by his exploits.
But why were none of you hungry then,   2
to seize and devour him as he torched our city?
Pleasant to hear but yielding sorrow later—
such is the counsel these ministers give, sire.
He who bridged the lord of waters in mere sport,   3
and landed with his army at Mount Subel*—
tell me brothers, is he just a man we will eat up?
All your declamations are but empty boasting!
Father, listen most attentively to my words   4
and do not reckon me to be a coward.
Men who hear and utter flattering speech
are legion in this world, whereas words
that are hard to listen to, yet most beneficial—   5
those who heed and speak them are rare, lord.
Hear my counsel: first, send emissaries,
then, handing over Sita, cultivate his favor.[17]

If, obtaining his wife, he turns back,   9
do not pursue the quarrel.
And if he does not, then steel yourself,
father, to fight him face to face on the field.

---

* Place of Ram's encampment.

१ यह मत जौं मानहु प्रभु मोरा ।
उभय प्रकार सुजसु जग तोरा ॥
सुत सन कह दसकंठ रिसाई ।
असि मति सठ केहिं तोहि सिखाई ॥

२ अबहीं ते उर संसय होई ।
बेनुमूल सुत भयहु घमोई ॥
सुनि पितु गिरा परुष अति घोरा ।
चला भवन कहि बचन कठोरा ॥

३ हित मत तोहि न लागत कैसें ।
काल बिबस कहुँ भेषज जैसें ॥
संध्या समय जानि दससीसा ।
भवन चलेउ निरखत भुज बीसा ॥

४ लंका सिखर उपर आगारा ।
अति बिचित्र तहँ होइ अखारा ॥
बैठ जाइ तेहिं मंदिर रावन ।
लागे किंनर गुन गन गावन ॥

५ बाजहिं ताल पखाउज बीना ।
नृत्य करहिं अपछरा प्रबीना ॥

१० सुनासीर सत सरिस सो संतत करइ बिलास ।
परम प्रबल रिपु सीस पर तद्यपि सोच न त्रास ॥

If you heed this advice of mine, lord,   1
either way, you will win fame in the world."
The ten-necked one spoke angrily to his son:
"Scoundrel, who schooled you in such wisdom?
Will doubt henceforth fill your heart, son,   2
so you become the rot that kills bamboo at its root?"[18]
Hearing his father's harsh and cruel words,
he went to his residence, uttering this rebuke:
"Beneficial advice has no more effect on you   3
than medicine on a doomed patient."
Knowing evening was approaching, Ravan
left for his abode, admiring his twenty arms.
At Lanka's highest point there was a palace   4
containing a most splendid amphitheater.
Ravan went and took a seat in that enclosure,
and demigods began singing the litany of his praise
to the sound of cymbals, drums, and *vīṇās*,[19]   5
while celestial nymphs expertly danced.

Like a hundred indolent Indras,[20]   10
he indulged in constant pleasure,
and though menaced by a supremely mighty foe,
felt neither worry nor fear.

१ इहाँ सुबेल सैल रघुबीरा ।
उतरे सेन सहित अति भीरा ॥
सिखर एक उतंग अति देखी ।
परम रम्य सम सुभ्र बिसेषी ॥

२ तहँ तरु किसलय सुमन सुहाए ।
लछिमन रचि निज हाथ डसाए ॥
ता पर रुचिर मृदुल मृगछाला ।
तेहिं आसन आसीन कृपाला ॥

३ प्रभु कृत सीस कपीस उछंगा ।
बाम दहिन दिसि चाप निषंगा ॥
दुहुँ कर कमल सुधारत बाना ।
कह लंकेस मंत्र लगि काना ॥

४ बड़भागी अंगद हनुमाना ।
चरन कमल चापत बिधि नाना ॥
प्रभु पाछें लछिमन बीरासन ।
कटि निषंग कर बान सरासन ॥

११क एहि बिधि कृपा रूप गुन धाम रामु आसीन ।
धन्य ते नर एहिं ध्यान जे रहत सदा लयलीन ॥

११ख पूरब दिसा बिलोकि प्रभु देखा उदित मयंक ।
कहत सबहि देखहु ससिहि मृगपति सरिस असंक ॥

24

Meanwhile, at Mount Subel, the Raghu hero   1
made camp, together with his immense host.
Spying one lofty summit,
delightful, level, and luminous,
and taking tender new leaves and flowers there,   2
Lakshman artfully spread them with his own hands,
and over them placed a fine, soft, deerskin
on which the merciful one took his seat.[21]
The Lord laid his head in the monkey monarch's lap,   3
his bow and quiver on his left and right sides,
and his lotus-like hands trued an arrow
while Vibhishan tendered counsel at his ear,
and the very fortunate Angad and Hanuman   4
devoted themselves to massaging his lovely feet.
Behind the Lord, Lakshman sat vigilant,[22]
quiver at his waist, bow and arrows in hand.

In this way, Lord Ram—abode of mercy,   11a
beauty, and virtue—sat resplendent.
Fortunate are they who remain absorbed
in constant, loving contemplation of this vision.[23]

Gazing eastward, the Lord   11b
beheld the rising lunar orb,
and said to them all, "Look at the moon—
fearless as a lion, the lord of beasts.

१   पूरब दिसि गिरिगुहा निवासी ।
      परम प्रताप तेज बल रासी ॥
      मत्त नाग तम कुंभ बिदारी ।
      ससि केसरी गगन बन चारी ॥

२   बिथुरे नभ मुकुताहल तारा ।
      निसि सुंदरी केर सिंगारा ॥
      कह प्रभु ससि महुँ मेचकताई ।
      कहहु काह निज निज मति भाई ॥

३   कह सुग्रीव सुनहु रघुराई ।
      ससि महुँ प्रगट भूमि कै झाँई ॥
      मारेउ राहु ससिहि कह कोई ।
      उर महँ परी स्यामता सोई ॥

४   कोउ कह जब बिधि रति मुख कीन्हा ।
      सार भाग ससि कर हरि लीन्हा ॥
      छिद्र सो प्रगट इंदु उर माहीं ।
      तेहि मग देखिअ नभ परिछाहीं ॥

५   प्रभु कह गरल बंधु ससि केरा ।
      अति प्रिय निज उर दीन्ह बसेरा ॥
      बिष संजुत कर निकर पसारी ।
      जारत बिरहवंत नर नारी ॥

१२क   कह हनुमंत सुनहु प्रभु ससि तुम्हार प्रिय दास ।
      तव मूरति बिधु उर बसति सोइ स्यामता अभास ॥

Dwelling in a cave in the eastern mountain,   1
a mass of supreme energy, intensity, and might,
he rips the swollen temples of dusk's crazed elephant[24]
to range as moon-lion in the forest of the firmament.
The stars in the sky are great, scattered pearls   2
for the sensual adornment of lady night.
But," said the Lord, "the darkness in the moon—
say what you each think it to be, brothers."
Sugriv said, "Raghu king, it is   3
earth's own shadow, manifest on the moon."
Someone said, "Demon Rahu assaulted the moon,
and darkness is the scar left on its heart."
Another said, "When the creator crafted Rati's* face,   4
he extracted the moon's essence,
cleaving a gap in the orb's breast
through which the dark sky's shadow is seen."
Then the Lord said, "Poison is the moon's brother,[25]   5
so dear to him that he harbors him in his heart.
Hence, his spreading rays, imbued with poison,
singe men and women plagued by separation."

At last, Hanuman declared, "The moon god   12a
is your beloved servant, lord,
and your form dwells in his very heart—
that darkness gives a glimpse of it."

---

* Wife of Kama.

१२ख पवन तनय के बचन सुनि बिहँसे रामु सुजान ।
दच्छिन दिसि अवलोकि प्रभु बोले कृपानिधान ॥

१ देखु बिभीषन दच्छिन आसा ।
घन घमंड दामिनी बिलासा ॥
मधुर मधुर गरजइ घन घोरा ।
होइ बृष्टि जनि उपल कठोरा ॥

२ कहत बिभीषन सुनहु कृपाला ।
होइ न तड़ित न बारिद माला ॥
लंका सिखर उपर आगारा ।
तहँ दसकंधर देख अखारा ॥

३ छत्र मेघडंबर सिर धारी ।
सोइ जनु जलद घटा अति कारी ॥
मंदोदरी श्रवन ताटंका ।
सोइ प्रभु जनु दामिनी दमंका ॥

४ बाजहिं ताल मृदंग अनूपा ।
सोइ रव मधुर सुनहु सुरभूपा ॥
प्रभु मुसुकान समुझि अभिमाना ।
चाप चढ़ाइ बान संधाना ॥

१३क छत्र मुकुट ताटंक तब हते एकहीं बान ।
सब के देखत महि परे मरमु न कोऊ जान ॥

28

Hearing the words of the wind's son,   12b
Ram, the all-knowing, smiled.
Then the Lord looked toward the south
and that treasury of mercy spoke again.

"Behold, Vibhishan—there in the south   1
are massed clouds and flashing lightning.
Those fearsome thunderheads rumble softly,
perhaps bringing heavy rain or even hail."
Vibhishan replied, "Merciful one,   2
those are neither cloudbanks nor lightning.
On Lanka's summit is a palatial enclosure;
there the ten-headed one enjoys entertainment.
The great, dark parasol placed over his head   3
is what looks like clouds, dense and black,
and Mandodari's glittering pendant earrings
shimmer like lightning flashes, lord.
The incomparable drums beating the rhythm,   4
protector of gods, produce that sweet rumbling."
Musing on Ravan's arrogance, the Lord smiled,
lifted his bow, and took aim.

With just one arrow, he severed   13a
the royal parasol, crown, and ear pendant.
In full view of all, they fell to the ground,
yet no one divined the cause.

१३ख अस कौतुक करि राम सर प्रबिसेउ आइ निषंग ।
रा␣वन सभा ससंक सब देखि महा रसभंग ॥

१ कंप न भूमि न मरुत बिसेषा ।
अस्त्र सस्त्र कछु नयन न देखा ॥
सोचहिं सब निज हृदय मझारी ।
असगुन भयउ भयंकर भारी ॥

२ दसमुख देखि सभा भय पाई ।
बिहसि बचन कह जुगुति बनाई ॥
सिरउ गिरे संतत सुभ जाही ।
मुकुट परे कस असगुन ताही ॥

३ सयन करहु निज निज गृह जाई ।
गवने भवन सकल सिर नाई ॥
मंदोदरी सोच उर बसेऊ ।
जब ते श्रवनपूर महि खसेऊ ॥

४ सजल नयन कह जुग कर जोरी ।
सुनहु प्रानपति बिनती मोरी ॥
कंत राम बिरोध परिहरहू ।
जानि मनुज जनि हठ मन धरहू ॥

१४ बिस्वरूप रघुबंस मनि करहु बचन बिस्वासु ।
लोक कल्पना बेद कर अंग अंग प्रति जासु ॥

Ram's arrow, having worked this wonder,   13b
returned and reentered his quiver.
Ravan's whole court was abashed to see
their lavish amusement spoiled.

The earth had not quaked, there was little wind,   1
and no eye had glimpsed any sort of weapon.
In their hearts, everyone thought
that it could only be a most awful omen.
But ten-headed Ravan, seeing his courtiers afraid,   2
laughed and concocted a clever speech:
"For one whose fallen heads brought an eternal boon,[26]
how can the fall of a crown be an ill augury?
Now, off to your respective abodes and to bed."   3
Bowing their heads, they all went home.
But Mandodari's heart was filled with worry
after her earring had fallen to the ground.
Her eyes tear-filled, with palms joined she said,   4
"Lord of my life, please listen to my plea:
give up your enmity toward Ram, husband.
Do not be obstinate, thinking him a mere man.

Believe my words: the jewel of the Raghus   14
is universal, omnipresent God,
whose every limb—as the Veda conceives—
is imbued with worlds.

१   पद पाताल सीस अज धामा ।
अपर लोक अँग अँग बिश्रामा ॥
भृकुटि बिलास भयंकर काला ।
नयन दिवाकर कच घन माला ॥

२   जासु घ्रान अस्विनीकुमारा ।
निसि अरु दिवस निमेष अपारा ॥
श्रवन दिसा दस बेद बखानी ।
मारुत स्वास निगम निज बानी ॥

३   अधर लोभ जम दसन कराला ।
माया हास बाहु दिगपाला ॥
आनन अनल अंबुपति जीहा ।
उतपति पालन प्रलय समीहा ॥

४   रोम राजि अष्टादस भारा ।
अस्थि सैल सरिता नस जारा ॥
उदर उदधि अधगो जातना ।
जगमय प्रभु का बहु कलपना ॥

१५क   अहंकार सिव बुद्धि अज मन ससि चित्त महान ।
मनुज बास सचराचर रूप राम भगवान ॥

१५ख   अस बिचारि सुनु प्रानपति प्रभु सन बयरु बिहाइ ।
प्रीति करहु रघुबीर पद मम अहिवात न जाइ ॥

His feet are the netherworlds, his brow Brahma's realm, 1
and all the other worlds abide in his limbs.
The play of his brows is fatal time,
his eye is the sun, his hair the massed clouds,
his nostrils are the twin Ashvin gods, 2
night and day, the recurring blinks of his eyelids.
His ears are the ten directions—so the Veda declares.
The wind is his breath, sacred lore his own voice,
his lip is greed, his fearsome teeth are Yama,* 3
his laughter is illusion, his arms the world-guardians,
his face is fire, his tongue the lord of waters,
and his activity is creation, preservation, annihilation.
The downy hairs on his limbs are myriad plant species, 4
his bones are mountains, rivers his web of veins,
his belly the ocean, his lower organs, torments of hell.[27]
But enough of such concepts—the Lord is all creation!

His ego is Shiva, his intelligence, unborn Brahma, 15a
his mind the moon, his cognition, great Vishnu.[28]
Embodying all beings, Ram—supreme God—
now abides in human form.

Consider all this, dear husband, and listen to me: 15b
abandon your hostility to the Lord
and adore the feet of the Raghu hero,
that I may not be widowed."

---

* God of death.

33

१ बिहँसा नारि बचन सुनि काना ।
अहो मोह महिमा बलवाना ॥
नारि सुभाउ सत्य सब कहहीं ।
अवगुन आठ सदा उर रहहीं ॥

२ साहस अनृत चपलता माया ।
भय अबिबेक असौच अदाया ॥
रिपु कर रूप सकल तैं गावा ।
अति बिसाल भय मोहि सुनावा ॥

३ सो सब प्रिया सहज बस मोरें ।
समुझि परा प्रसाद अब तोरें ॥
जानिउँ प्रिया तोरि चतुराई ।
एहि बिधि कहहु मोरि प्रभुताई ॥

४ तव बतकही गूढ़ मृगलोचनि ।
समुझत सुखद सुनत भय मोचनि ॥
मंदोदरि मन महुँ अस ठयऊ ।
पियहि काल बस मतिभ्रम भयऊ ॥

१६क एहि बिधि करत बिनोद बहु प्रात प्रगट दसकंध ।
सहज असंक लंकपति सभाँ गयउ मद अंध ॥

१६ख फूलइ फरइ न बेत जदपि सुधा बरषहिं जलद ।
मूरुख हृदयँ न चेत जौं गुर मिलहिं बिरंचि सम ॥

34

When he heard his wife's words, Ravan guffawed—   1
"How great is the power of delusion!
Truly does everyone say of women's nature[29]
that their hearts always harbor eight defects:
rashness, falsehood, fickleness, deceit,   2
cowardice, imprudence, impurity, and cruelty.
You recited a whole litany on my enemy's form,
trying to give me a good scare.
But all that you describe, dear, is firmly in my grip,   3
and now, thanks to you, I realize this.
Indeed, I grasp your cleverness, dear wife,
in using this pretext to proclaim my majesty!
Your prattling, doe-eyed one, is in fact profound,   4
pleasing to muse on and emboldening to hear."[30]
In her heart, Mandodari now grew certain
that her husband was deluded by impending doom.

Thus ten-necked Ravan amused himself   16a
in numerous ways till morning broke.
Then that lord of Lanka, fearless by nature
and blinded by arrogance, strode into his court.

The cane plant never fruits or flowers   16b
even if clouds shower it with ambrosia,
nor can a fool's heart gain knowledge,
though he finds a guru like Brahma himself.[31]

१   इहाँ प्रात जागे रघुराई ।
पूछा मत सब सचिव बोलाई ॥
कहहु बेगि का करिअ उपाई ।
जामवंत कह पद सिरु नाई ॥

२   सुनु सर्बग्य सकल उर बासी ।
बुधि बल तेज धर्म गुन रासी ॥
मंत्र कहउँ निज मति अनुसारा ।
दूत पठाइअ बालिकुमारा ॥

३   नीक मंत्र सब के मन माना ।
अंगद सन कह कृपानिधाना ॥
बालितनय बुधि बल गुन धामा ।
लंका जाहु तात मम कामा ॥

४   बहुत बुझाइ तुम्हहि का कहउँ ।
परम चतुर मैं जानत अहउँ ॥
काजु हमार तासु हित होई ।
रिपु सन करेहु बतकही सोई ॥

१७क   प्रभु अग्या धरि सीस चरन बंदि अंगद उठेउ ।
सोइ गुन सागर ईस राम कृपा जा पर करहु ॥

१७ख   स्वयं सिद्ध सब काज नाथ मोहि आदरु दियउ ।
अस बिचारि जुबराज तन पुलकित हरषित हियउ ॥

Meanwhile, the Raghu king awoke at dawn   1
and summoned his counselors to ask their advice:
"Tell me at once what strategy to adopt."
Bowing at his feet, Jambavan said,
"Omniscient one, abiding in all hearts,   2
treasury of wisdom, might, glory, dharma, and merit—
I offer this counsel according to my wit:
Send Bali's son as your emissary."
This sound advice appealed to everyone,   3
and the sea of mercy spoke to Angad:
"Son of Bali, abode of knowledge, power, and virtue—
go to Lanka, dear lad, on my mission.
No need for me to give you much instruction,   4
for I know you to be highly astute.
To secure our purpose and his own good,
converse as necessary with the enemy."

Humbly accepting the Lord's command   17a
and bowing at his feet, Angad rose
and said, "That one alone is a sea of virtue,
Lord Ram, on whom you bestow your grace."

"Our master, whose tasks are all self-fulfilled,   17b
has shown me such respect!"
Musing on this, the crown prince
thrilled with heartfelt delight.

१ बंदि चरन उर धरि प्रभुताई ।
   अंगद चलेउ सबहि सिरु नाई ॥
   प्रभु प्रताप उर सहज असंका ।
   रन बाँकुरा बालिसुत बंका ॥

२ पुर पैठत रावन कर बेटा ।
   खेलत रहा सो होइ गै भेटा ॥
   बातहिं बात करष बढ़ि आई ।
   जुगल अतुल बल पुनि तरुनाई ॥

३ तेहिं अंगद कहुँ लात उठाई ।
   गहि पद पटकेउ भूमि भवाँई ॥
   निसिचर निकर देखि भट भारी ।
   जहँ तहँ चले न सकहिं पुकारी ॥

४ एक एक सन मरमु न कहहीं ।
   समुझि तासु बध चुप करि रहहीं ॥
   भयउ कोलाहल नगर मझारी ।
   आवा कपि लंका जेहिं जारी ॥

५ अब धौं कहा करिहि करतारा ।
   अति सभीत सब करहिं बिचारा ॥
   बिनु पूछें मगु देहिं दिखाई ।
   जेहि बिलोक सोइ जाइ सुखाई ॥

१८ गयउ सभा दरबार तब सुमिरि राम पद कंज ।
    सिंह ठवनि इत उत चितव धीर बीर बल पुंज ॥

Bowing at Ram's feet and placing his glory in his heart,   1
Angad saluted them all, and departed.
The Lord's might in his heart and innately fearless,
Bali's formidable son was adept in combat.
As he entered the city, one of Ravan's sons   2
was sporting there and encountered him.[32]
They exchanged words with growing ire,
for both were matchlessly strong, strapping youths.
As the Lankan lifted a leg to kick him, Angad   3
seized it, spun him round, and slammed him to earth.
Seeing such a champion, the night-stalkers there
fled in all directions, afraid to even cry out
or admit to one another that their prince   4
was slain; though they knew, they kept silent.
But in the city, panic erupted:
"That monkey who burned Lanka is back!
Now who knows what mischief fate will play?"   5
So they all thought, and were in utter terror.
Without his asking, they directed Angad to the court,
and whoever he glanced at froze in fear.

He went to the door of the royal assembly,   18
recollecting Ram's lotus-like feet,
and with the stance of a proud lion, the stalwart
and mighty hero glanced this way and that.

१	तुरत निसाचर एक पठावा ।
	समाचार रावनहि जनावा ॥
	सुनत बिहँसि बोला दससीसा ।
	आनहु बोलि कहाँ कर कीसा ॥

२	आयसु पाइ दूत बहु धाए ।
	कपिकुंजरहि बोलि लै आए ॥
	अंगद दीख दसानन बैसें ।
	सहित प्रान कज्जलगिरि जैसें ॥

३	भुजा बिटप सिर सृंग समाना ।
	रोमावली लता जनु नाना ॥
	मुख नासिका नयन अरु काना ।
	गिरि कंदरा खोह अनुमाना ॥

४	गयउ सभाँ मन नेकु न मुरा ।
	बालितनय अतिबल बाँकुरा ॥
	उठे सभासद कपि कहुँ देखी ।
	रावन उर भा क्रोध बिसेषी ॥

१९	जथा मत्त गज जूथ महुँ पंचानन चलि जाइ ।
	राम प्रताप सुमिरि मन बैठ सभाँ सिरु नाइ ॥

१	कह दसकंठ कवन तैं बंदर ।
	मैं रघुबीर दूत दसकंधर ॥
	मम जनकहि तोहि रही मिताई ।
	तव हित कारन आयउँ भाई ॥

Losing no time, he sent a night-stalker   1
to announce his arrival to Ravan.
At this, the ten-headed one laughed loudly and said,
"Bring him, and we'll see from where this monkey hails."
At his command, many servants scurried off   2
to bring in that bull elephant of monkeys.
To Angad's eyes, the ten-faced lord seated there
looked like a living, breathing mountain of soot,
with arms like trees, heads like craggy summits,   3
the hair of his pores like countless vines;
his mouths, nostrils, eyes, and ears
seemed like its caves and fissures.
But on entering his assembly hall,   4
Bali's mighty, audacious son did not even flinch.[33]
Seeing the monkey, the courtiers spontaneously arose,
and this particularly enraged Ravan.

As when a lordly lion saunters into the midst   19
of a herd of maddened elephants,
just so, meditating in his heart on Ram's glory,
and nodding to the assembly, Angad sat down.[34]

"Who are you, monkey?" Ravan demanded.   1
Angad said, "I am the Raghu hero's emissary, Ten-neck.
There was friendship between my father and you,
and so I have come, brother, for your own good.

२ उत्तम कुल पुलस्ति कर नाती ।
सिव बिरंचि पूजेहु बहु भाँती ॥
बर पायहु कीन्हेहु सब काजा ।
जीतेहु लोकपाल सब राजा ॥

३ नृप अभिमान मोह बस किंबा ।
हरि आनिहु सीता जगदंबा ॥
अब सुभ कहा सुनहु तुम्ह मोरा ।
सब अपराध छमिहि प्रभु तोरा ॥

४ दसन गहहु तृन कंठ कुठारी ।
परिजन सहित संग निज नारी ॥
सादर जनकसुता करि आगें ।
एहि बिधि चलहु सकल भय त्यागें ॥

२० प्रनतपाल रघुबंसमनि त्राहि त्राहि अब मोहि ।
आरत गिरा सुनत प्रभु अभय करैगो तोहि ॥

१ रे कपिपोत बोलु संभारी ।
मूढ़ न जानेहि मोहि सुरारी ॥
कहु निज नाम जनक कर भाई ।
केहि नातें मानिए मिताई ॥

२ अंगद नाम बालि कर बेटा ।
तासों कबहुँ भई ही भेटा ॥
अंगद बचन सुनत सकुचाना ।
रहा बालि बानर मैं जाना ॥

Of noble lineage and grandson of sage Pulastya, 2
you richly propitiated Shiva and Brahma.
You obtained boons and achieved all your ends,
defeating the world-guardians and hosts of kings.
Then, from royal arrogance or in delusion's grip, 3
you kidnaped Sita, mother of the universe.
But now listen to my beneficial advice
and the Lord will yet forgive all your crimes:
Take straw in your teeth, hang an ax round your neck,[35] 4
and accompanied by all your relations and wives,
with Janak's daughter placed respectfully in front,
go to him, abandoning all apprehensions, and say,

'Guardian of asylum seekers, gem of Raghus— 20
protect me, protect me now!'
As soon as he hears your anguished cry,
the Lord will surely allay your fears."

Ravan replied, "Watch what you say, monkey whelp! 1
Don't you know me, fool, as foe of the gods?
Say your name, brother, and that of your father,
and by what connection you claim my friendship."
"My name is Angad and I am the son of Bali, 2
with whom, at some point, I believe you met?"[36]
At Angad's words, Ravan was startled, but said,
"I do recall there being a monkey named Bali.

३ अंगद तहीं बालि कर बालक ।
उपजेहु बंस अनल कुल घालक ॥
गर्भ न गयहु ब्यर्थ तुम्ह जायहु ।
निज मुख तापस दूत कहायहु ॥

४ अब कहु कुसल बालि कहँ अहई ।
बिहँसि बचन तब अंगद कहई ॥
दिन दस गएँ बालि पहिं जाई ।
बूझेहु कुसल सखा उर लाई ॥

५ राम बिरोध कुसल जसि होई ।
सो सब तोहि सुनाइहि सोई ॥
सुनु सठ भेद होइ मन ताकें ।
श्रीरघुबीर हृदय नहिं जाकें ॥

२१ हम कुल घालक सत्य तुम्ह कुल पालक दससीस ।
अंधउ बधिर न अस कहहिं नयन कान तव बीस ॥

१ सिव बिरंचि सुर मुनि समुदाई ।
चाहत जासु चरन सेवकाई ॥
तासु दूत होइ हम कुल बोरा ।
अइसिहुँ मति उर बिहर न तोरा ॥

२ सुनि कठोर बानी कपि केरी ।
कहत दसानन नयन तरेरी ॥
खल तव कठिन बचन सब सहउँ ।
नीति धर्म मैं जानत अहउँ ॥

But can you be the child of Bali, Angad—   3
born to be the ruin of your clan, fire in its bamboo grove?
Better you were stillborn than uselessly spawned
to announce yourself as errand boy of an ascetic.
But tell me—how is Bali now, and where?"   4
Angad laughed at this and replied,
"In a matter of days, when you go where Bali is,
give your friend a hug and inquire of his welfare—
such welfare as comes from opposing Ram;   5
indeed, he will tell you all about that!
Listen to me, fool: you can only sow doubt in one
whose heart does not harbor the Raghu hero.

Truly, to say that I defame my lineage   21
while you defend yours, Ten-head,
not even the blind and deaf would dare—   ·
and you have twenty eyes and ears.

He at whose feet Shiva, Brahma, and hosts   1
of gods and sages yearn to worship,
to think that, as his messenger, I defame
my clan—doesn't it tear your breast apart?"[37]
Hearing the monkey's harsh words,   2
the ten-faced lord glared at him and said,
"I put up with all your insults, scoundrel,
only due to my knowledge of ethics and dharma."

३ कह कपि धर्मसीलता तोरी ।
हमहुँ सुनी कृत पर त्रिय चोरी ॥
देखी नयन दूत रखवारी ।
बूड़ि न मरहु धर्म ब्रतधारी ॥

४ कान नाक बिनु भगिनि निहारी ।
छमा कीन्हि तुम्ह धर्म बिचारी ॥
धर्मसीलता तव जग जागी ।
पावा दरसु हमहुँ बड़भागी ॥

२२क जनि जल्पसि जड़ जंतु कपि सठ बिलोकु मम बाहु ।
लोकपाल बल बिपुल ससि ग्रसन हेतु सब राहु ॥

२२ख पुनि नभ सर मम कर निकर कमलन्हि पर करि बास ।
सोभत भयउ मराल इव संभु सहित कैलास ॥

१ तुम्हरे कटक माझ सुनु अंगद ।
मो सन भिरिहि कवन जोधा बद ॥
तव प्रभु नारि बिरहँ बलहीना ।
अनुज तासु दुख दुखी मलीना ॥

२ तुम्ह सुग्रीव कूलद्रुम दोऊ ।
अनुज हमार भीरु अति सोऊ ॥
जामवंत मंत्री अति बूढ़ा ।
सो कि होइ अब समरारूढ़ा ॥

The monkey said, "Ah, your ethical standards—   3
I heard about them: how you stole another's wife.
And how you safeguard emissaries has also been seen.[38]
Upholder of dharma! Why don't you drown yourself?
Seeing your sister without her nose and ears,   4
you forgave it, no doubt reflecting on dharma.
Your high moral code is world renowned,
and how lucky I am to see you in person!"

"Stupid monkey vermin," said Ravan, "stop chattering   22a
and just look, fool, at these arms of mine—
all eclipse-demons for seizing the moons
of the immense might of the guardians of space.

Moreover, on the firmament's lake,   22b
my many arms were the clustered lotuses
that harbored Shambhu* and Mount Kailash, too,
like a serenely floating *haṃsa* bird.[39]

Listen, Angad, in the whole of your army—   1
just tell me—what warrior can take me on?
Your lord is weak from pining for his woman,
his brother, wan and depressed by his sorrow,
you and Sugriv are trees clinging to an eroding shore,   2
and my own little brother, an utter coward.
Counselor Jambavan is an old dotard;
is he now up to venturing onto the field of war?

---

* Shiva.

३ सिल्पिकर्म जानहिं नल नीला ।
है कपि एक महा बलसीला ॥
आवा प्रथम नगरु जेहिं जारा ।
सुनत बचन कह बालिकुमारा ॥

४ सत्य बचन कहु निसिचर नाहा ।
साँचेहुँ कीस कीन्ह पुर दाहा ॥
रावन नगर अल्प कपि दहई ।
सुनि अस बचन सत्य को कहई ॥

५ जो अति सुभट सराहेहु रावन ।
सो सुग्रीव केर लघु धावन ॥
चलइ बहुत सो बीर न होई ।
पठवा खबरि लेन हम सोई ॥

२३क सत्य नगरु कपि जारेउ बिनु प्रभु आयसु पाइ ।
फिरि न गयउ सुग्रीव पहिं तेहिं भय रहा लुकाइ ॥

२३ख सत्य कहहि दसकंठ सब मोहि न सुनि कछु कोह ।
कोउ न हमारें कटक अस तो सन लरत जो सोह ॥

२३ग प्रीति बिरोध समान सन करिअ नीति असि आहि ।
जौं मृगपति बध मेडुकन्हि भल कि कहइ कोउ ताहि ॥

48

Nal and Nil know how to build things,[40]   3
and yes, there is one monkey who is very strong:
the one who came before and torched the town."
When he heard this speech, Bali's son declared,
"Tell the truth, now, lord of night-stalkers—   4
did a mere beast really burn your city?
That a lowly monkey set Ravan's capital ablaze—
who would give credence to such a claim?
The one you praised as a mighty warrior, Ravan,   5
is merely one of Sugriv's minor errand boys,[41]
who runs around a lot, but is hardly a hero!
We sent him only to bring back intelligence.

Did that monkey truly burn your city,   23a
moreover, without our lord's permission?
This explains why he never returned to Sugriv—
he is hiding somewhere out of fear![42]

Everything you have said is true, Ten-neck,   23b
and I am not the least annoyed at hearing it.
There is indeed no one in our army
who could gain fame by taking you on.

Make love and war only with your equals—   23c
that is sound policy.
If a lion slaughters a bunch of frogs,
will anyone commend him for it?

२३घ जद्यपि लघुता राम कहुँ तोहि बधें बड़ दोष ।
तदपि कठिन दसकंठ सुनु छत्र जाति कर रोष ॥

२३ङ बक्र उक्ति धनु बचन सर हृदय दहेउ रिपु कीस ।
प्रतिउत्तर सड़सिन्ह मनहुँ काढ़त भट दससीस ॥

२३च हँसि बोलेउ दसमौलि तब कपि कर बड़ गुन एक ।
जो प्रतिपालइ तासु हित करइ उपाय अनेक ॥

१ धन्य कीस जो निज प्रभु काजा ।
जहँ तहँ नाचइ परिहरि लाजा ॥
नाचि कूदि करि लोग रिझाई ।
पति हित करइ धर्म निपुनाई ॥

२ अंगद स्वामिभक्त तव जाती ।
प्रभु गुन कस न कहसि एहि भाँती ॥
मैं गुन गाहक परम सुजाना ।
तव कटु रटनि करउँ नहिं काना ॥

३ कह कपि तव गुन गाहकताई ।
सत्य पवनसुत मोहि सुनाई ॥
बन बिधंसि सुत बधि पुर जारा ।
तदपि न तेहिं कछु कृत अपकारा ॥

Although it is beneath Ram's dignity   23d
to slay you, and a great sin,[43]
still—mark my words, Ten-neck—
the wrath of the warrior class is awful."

Shot from the monkey's bow of sarcasm,   23e
these word-arrows set his enemy's heart ablaze.
But the redoubtable ten-head gave a retort
that was like pincers to extract them.

With a laugh, Ravan then quipped,   23f
"Monkeys do have one sterling quality:
whoever feeds and cares for them,
they serve in all sorts of ways.

A monkey earns merit who, for his master's sake,[44]   1
performs anywhere, abandoning all shame.
Dancing and capering, he captivates people
and benefits his master—such adroitness is his dharma.
Your species is innately servile, Angad,   2
so how can you not sing your lord's praises in this way?
Since I appreciate virtues and am supremely wise
I give no ear to your tiresome, repeated insults."
The monkey replied, "Your appreciation of virtue—   3
how true! The son of the wind* told me all about that.
He wrecked your grove, slew your son, burned your city—
yet none of this seemed to you the least disservice.

---

* Hanuman.

४ सोइ बिचारि तव प्रकृति सुहाई ।
दसकंधर मैं कीन्हि ढिठाई ॥
देखेउँ आइ जो कछु कपि भाषा ।
तुम्हरें लाज न रोष न माखा ॥

५ जौं असि मति पितु खाए कीसा ।
कहि अस बचन हँसा दससीसा ॥
पितहि खाइ खातेउँ पुनि तोही ।
अबहीं समुझि परा कछु मोही ॥

६ बालि बिमल जस भाजन जानी ।
हतउँ न तोहि अधम अभिमानी ॥
कहु रावन रावन जग केते ।
मैं निज श्रवन सुने सुनु जेते ॥

७ बलिहि जितन एक गयउ पताला ।
राखेउ बाँधि सिसुन्ह हयसाला ॥
खेलहिं बालक मारहिं जाई ।
दया लागि बलि दीन्ह छोड़ाई ॥

८ एक बहोरि सहसभुज देखा ।
धाइ धरा जिमि जंतु बिसेषा ॥
कौतुक लागि भवन लै आवा ।
सो पुलस्ति मुनि जाइ छोड़ावा ॥

52

Reckoning on your benevolent nature,   4
Ten-neck, I have ventured to be a little bold.
Coming here, I see that everything the monkey said is
      true—
you have no shame, anger, or even irritation."
"Monkey," Ravan retorted, "with such wit, no wonder   5
you ate your own father!" At this, all ten heads laughed.[45]
"If I ate my father, I would eat you next,
except that I just remembered something else—
I take you to be a reminder of Bali's pure renown,   6
and so do not slay you, vile and arrogant though you are.
But say Ravan—how many of you are there in the world?
I will tell you about the ones of whom I've heard; listen—
one went to the netherworld to defeat demon Bali,[46]   7
but Bali's kids tied him up and put him in the stable.
The little ones used to go and pummel him in their play,
till Bali took pity on him and set him free.
Then there was the one King Thousand-arm spotted,   8
chased after, and caught, thinking him an odd creature.
He brought him home for his own amusement,
but Sage Pulastya* went and got him released.

---

* Ravan's grandfather.

२४   एक कहत मोहि सकुच अति रहा बालि कीं काँख ।
      इन्ह महुँ रावन तैं कवन सत्य बदहि तजि माख ॥

१   सुनु सठ सोइ रावन बलसीला ।
      हरगिरि जान जासु भुज लीला ॥
      जान उमापति जासु सुराई ।
      पूजेउँ जेहि सिर सुमन चढ़ाई ॥
२   सिर सरोज निज करन्हि उतारी ।
      पूजेउँ अमित बार त्रिपुरारी ॥
      भुज बिक्रम जानहिं दिगपाला ।
      सठ अजहूँ जिन्ह कें उर साला ॥
३   जानहिं दिग्गज उर कठिनाई ।
      जब जब भिरउँ जाइ बरिआई ॥
      जिन्ह के दसन कराल न फूटे ।
      उर लागत मूलक इव टूटे ॥
४   जासु चलत डोलति इमि धरनी ।
      चढ़त मत्त गज जिमि लघु तरनी ॥
      सोइ रावन जग बिदित प्रतापी ।
      सुनेहि न श्रवन अलीक प्रलापी ॥

२५   तेहि रावन कहँ लघु कहसि नर कर करसि बखान ।
      रे कपि बर्बर खर्ब खल अब जाना तव ग्यान ॥

And there was one of whom I am too embarrassed   24
to speak, since he was held fast in Bali's armpit![47]
Which of these Ravans might you be?
Just tell me the truth and don't get miffed."

"Listen, fool," said the other, "I am that mighty Ravan   1
whose arms' mere play Shiva's summit knows well,[48]
and whose unflinching courage Uma's lord learned
from my flower-like offering of my heads in worship.
Plucking the lotuses of my heads with my own hands,   2
I propitiated, time and again, the triple cities' foe.
And the world-guardians know my arms' prowess,
numbskull, whose breasts still smart from their wounds.
The cosmic elephants know the hardness of my chest,   3
for whenever I took them on in earnest
their sharp tusks could never penetrate it—
hitting this chest, they snapped like radish roots!
The one at whose every footfall earth shakes   4
like a little boat boarded by an enraged elephant—
that Ravan am I, of world-renowned glory,
babbler of falsehoods! Haven't your ears heard of me?

That very Ravan you would belittle   25
while you magnify a mere man.
Now I see—nasty, uncouth dwarf of a monkey—
just how much intelligence you have."

१ सुनि अंगद सकोप कह बानी ।
बोलु सँभारि अधम अभिमानी ॥
सहसबाहु भुज गहन अपारा ।
दहन अनल सम जासु कुठारा ॥

२ जासु परसु सागर खर धारा ।
बूड़े नृप अगनित बहु बारा ॥
तासु गर्ब जेहि देखत भागा ।
सो नर क्यों दससीस अभागा ॥

३ राम मनुज कस रे सठ बंगा ।
धन्वी कामु नदी पुनि गंगा ॥
पसु सुरधेनु कल्पतरु रूखा ।
अन्न दान अरु रस पीयूषा ॥

४ बैनतेय खग अहि सहसानन ।
चिंतामनि पुनि उपल दसानन ॥
सुनु मतिमंद लोक बैकुंठा ।
लाभ कि रघुपति भगति अकुंठा ॥

२६ सेन सहित तव मान मथि बन उजारि पुर जारि ।
कस रे सठ हनुमान कपि गयउ जो तव सुत मारि ॥

१ सुनु रावन परिहरि चतुराई ।
भजसि न कृपासिंधु रघुराई ॥
जौं खल भएसि राम कर द्रोही ।
ब्रह्म रुद्र सक राखि न तोही ॥

At this, Angad spoke out in anger—   1
"Watch what you say, arrogant villain!
Sahasrabahu's thousand arms were a veritable forest,
but he whose ax was like a fire to consume it,[*]
and whose ax blade was a turbulent ocean current[49]   2
in which legions of kings repeatedly drowned—
his own pride fled away at the mere sight of the one
whom you are calling a man, wretched Ten-neck.[50]
Impertinent imbecile! Is Ram but a human being?   3
Is Kama just another bowman, Ganga a mere river,
the divine cow livestock, the wishing tree a crude shrub?
Is sustenance mere charity, ambrosia ordinary juice?[51]
Is Garuda just a bird, thousand-headed Shesh a snake,   4
and the alchemy stone only a pebble, Ten-face?
You dull-witted one—is Vaikunth[†] just any old realm,
or firm devotion to the Raghu lord a worldly windfall?

And he who left here, having shaken your pride,   26
devastated your grove, burned your city,
and slain your own son—is that Hanuman,
you fool, merely another monkey?

Abandon all wiles and listen to me, Ravan: 1
why not worship the Raghu king?
For if you are an enemy of Ram, scoundrel,
not even Brahma and Shiva can save you.

---

[*] Parashuram, Vishnu's sixth avatar.
[†] Vishnu's heaven.

२ मूढ़ बृथा जनि मारसि गाला ।
राम बयर अस होइहि हाला ॥
तव सिर निकर कपिन्ह के आगें ।
परिहहिं धरनि राम सर लागें ॥

३ ते तव सिर कंदुक सम नाना ।
खेलिहहिं भालु कीस चौगाना ॥
जबहिं समर कोपिहि रघुनायक ।
छुटिहहिं अति कराल बहु सायक ॥

४ तब कि चलिहि अस गाल तुम्हारा ।
अस बिचारि भजु राम उदारा ॥
सुनत बचन रावन परजरा ।
जरत महानल जनु घृत परा ॥

२७ कुंभकरन अस बंधु मम सुत प्रसिद्ध सक्रारि ।
मोर पराक्रम नहिं सुनेहि जितेउँ चराचर झारि ॥

१ सठ साखामृग जोरि सहाई ।
बाँधा सिंधु इहइ मनुसाई ॥
नाघहिं खग अनेक बारीसा ।
सूर न होहिं ते सुनु सब कीसा ॥

२ मम भुज सागर बल जल पूरा ।
जहँ बूड़े बहु सुर नर सूरा ॥
बीस पयोधि अगाध अपारा ।
को अस बीर जो पाइहि पारा ॥

Stop your empty boasting, fool,   2
for, opposing Ram, this will be your fate:
before the monkeys' eyes, your stack of heads
will plummet to earth, struck by Ram's arrows,
and using your many skulls as balls,   3
those bears and monkeys will play polo![52]
When the Raghu lord becomes enraged in battle
and releases his myriad deadly arrows,
what good will this boasting of yours do?   4
Pondering this, worship Ram, the beneficent."
Hearing these words, Ravan flared up
like a roaring blaze on which ghee is poured.

"I have the likes of Kumbhakaran for a brother,   27
and Indra's famous foe* for my son.
And you must not have heard of my valor,
with which I conquered all created beings.

Fool, with the aid of assembled tree vermin,   1
your master bridged the sea—such is his manliness!
But countless birds cross over that lord of waters,
and it hardly makes them all heroes, monkey.[53]
My every arm is an ocean, filled with water of might   2
in which many divine and human champions drowned.
And there are twenty such seas, fathomless and vast—
who will be hero enough to get across them?

---

* Meghnad, also known as Indrajit.

59

३ दिगपालन्ह मैं नीर भरावा ।
भूप सुजस खल मोहि सुनावा ॥
जौं पै समर सुभट तव नाथा ।
पुनि पुनि कहसि जासु गुन गाथा ॥

४ तौ बसीठ पठवत केहि काजा ।
रिपु सन प्रीति करत नहिं लाजा ॥
हरगिरि मथन निरखु मम बाहू ।
पुनि सठ कपि निज प्रभुहि सराहू ॥

२८ सूर कवन रावन सरिस स्वकर काटि जेहिं सीस ।
हुने अनल अति हरष बहु बार साखि गौरीस ॥

१ जरत बिलोकेउँ जबहिं कपाला ।
बिधि के लिखे अंक निज भाला ॥
नर कें कर आपन बध बाँची ।
हसेउँ जानि बिधि गिरा असाँची ॥

२ सोउ मन समुझि त्रास नहिं मोरें ।
लिखा बिरंचि जरठ मति भोरें ॥
आन बीर बल सठ मम आगें ।
पुनि पुनि कहसि लाज पति त्यागें ॥

३ कह अंगद सलज्ज जग माहीं ।
रावन तोहि समान कोउ नाहीं ॥
लाजवंत तव सहज सुभाऊ ।
निज मुख निज गुन कहसि न काऊ ॥

I have made the world-guardians haul my water,　　　　3
and you, wretch, extol to me an earthly king's fame!
If your master is really a stalwart in battle—
he whose merits you so tiresomely declare—
then why does he need to send an emissary?　　　　4
Is he not ashamed to be conciliatory with a foe?
Gaze on my arms that shook Shiva's summit,
and then, fool monkey, dare praise your lord again!

What hero can compare to Ravan,　　　　28
who lopped off his heads with his own hands,
and with utter joy offered them in the sacred fire
time and again, as Gauri's lord* is witness?

As I watched my own skulls burning,　　　　1
I saw what the creator had written on my brows.[54]
Reading of my death by a man's hand,
I laughed, knowing fate's dictate to be false.
Even recalling that, I have no fear, knowing　　　　2
senile old Brahma was confused when he wrote it.
Yet in front of me, fool, you rant of another hero's might,
time and again, abandoning all modesty and restraint."
Angad replied, "When it comes to modesty,　　　　3
no one in this world equals you, Ravan.
Being modest comes so naturally to you—
you yourself never speak of your own virtues.

---

* Shiva.

४   सिर अरु सैल कथा चित रही ।
ताते बार बीस तैं कही ॥
सो भुजबल राखेहु उर घाली ।
जीतेहु सहसबाहु बलि बाली ॥

५   सुनु मतिमंद देहि अब पूरा ।
काटें सीस कि होइअ सूरा ॥
इंद्रजालि कहुँ कहिअ न बीरा ।
काटइ निज कर सकल सरीरा ॥

२९   जरहिं पतंग मोह बस भार बहहिं खर बृंद ।
ते नहिं सूर कहावहिं समुझि देखु मतिमंद ॥

१   अब जनि बतबढ़ाव खल करही ।
सुनु मम बचन मान परिहरही ॥
दसमुख मैं न बसीठीं आयउँ ।
अस बिचारि रघुबीर पठायउँ ॥

२   बार बार अस कहइ कृपाला ।
नहिं गजारि जसु बधें सृकाला ॥
मन महुँ समुझि बचन प्रभु केरे ।
सहेउँ कठोर बचन सठ तेरे ॥

३   नाहिं त करि मुख भंजन तोरा ।
लै जातेउँ सीतहि बरजोरा ॥
जानेउँ तव बल अधम सुरारी ।
सूनें हरि आनिहि परनारी ॥

62

The tale of cut heads and hefted hilltop obsesses you,   4
true, and so you've told it at least twenty times.
But you discreetly hid that strength of your arms
by which you bested Sahasrabahu, Bali, and my father.[55]
Now listen, dunce, and answer me this: 5
does lopping off his head make anyone a hero?
A conjurer is never said to be heroic,
though he slices through his whole body.

Impelled by delusion, moths get incinerated,   29
and packs of asses transport heavy burdens,
but all these are never said to be heroic,
dullard—observe this and wise up.

Now, scoundrel, stop prolonging this argument   1
and heed my words, abandoning your arrogance.
I have not come as a negotiator, Ten-head.
Rather, the Raghu hero sent me with this thought,
for so that merciful one always says: 2
'It does not befit a lion to slay a lowly jackal.'
Only because I recall those words of the Lord
have I suffered your stinging speeches, fool.
Otherwise, I would just smash your faces   3
and forcibly take back Sita.
I fathomed your real strength, vile foe of gods,
when you snatched away another's wife on the sly.

४ तैं निसिचरपति गर्ब बहूता ।
मैं रघुपति सेवक कर दूता ॥
जौं न राम अपमानहि डरऊँ ।
तोहि देखत अस कौतुक करऊँ ॥

३० तोहि पटकि महि सेन हति चौपट करि तव गाउँ ।
तव जुबतिन्ह समेत सठ जनकसुतहि लै जाउँ ॥

१ जौं अस करौं तदपि न बड़ाई ।
मुएहि बधें नहिं कछु मनुसाई ॥
कौल कामबस कृपिन बिमूढ़ा ।
अति दरिद्र अजसी अति बूढ़ा ॥

२ सदा रोगबस संतत क्रोधी ।
बिष्नु बिमुख श्रुति संत बिरोधी ॥
तनु पोषक निंदक अघ खानी ।
जीवत सव सम चौदह प्रानी ॥

३ अस बिचारि खल बधउँ न तोही ।
अब जनि रिस उपजावसि मोही ॥
सुनि सकोप कह निसिचर नाथा ।
अधर दसन दसि मीजत हाथा ॥

४ रे कपि अधम मरन अब चहसी ।
छोटे बदन बात बड़ि कहसी ॥
कटु जल्पसि जड़ कपि बल जाकें ।
बल प्रताप बुधि तेज न ताकें ॥

64

You may be lord of night-stalkers and mightily proud,   4
but I am emissary of the servant of the Raghu lord,
and were I not afraid of disrespecting Ram,
I would, before your very eyes, perform certain feats:

slam you to the ground, slaughter your troops,   30
turn your little hamlet upside down
and make off with all your women,
scoundrel, along with Janak's daughter!*

And even if I did this, it would not bring me glory,   1
for there is no valor in killing the already dead.
A Tantric, one crazed by lust, a miser or an imbecile,[56]
an utter pauper, one who is disreputable or very aged,
an incurable invalid, one who is always angry,   2
a foe of Vishnu, or one opposed to the Veda and holy ones,
one who pampers his body, a slanderer, or great sinner—
these fourteen beings are like living corpses.
Considering this, villain, I do not slay you,   3
so do not provoke my wrath now."
When he heard this, the enraged lord of demons spoke,
biting his lips and kneading his hands:
"Vile monkey, now you really must want to die,   4
and that's why your little mouth runs over so!
He by whose strength you babble insults, stupid beast,
has no real might or courage, no wisdom or energy.

---

* Sita.

३१क   अगुन अमान जानि तेहि दीन्ह पिता बनबास ।
     सो दुख अरु जुबती बिरह पुनि निसि दिन मम त्रास ॥

३१ख   जिन्ह के बल कर गर्ब तोहि अइसे मनुज अनेक ।
     खाहिं निसाचर दिवस निसि मूढ़ समुझु तजि टेक ॥

१   जब तेहिं कीन्हि राम कै निंदा ।
    क्रोधवंत अति भयउ कपिंदा ॥
    हरि हर निंदा सुनइ जो काना ।
    होइ पाप गोघात समाना ॥

२   कटकटान कपिकुंजर भारी ।
    दुहु भुजदंड तमकि महि मारी ॥
    डोलत धरनि सभासद खसे ।
    चले भाजि भय मारुत ग्रसे ॥

३   गिरत सँभारि उठा दसकंधर ।
    भूतल परे मुकुट अति सुंदर ॥
    कछु तेहिं लै निज सिरन्हि सँवारे ।
    कछु अंगद प्रभु पास पबारे ॥

४   आवत मुकुट देखि कपि भागे ।
    दिनहीं लूक परन बिधि लागे ॥
    की रावन करि कोप चलाए ।
    कुलिस चारि आवत अति धाए ॥

Knowing he lacked all virtue and stature,[57]   31a
his father sent him into forest exile.
Hence he's depressed, plus pining for his woman,
and on top of that, in terror of me night and day.

He in whose strength you take such pride—   31b
countless men of his sort
are devoured daily by my night-stalkers.
Grasp this, fool, and drop your obstinacy."

When Ravan spoke insultingly of Ram,   1
that lord of monkeys became furious,
for one who listens to slander of Vishnu or Shiva
incurs sin equal to that of slaughtering a cow.
The great monkey bared his teeth in rage[58]   2
and, in fury, thrust his two mighty arms to the floor.
The earth shook, and courtiers toppled from their seats
and fled, seized by the spirit of terror.
Ten-necked Ravan steadied himself and rose,   3
but his gorgeous crowns crashed to the ground.
He grabbed some and replaced them on his heads,
but some Angad seized and hurled toward the Lord.
Seeing these crowns coming, the monkeys fled, crying,   4
"Brahma, have shooting stars started falling by day,
or has Ravan in his awful rage
loosed four thunderbolts that hurtle our way?"

५   कह प्रभु हँसि जनि हृदयँ डेराहू ।
लूक न असनि केतु नहिं राहू ॥
ए किरीट दसकंधर केरे ।
आवत बालितनय के प्रेरे ॥

३२क   तरकि पवनसुत कर गहे आनि धरे प्रभु पास ।
कौतुक देखहिं भालु कपि दिनकर सरिस प्रकास ॥

३२ख   उहाँ सकोपि दसानन सब सन कहत रिसाइ ।
धरहु कपिहि धरि मारहु सुनि अंगद मुसुकाइ ॥

१   एहि बधि बेगि सुभट सब धावहु ।
खाहु भालु कपि जहँ जहँ पावहु ॥
मर्कटहीन करहु महि जाई ।
जिअत धरहु तापस द्वौ भाई ॥

२   पुनि सकोप बोलेउ जुबराजा ।
गाल बजावत तोहि न लाजा ॥
मरु गर काटि निलज कुलघाती ।
बल बिलोकि बिहरति नहिं छाती ॥

३   रे त्रिय चोर कुमारग गामी ।
खल मल रासि मंदमति कामी ॥
सन्यपात जल्पसि दुर्बादा ।
भएसि कालबस खल मनुजादा ॥

The Lord smiled and said, "Don't be frightened. 5
These are no meteors or lightning, not Ketu or Rahu.[59]
They are diadems of ten-necked Ravan,
sent this way by Bali's son!"

The son of the wind leaped up, caught them, 32a
and brought them before the Lord.
All the bears and monkeys gazed in wonder
at their sun-like brilliance.

Meanwhile, the enraged ten-headed one 32b
bellowed furiously at all in attendance—
"Seize that monkey and slay him!"
Angad heard this and merely smiled.

"And rush out, all you warriors, right now; 1
devour bears and monkeys wherever you find them.
Go and rid the earth of monkeys,
but seize those two mendicant brothers alive."
Then the crown prince of monkeys spoke angrily: 2
"Empty boasting causes you no embarrassment,
shameless scourge of your line, so slit your own throats
    and die.
Didn't your heart fail on seeing my strength?[60]
Woman-stealer, walker on the path of evil, 3
thoroughly defiled villain, lustful dullard—
you babble foul nonsense in your delirium,
wicked demon, for you are in death's snare.

४ याको फलु पावहिगो आगें ।
बानर भालु चपेटन्हि लागें ॥
रामु मनुज बोलत असि बानी ।
गिरिहिं न तव रसना अभिमानी ॥
५ गिरिहहिं रसना संसय नाहीं ।
सिरन्हि समेत समर महि माहीं ॥

३३क सो नर क्यों दसकंध बालि बध्यो जेहिं एक सर ।
बीसहुँ लोचन अंध धिग तव जन्म कुजाति जड़ ॥

३३ख तव सोनित कीं प्यास तृषित राम सायक निकर ।
तजउँ तोहि तेहि त्रास कटु जल्पक निसिचर अधम ॥

१ मैं तव दसन तोरिबे लायक ।
आयसु मोहि न दीन्ह रघुनायक ॥
असि रिस होति दसउ मुख तोरौं ।
लंका गहि समुद्र महँ बोरौं ॥
२ गूलरि फल समान तव लंका ।
बसहु मध्य तुम्ह जंतु असंका ॥
मैं बानर फल खात न बारा ।
आयसु दीन्ह न राम उदारा ॥

You will shortly taste the fruit of this,   4
when the monkeys and bears start slapping you around.
To call Ram a mere man—when you say such words,
arrogant one, don't your tongues fall out?
Oh, but they will fall, no doubt about it,   5
along with your heads, on the field of war.

Can he be but a man, Ten-head,   33a
who slew Bali with a single arrow?
Blind for all of your twenty eyes,
you are a lowborn dunce, spawned in vain.

The swarm of Ram's arrows   33b
are thirsting for your blood,
and I spare you, vile, foul-mouthed demon,
only for fear of disappointing them.

I am quite capable of breaking your teeth,   1
but the Raghu master gave me no such order.
I am mad enough to smash your ten faces,
snatch up your island, and sink it in the sea.
Your Lanka is like a ripe wild fig   2
which you all infest as smug vermin.
Being a monkey, I would swallow it in no time,
but high-minded Ram gave no such mandate."

३ जुगुति सुनत रावन मुसुकाई ।
   मूढ़ सिखिहि कहँ बहुत झुठाई ॥
   बालि न कबहुँ गाल अस मारा ।
   मिलि तपसिन्ह तैं भएसि लबारा ॥

४ साँचेहुँ मैं लबार भुज बीहा ।
   जौं न उपारिउँ तव दस जीहा ॥
   समुझि राम प्रताप कपि कोपा ।
   सभा माझ पन करि पद रोपा ॥

५ जौं मम चरन सकसि सठ टारी ।
   फिरहिं रामु सीता मैं हारी ॥
   सुनहु सुभट सब कह दससीसा ।
   पद गहि धरनि पछारहु कीसा ॥

६ इंद्रजीत आदिक बलवाना ।
   हरषि उठे जहँ तहँ भट नाना ॥
   झपटहिं करि बल बिपुल उपाई ।
   पद न टरइ बैठहिं सिरु नाई ॥

७ पुनि उठि झपटहिं सुर आराती ।
   टरइ न कीस चरन एहि भाँती ॥
   पुरुष कुजोगी जिमि उरगारी ।
   मोह बिटप नहिं सकहिं उपारी ॥

३४क कोटिन्ह मेघनाद सम सुभट उठे हरषाइ ।
      झपटहिं टरै न कपि चरन पुनि बैठहिं सिर नाइ ॥

Ravan smiled at his verbal wit, and said,   3
"Where did you learn so many falsehoods, fool?
Bali never used to carry on like this,
but falling in with mendicants, you've become a prattler."
Angad answered, "I will truly be a prattler, Twenty-arms,   4
if I do not tear out all ten of your tongues."
Then, recalling Ram's majesty, the enraged monkey
planted his foot determinedly in that hall, and vowed,
"Scoundrels, if you can move this foot of mine,   5
Ram will turn back and I will have lost Sita!"[61]
"Did you hear that, all you heroes?" roared Ravan.
"Grab the monkey's foot and fling him to the ground."
Indrajit* and countless other powerful warriors   6
gleefully rose from their places on all sides
to pounce on Angad, exerting their full strength and skills.
But the foot would not budge, and they sat down, heads
      bowed.
Then those enemies of the gods arose and fell on him   7
      again,
but they could no more move that monkey's foot,
foe of serpents, than a false, sense-addled yogi[62]
can uproot delusion's mighty tree.

Millions of stalwart warriors, each equal to Meghnad,   34a
merrily rose and set upon him.
But the monkey's foot did not even flinch,
and so they sat down again, shamefaced.

---

* Ravan's eldest son, also called Meghnad.

३४ख भूमि न छाँड़त कपि चरन देखत रिपु मद भाग ।
कोटि बिघ्न ते संत कर मन जिमि नीति न त्याग ॥

१ कपि बल देखि सकल हियँ हारे ।
उठा आपु कपि कें परचारे ॥
गहत चरन कह बालिकुमारा ।
मम पद गहें न तोर उबारा ॥

२ गहसि न राम चरन सठ जाई ।
सुनत फिरा मन अति सकुचाई ॥
भयउ तेजहत श्री सब गई ।
मध्य दिवस जिमि ससि सोहई ॥

३ सिंघासन बैठेउ सिर नाई ।
मानहुँ संपति सकल गँवाई ॥
जगदातमा प्रानपति रामा ।
तासु बिमुख किमि लह बिश्रामा ॥

४ उमा राम की भृकुटि बिलासा ।
होइ बिस्व पुनि पावइ नासा ॥
तृन ते कुलिस कुलिस तृन करई ।
तासु दूत पन कहु किमि टरई ॥

५ पुनि कपि कही नीति बिधि नाना ।
मान न ताहि कालु निअराना ॥
रिपु मद मथि प्रभु सुजसु सुनायो ।
यह कहि चल्यो बालि नृप जायो ॥

The foot of the monkey never left the ground—   34b
seeing this, his foes lost their pride—
just as the mind of a saintly one, though faced
with countless obstacles, never abandons virtue.

Witnessing the monkey's might, all were disheartened.   1
Then, challenged by Angad, Ravan himself arose.
But when he grasped his foot, Bali's son declared,
"Clutching at this foot of mine will never save you,
scoundrel—why not go and take hold of Ram's feet?"   2
At this, Ravan shrank away, deeply embarrassed,
all his grandeur and royal radiance dulled,[63]
as when the moon shows but palely at midday.
Heads drooping, he went and sat on his lion throne,   3
looking as if he had lost his whole fortune.
Ram is the universal self, lord of life's breaths,
so how can one opposed to him find peace?
Uma, by the mere play of Ram's brows   4
the world comes to be, then meets its annihilation.
He can make a wisp of straw a thunderbolt, and vice versa;
so tell me, how could his messenger's vow be broken?
Once more, the monkey expounded sound statecraft,   5
but he whose death was near paid it no heed.
And so, having smashed the enemy's pride and proclaimed
the Lord's fame, King Bali's son left, declaring—

६ हतौं न खेत खेलाइ खेलाई ।
तोहि अबहिं का करौं बड़ाई ॥
प्रथमहिं तासु तनय कपि मारा ।
सो सुनि रावन भयउ दुखारा ॥

७ जातुधान अंगद पन देखी ।
भय ब्याकुल सब भए बिसेषी ॥

३५क रिपु बल धरषि हरषि कपि बालितनय बल पुंज ।
पुलक सरीर नयन जल गहे राम पद कंज ॥

३५ख साँझ जानि दसकंधर भवन गयउ बिलखाइ ।
मंदोदरीं रावनहि बहुरि कहा समुझाइ ॥

१ कंत समुझि मन तजहु कुमतिही ।
सोह न समर तुम्हहि रघुपतिही ॥
रामानुज लघु रेख खचाई ।
सोउ नहिं नाघेहु असि मनुसाई ॥

२ पिय तुम्ह ताहि जितब संग्रामा ।
जाके दूत केर यह कामा ॥
कौतुक सिंधु नाघि तव लंका ।
आयउ कपि केहरी असंका ॥

"Since I cannot yet hunt you down on the field,   6
what point in further boasting just now?"
When Ravan heard that, earlier, the monkey had slain
one of his sons, he grew still more depressed,
and all the demons who had witnessed Angad's vow   7
became distracted with terror.

Having subdued the enemy's might, that monkey,   35a
Bali's son, in great delight,
his body thrilling and with tear-filled eyes
clasped Ram's holy feet.

Knowing it was dusk, the ten-necked lord   35b
mournfully repaired to his apartments,
where, once more, Mandodari spoke out
to Ravan in admonition.[64]

"Give up your folly, husband, reflect on this: 1
battle with the Raghu lord won't enhance your glory.
Ram's little brother drew a mere line in the dust,
and you couldn't cross that, for all your manhood.[65]
How, dear husband, will you defeat in battle   2
one whose emissary performed such feats as these:
he easily leaped the sea and came brazenly,
a lion among monkeys, into your Lanka.

३   रखवारे हति बिपिन उजारा ।
देखत तोहि अच्छ तेहिं मारा ॥
जारि सकल पुर कीन्हेसि छारा ।
कहाँ रहा बल गर्ब तुम्हारा ॥

४   अब पति मृषा गाल जनि मारहु ।
मोर कहा कछु हृदयँ बिचारहु ॥
पति रघुपतिहि नृपति जनि मानहु ।
अग जग नाथ अतुलबल जानहु ॥

५   बान प्रताप जान मारीचा ।
तासु कहा नहिं मानेहि नीचा ॥
जनक सभाँ अगनित भूपाला ।
रहे तुम्हउ बल अतुल बिसाला ॥

६   भंजि धनुष जानकी बिआही ।
तब संग्राम जितेहु किन ताही ॥
सुरपति सुत जानइ बल थोरा ।
राखा जिअत आँखि गहि फोरा ॥

७   सूपनखा कै गति तुम्ह देखी ।
तदपि हृदयँ नहिं लाज बिसेषी ॥

३६   बधि बिराध खर दूषनहि लीलाँ हत्यो कबंध ।
बालि एक सर मार्यो तेहि जानहु दसकंध ॥

He slew your guards, wrecked your grove,   3
killed prince Akshay right under your nose,[66]
and burned your whole city to ashes.
Where, then, was this conceit in your strength?
So now, husband, do not spout boasts in vain   4
but give some thought to what I am saying.
Do not reckon the Raghu lord a mere king of men;
know him as the incomparably mighty master of all
    beings!
Marich knew well the power of his arrow,   5
but you would not heed the poor fellow's advice.[67]
Countless kings came to Janak's assembly,
and you were there too, in all your vaunted might.
When he broke the bow and wedded Janaki,   6
why didn't you best him in battle there and then?
Indra's son learned a little about the power of Ram,
who caught him and put out his eye, but spared his life.[68]
Yet even when you saw Shurpanakha's condition,   7
your heart was not particularly shamed.

The slayer of Viradh, of Khar and Dushan,   36
who killed Kabandh in mere sport
and slew Bali with a single arrow—
realize who he is, my ten-necked lord!

१ जेहिं जलनाथ बँधायउ हेला ।
   उतरे प्रभु दल सहित सुबेला ॥
   कारुनीक दिनकर कुल केतू ।
   दूत पठायउ तव हित हेतू ॥

२ सभा माझ जेहिं तव बल मथा ।
   करि बरूथ महुँ मृगपति जथा ॥
   अंगद हनुमत अनुचर जाके ।
   रन बाँकुरे बीर अति बाँके ॥

३ तेहि कहँ पिय पुनि पुनि नर कहहू ।
   मुधा मान ममता मद बहहू ॥
   अहह कंत कृत राम बिरोधा ।
   काल बिबस मन उपज न बोधा ॥

४ काल दंड गहि काहु न मारा ।
   हरइ धर्म बल बुद्धि बिचारा ॥
   निकट काल जेहि आवत साईं ।
   तेहि भ्रम होइ तुम्हारिहि नाईं ॥

३७ दुइ सुत मरे दहेउ पुर अजहुँ पूर पिय देहु ।
    कृपासिंधु रघुनाथ भजि नाथ बिमल जसु लेहु ॥

१ नारि बचन सुनि बिसिख समाना ।
   सभाँ गयउ उठि होत बिहाना ॥
   बैठ जाइ सिंघासन फूली ।
   अति अभिमान त्रास सब भूली ॥

80

That lord who playfully bridged the king of waters,   1
and landed, with his army, on Mount Subel,
that merciful one, proud ensign of the solar clan,
dispatched a messenger for your sake
who, before your court, subdued your might   2
like a lordly lion amid a herd of elephants.
He who has servants like Angad and Hanuman—
formidable heroes, most dexterous in battle—
him, my dear, you repeatedly call 'a mere man,'   3
and vainly flaunt pride, egoism, and arrogance.
Alas, husband! You have challenged Ram
and are in death's grip, so your mind is oblivious.
Death does not seize a club to slay anyone,   4
but steals his virtue, strength, wit, and wisdom,
and one whose end is very near, my lord,
becomes confused, just as you are.

Our two sons were killed, our city burned—   37
but now, dear, put an end to this.
Worship the Raghu king, ocean of mercy,
master, and win stainless renown."

He listened to his wife's arrow-like words,   1
but when day dawned, rose and returned to court
to sit on his grand throne, puffed up
with supreme arrogance and forgetful of all fear.

२   इहाँ राम अंगदहि बोलावा ।
आइ चरन पंकज सिरु नावा ॥
अति आदर समीप बैठारी ।
बोले बिहँसि कृपाल खरारी ॥

३   बालितनय कौतुक अति मोही ।
तात सत्य कहु पूछउँ तोही ॥
रावनु जातुधान कुल टीका ।
भुज बल अतुल जासु जग लीका ॥

४   तासु मुकुट तुम्ह चारि चलाए ।
कहहु तात कवनी बिधि पाए ॥
सुनु सर्बग्य प्रनत सुखकारी ।
मुकुट न होहिं भूप गुन चारी ॥

५   साम दान अरु दंड बिभेदा ।
नृप उर बसहिं नाथ कह बेदा ॥
नीति धर्म के चरन सुहाए ।
अस जियँ जानि नाथ पहिं आए ॥

३८क   धर्महीन प्रभु पद बिमुख काल बिबस दससीस ।
तेहि परिहरि गुन आए सुनहु कोसलाधीस ॥

३८ख   परम चतुरता श्रवन सुनि बिहँसे रामु उदार ।
समाचार पुनि सब कहे गढ़ के बालिकुमार ॥

Meanwhile, Ram called for Angad,   2
who came and bowed at his holy feet.
With great respect, seating him close by,
the merciful one, Khar's foe, smiled and said,
"Son of Bali, I am astonished and curious,   3
and so I ask you—tell me truly, brother:
Ravan is the overlord of the demon clan,
whose incomparably strong arms are world renowned,
yet you sent off four of his own crowns!   4
Tell me, brother—however did you obtain them?"
Angad answered, "All-knowing one, delight of devotees—
they were no crowns, but the four kingly virtues
of conciliation, charity, righteous force, and stratagem,[69]   5
which abide in a ruler's heart, lord, as the Veda declares.
These four noble legs of the dharma of statecraft,
have come to you, master, knowing this:[70]

that Ten-head is bereft of dharma, averse   38a
to the Lord's feet, and ensnared by death.
Abandoning him, those virtues have come
to you, king of Kosala."

Hearing the great ingenuity of this speech,   38b
good-hearted Ram smiled graciously,
and then Bali's son gave a full report
on the enemy's stronghold.

The Battle

१ रिपु के समाचार जब पाए ।
   राम सचिव सब निकट बोलाए ॥
   लंका बाँके चारि दुआरा ।
   केहि बिधि लागिअ करहु बिचारा ॥

२ तब कपीस रिच्छेस बिभीषन ।
   सुमिरि हृदयँ दिनकर कुल भूषन ॥
   करि बिचार तिन्ह मंत्र दृढ़ावा ।
   चारि अनी कपि कटकु बनावा ॥

३ जथाजोग सेनापति कीन्हे ।
   जूथप सकल बोलि तब लीन्हे ॥
   प्रभु प्रताप कहि सब समुझाए ।
   सुनि कपि सिंघनाद करि धाए ॥

४ हरषित राम चरन सिर नावहिं ।
   गहि गिरि सिखर बीर सब धावहिं ॥
   गर्जहिं तर्जहिं भालु कपीसा ।
   जय रघुबीर कोसलाधीसा ॥

५ जानत परम दुर्ग अति लंका ।
   प्रभु प्रताप कपि चले असंका ॥
   घटाटोप करि चहुँ दिसि घेरी ।
   मुखहिं निसान बजावहिं भेरी ॥

३९ जयति राम जय लछिमन जय कपीस सुग्रीव ।
    गर्जहिं सिंहनाद कपि भालु महा बल सींव ॥

When he had received intelligence of the foe, 1
Ram summoned all his counselors and said,
"Lanka has four formidable gates;
consider how to lay siege to them."
Then the monkey and bear kings, with Vibhishan, 2
hearts focused on the jewel of the solar line,
pondered and arrived at the strategy
of forming their simian host into four divisions,
to which they appointed suitable generals. 3
Then they summoned all their commanders
and admonished them to recall the Lord's might.
The monkeys heard and rushed forth, roaring like lions.
Joyously, they bowed their heads at Ram's feet, 4
then, seizing mountaintops, the heroes surged forward.
Bellowing and reviling the foe, those bears and monkeys
shouted, "Victory to the Raghu hero, Kosala's king!"
Knowing Lanka to be an impregnable fortress, 5
they advanced fearlessly by the power of the Lord.
Like dense clouds, they hemmed the city on all sides,
emitting cries like resounding war drums.

"Victory to Ram, victory to Lakshman, 39
and victory to Sugriv, king of monkeys!"
Such were the lion-like roars of those simians
and bears, paragons of might.

१ लंकाँ भयउ कोलाहल भारी ।
सुना दसानन अति अहँकारी ॥
देखहु बनरन्ह केरि ढिठाई ।
बिहँसि निसाचर सेन बोलाई ॥

२ आए कीस काल के प्रेरे ।
छुधावंत सब निसिचर मेरे ॥
अस कहि अट्टहास सठ कीन्हा ।
गृह बैठें अहार बिधि दीन्हा ॥

३ सुभट सकल चारिहुँ दिसि जाहू ।
धरि धरि भालु कीस सब खाहू ॥
उमा रावनहि अस अभिमाना ।
जिमि टिट्टिभ खग सूत उताना ॥

४ चले निसाचर आयसु मागी ।
गहि कर भिंडिपाल बर साँगी ॥
तोमर मुद्गर परसु प्रचंडा ।
सूल कृपान परिघ गिरिखंडा ॥

५ जिमि अरुनोपल निकर निहारी ।
धावहिं सठ खग मांस अहारी ॥
चोंच भंग दुख तिन्हहि न सूझा ।
तिमि धाए मनुजाद अबूझा ॥

४० नानायुध सर चाप धर जातुधान बल बीर ।
कोट कँगूरन्हि चढ़ि गए कोटि कोटि रनधीर ॥

A great commotion broke out in Lanka,   1
but when he heard it, Ten-head said arrogantly,
"Just look at the impudence of those apes,"
and laughing, summoned his night-stalker legions.
"These monkeys have come, driven by their doom,   2
and all my night-roaming demons are famished."
Then, roaring with laughter, the villain declared,
"Destiny delivers our meals while we sit at home.
Go forth, all you warriors, in the four directions,   3
seize those bears and monkeys, and devour them all."
Shiva said, "Uma, in his deluded arrogance, Ravan
was like the lapwing bird, which sleeps upside-down."[1]
At his command, the night-stalkers streamed forth   4
bearing slingshots and pointed javelins,
lances, maces, sharpened battle-axes,
spears, short swords, pikes, and boulders.[2]
As when, spying a field of reddish-colored rocks,   5
carnivorous birds foolishly fall upon them,
heedless of the pain of breaking their beaks,
just so did the crazed demons race forward.

Bearing all sorts of weapons and armed   40
with arrows and bows, mighty demon heroes,
steadfast in battle, in their tens of millions
climbed onto the ramparts of the fort.

१ कोट कँगूरन्हि सोहहिं कैसे ।
मेरु के सृंगनि जनु घन बैसे ॥
बाजहिं ढोल निसान जुझाऊ ।
सुनि धुनि होइ भटन्हि मन चाऊ ॥

२ बाजहिं भेरि नफीरि अपारा ।
सुनि कादर उर जाहिं दरारा ॥
देखिन्ह जाइ कपिन्ह के ठट्टा ।
अति बिसाल तनु भालु सुभट्टा ॥

३ धावहिं गनहिं न अवघट घाटा ।
पर्बत फोरि करहिं गहि बाटा ॥
कटकटाहिं कोटिन्ह भट गर्जहिं ।
दसन ओठ काटहिं अति तर्जहिं ॥

४ उत रावन इत राम दोहाई ।
जयति जयति जय परी लराई ॥
निसिचर सिखर समूह ढहावहिं ।
कूदि धरहिं कपि फेरि चलावहिं ॥

The ramparts and parapets now appeared like   1
Mount Meru's summits wreathed in dark clouds.
Kettledrums and other martial instruments boomed,
exciting the hearts of heroes.
Countless drums and reeds were played   2
with a sound to rend the hearts of cowards.
Now the demons beheld that horde
of huge-bodied monkey and bear warriors
rushing forward, heedless of the rough terrain—   3
they just tore off mountaintops to make a path.
Gnashing their teeth, those millions of soldiers roared,[3]
bit their lips, and yelled in furious challenge.
There Ravan, and here Ram was loudly hailed,   4
and amid cries of "Victory! Victory!" battle was joined.
The demons sent down a barrage of craggy boulders,
but the monkeys leaped up, seized them, and threw them
    back.

५   धरि कुधर खंड प्रचंड मर्कट
भालु गढ़ पर डारहीं ।
झपटहिं चरन गहि पटकि महि भजि
चलत बहुरि पचारहीं ॥
अति तरल तरुन प्रताप तरपहिं
तमकि गढ़ चढ़ि चढ़ि गए ।
कपि भालु चढ़ि मंदिरन्ह जहँ तहँ
राम जसु गावत भए ॥

४१   एकु एकु निसिचर गहि पुनि कपि चले पराइ ।
ऊपर आपु हेठ भट गिरहिं धरनि पर आइ ॥

१   राम प्रताप प्रबल कपिजूथा ।
मर्दहिं निसिचर सुभट बरूथा ॥
चढ़े दुर्ग पुनि जहँ तहँ बानर ।
जय रघुबीर प्रताप दिवाकर ॥

२   चले निसाचर निकर पराई ।
प्रबल पवन जिमि घन समुदाई ॥
हाहाकार भयउ पुर भारी ।
रोवहिं बालक आतुर नारी ॥

३   सब मिलि देहिं रावनहिं गारी ।
राज करत एहिं मृत्यु हँकारी ॥
निज दल बिचल सुनी तेहिं काना ।
फेरि सुभट लंकेस रिसाना ॥

Seizing chunks of mountain, the raging monkeys[4]   5
and bears hurled them at the fortress.
Pouncing, they seized foes by the feet and slammed them
to the ground, and then ran off, roaring in challenge.
Extremely agile, young, and strong, and fired with rage,
those monkeys and bears climbed relentlessly
onto the citadel, and then onto houses, too,
everywhere proclaiming Ram's glorious renown.

Then each monkey, seizing a night-stalker,   41
leaped downward once more—
himself on top, his soldier-foe beneath—
and plunged to earth.

Empowered by Ram's might, the monkey legions   1
decimated hordes of demonic warriors
and, clambering onto the fort again from all sides,
shouted, "Victory to the Raghu hero, sun of splendor!"
The night-stalkers turned and fled pell-mell,   2
like cloudbanks driven by a powerful wind.
Great cries of lamentation arose in the city
as anguished women and children sobbed.[5]
With one voice, they all began cursing Ravan: 3
"Even while he reigns, he obstinately invites doom!"
When he got word of his army's disarray,
the enraged lord of Lanka sent his stalwarts back,

४ जो रन बिमुख सुना मैं काना ।
सो मैं हतब कराल कृपाना ॥
सर्बसु खाइ भोग करि नाना ।
समर भूमि भए बल्लभ प्राना ॥

५ उग्र बचन सुनि सकल डेराने ।
चले क्रोध करि सुभट लजाने ॥
सन्मुख मरन बीर कै सोभा ।
तब तिन्ह तजा प्रान कर लोभा ॥

४२ बहु आयुध धर सुभट सब भिरहिं पचारि पचारि ।
ब्याकुल किए भालु कपि परिघ त्रिसूलन्हि मारि ॥

१ भय आतुर कपि भागन लागे ।
जद्यपि उमा जीतिहहिं आगे ॥
कोउ कह कहँ अंगद हनुमंता ।
कहँ नल नील दुबिद बलवंता ॥

२ निज दल बिकल सुना हनुमाना ।
पच्छिम द्वार रहा बलवाना ॥
मेघनाद तहँ करइ लराई ।
टूट न द्वार परम कठिनाई ॥

३ पवनतनय मन भा अति क्रोधा ।
गर्जेउ प्रबल काल सम जोधा ॥
कूदि लंक गढ़ ऊपर आवा ।
गहि गिरि मेघनाद कहुँ धावा ॥

saying, "Anyone whom I hear of fleeing battle,   4
I will personally gut with my sharpest dagger.
You lapped up my largesse, enjoyed every comfort;
now, on the field, you cherish your own breath?"
When they heard these harsh words, all the soldiers,   5
frightened and ashamed, went back with renewed rage.
Thinking, "A hero's glory is to die in close combat,"
they relinquished all attachment to their lives.

Seizing diverse weapons and bellowing challenges,   42
those warriors all fell to fighting
the bears and monkeys, harassing them
with blows of their iron cudgels and tridents.

Seized with terror, the monkeys started to flee—   1
"Although, Uma," Shiva said, "they will eventually win."[6]
Some cried, "Where is Angad?" or "Where is Hanuman?"
"Where are the mighty Nal, Nil, and Dvivid?"
When Hanuman heard of the dismay of his troops,   2
that powerful one was at the western gate,
where he was doing battle with Meghnad,
but the gate did not fall, and there was great danger.
Then the son of the wind grew utterly enraged,   3
and roaring like all-powerful Death, that warrior
leaped atop the wall of Lanka's fortress,
seized a mountain peak, and charged at Meghnad.

४   भंजेउ रथ सारथी निपाता ।
     ताहि हृदय महुँ मारेसि लाता ॥
     दुसरें सूत बिकल तेहि जाना ।
     स्यंदन घालि तुरत गृह आना ॥

४३   अंगद सुना पवनसुत गढ़ पर गयउ अकेल ।
     रन बाँकुरा बालिसुत तरकि चढ़ेउ कपि खेल ॥

१   जुद्ध बिरुद्ध क्रुद्ध द्वौ बंदर ।
     राम प्रताप सुमिरि उर अंतर ॥
     रावन भवन चढ़े द्वौ धाई ।
     करहिं कोसलाधीस दोहाई ॥

२   कलस सहित गहि भवनु ढहावा ।
     देखि निसाचरपति भय पावा ॥
     नारि बृंद कर पीटहिं छाती ।
     अब दुइ कपि आए उतपाती ॥

३   कपिलीला करि तिन्हहि डेरावहिं ।
     रामचंद्र कर सुजसु सुनावहिं ॥
     पुनि कर गहि कंचन के खंभा ।
     कहेन्हि करिअ उतपात अरंभा ॥

४   गर्जि परे रिपु कटक मझारी ।
     लागे मर्दें भुज बल भारी ॥
     काहुहि लात चपेटन्हि केहू ।
     भजहु न रामहि सो फल लेहू ॥

96

He smashed his chariot, slew its driver,   4
and planted a mighty kick in the demon's chest.
A second driver, realizing the prince's distress,
put him in his chariot and rushed him home.

Angad heard that the son of the wind   43
had ventured alone onto the battlements.
Then Bali's son, too, adept in warfare,
mounted them with a playful simian leap.

Both monkeys, inflamed by battle passion,   1
yet inwardly meditating on Ram's majesty,
charged forward and climbed onto Ravan's palace,
proclaiming the victory of Kosala's king.
Seizing it by its spires, they toppled the building,   2
and to see this gave the night-stalker ruler a scare.
His women beat their breasts and wailed,
"Now two of those dreadful monkeys have come!"
Terrifying them with simian antics,   3
the two extolled the glory of Ramchandra.
Then they took hold of some gilded columns
and said, "Let's start wreaking real havoc."
Roaring, they plunged into enemy ranks   4
and began slaying them with their mighty arms.
Kicking some and slapping others, they said,
"Take your reward for not worshiping Ram!"

४४ एक एक सों मर्दहिं तोरि चलावहिं मुंड ।
राबन आगें परहिं ते जनु फूटहिं दधि कुंड ॥

१ महा महा मुखिआ जे पावहिं ।
ते पद गहि प्रभु पास चलावहिं ॥
कहइ बिभीषनु तिन्ह के नामा ।
देहिं राम तिन्हहू निज धामा ॥

२ खल मनुजाद द्विजामिष भोगी ।
पावहिं गति जो जाचत जोगी ॥
उमा राम मृदुचित करुनाकर ।
बयर भाव सुमिरत मोहि निसिचर ॥

३ देहिं परम गति सो जियँ जानी ।
अस कृपाल को कहहु भवानी ॥
अस प्रभु सुनि न भजहिं भ्रम त्यागी ।
नर मतिमंद ते परम अभागी ॥

४ अंगद अरु हनुमंत प्रबेसा ।
कीन्ह दुर्ग अस कह अवधेसा ॥
लंका द्वौ कपि सोहहिं कैसें ।
मथहिं सिंधु दुइ मंदर जैसें ॥

४५ भुज बल रिपु दल दलमलि देखि दिवस कर अंत ।
कूदे जुगल बिगत श्रम आए जहँ भगवंत ॥

Smashing one demon against another,   44
they tore off their heads, then pitched them
so they landed right in front of Ravan,
where they burst like big clay pots of curd.

Finding demon generals, they seized them   1
by their feet and hurled them before the Lord.
Vibhishan identified them all by name,
and Ram admitted them to his own blessed abode.
Vile man-eaters, who feasted on twice-born flesh,   2
obtained that state for which yogis plead.
Shiva said, "Ram is tenderhearted and merciful, Uma,
and thought, 'In animosity, these demons remember me.'[7]
Reflecting thus, he gave them the supreme state—   3
tell me, Bhavani, who else is so compassionate?
Hearing this of the Lord, one who does not shed illusion
and worship him is an utterly luckless dolt."
"Angad and Hanuman have managed to enter   4
the citadel"—so the master of Avadh declared.
There in Lanka the two monkeys looked as splendid
as dual Mount Mandaras churning the milky sea.[8]

Having smashed enemy forces with the might   45
of their arms, and seeing that day was waning,
the two leaped down with untired ease
and came to where the blessed Lord was.

१ प्रभु पद कमल सीस तिन्ह नाए ।
देखि सुभट रघुपति मन भाए ॥
राम कृपा करि जुगल निहारे ।
भए बिगतश्रम परम सुखारे ॥

२ गए जानि अंगद हनुमाना ।
फिरे भालु मर्कट भट नाना ॥
जातुधान प्रदोष बल पाई ।
धाए करि दससीस दोहाई ॥

३ निसिचर अनी देखि कपि फिरे ।
जहँ तहँ कटकटाइ भट भिरे ॥
द्वौ दल प्रबल पचारि पचारी ।
लरत सुभट नहिं मानहिं हारी ॥

४ महाबीर निसिचर सब कारे ।
नाना बरन बलीमुख भारे ॥
सबल जुगल दल समबल जोधा ।
कौतुक करत लरत करि क्रोधा ॥

५ प्राबिट सरद पयोद घनेरे ।
लरत मनहु मारुत के प्रेरे ॥
अनिप अकंपन अरु अतिकाया ।
बिचलत सेन कीन्हि इन्ह माया ॥

६ भयउ निमिष महँ अति अँधिआरा ।
बृष्टि होइ रुधिरोपल छारा ॥

100

They bowed their heads at his holy feet,   1
and the Raghu lord rejoiced to see these champions.
As Ram gazed compassionately on the pair,
they became free of fatigue and blissfully happy.
Knowing that Angad and Hanuman had left,   2
countless bear and monkey soldiers turned back,
but the demons, gaining strength as day waned,[9]
charged again, proclaiming their ten-headed king's glory.
Seeing the night-stalker legions, the monkeys returned,   3
and warriors clashed everywhere, gnashing their teeth.
Both sides, equally powerful, roared in challenge,
and the dueling champions never admitted defeat.
The night-stalker heroes were all swarthy-limbed,   4
the simians, huge and multicolored.
Both armies were strong, with warriors of equal might,
and fought, in their rage, with reckless heroism,
as if dark monsoon clouds and multihued ones of Sharad[10] 5
were clashing, driven by powerful winds.
The demon generals Akampan and Atikay,[11]
their army faltering, resorted to magic.
In an instant, it became pitch-black   6
and began to rain blood, stone, and ash.

४६ देखि निबिड़ तम दसहुँ दिसि कपिदल भयउ खभार ।
एकहि एक न देखई जहँ तहँ करहिं पुकार ॥

१ सकल मरमु रघुनायक जाना ।
लिए बोलि अंगद हनुमाना ॥
समाचार सब कहि समुझाए ।
सुनत कोपि कपिकुंजर धाए ॥

२ पुनि कृपाल हँसि चाप चढ़ावा ।
पावक सायक सपदि चलावा ॥
भयउ प्रकास कतहुँ तम नाहीं ।
ग्यान उदयँ जिमि संसय जाहीं ॥

३ भालु बलीमुख पाइ प्रकासा ।
धाए हरष बिगत श्रम त्रासा ॥
हनूमान अंगद रन गाजे ।
हाँक सुनत रजनीचर भाजे ॥

४ भागत भट पटकहिं धरि धरनी ।
करहिं भालु कपि अद्भुत करनी ॥
गहि पद डारहिं सागर माहीं ।
मकर उरग झष धरि धरि खाहीं ॥

४७ कछु मारे कछु घायल कछु गढ़ चढ़े पराइ ।
गर्जहिं भालु बलीमुख रिपु दल बल बिचलाइ ॥

Seeing utter darkness in the ten directions,   46
the monkey army fell into a panic.
Unable to see one another,
they called frantically in every direction.

But the Raghu master knew the whole secret.   1
He summoned Angad and Hanuman
and explained it all to them.
When they heard, the mighty monkeys
    rushed off, enraged.
Then the merciful one laughed, raised his bow,   2
and quickly released a fiery arrow.
There was dazzling light, darkness was no more—
as when wisdom dawns, doubt departs.
Regaining light, the bears and monkeys   3
advanced happily, free of fatigue and fear.
Hanuman and Angad roared on the field,
and just hearing their battle cry, the demons fled.
Catching the fleeing troops, knocking them to the ground, 4
the bears and monkeys performed marvelous deeds:
seizing their feet, they hurled them into the sea,
where crocodiles, serpents, and sharks caught and ate
    them.[12]

Some were slaughtered, some badly wounded,   47
some ran away and clambered into the fort.
The bears and monkeys bellowed in triumph,
having scattered, by their might, the foe's army.

१ निसा जानि कपि चारिउ अनी ।
आए जहाँ कोसला धनी ॥
राम कृपा करि चितवा सबही ।
भए बिगतश्रम बानर तबही ॥

२ उहाँ दसानन सचिव हँकारे ।
सब सन कहेसि सुभट जे मारे ॥
आधा कटकु कपिन्ह संघारा ।
कहहु बेगि का करिअ बिचारा ॥

३ माल्यवंत अति जरठ निसाचर ।
रावन मातु पिता मंत्री बर ॥
बोला बचन नीति अति पावन ।
सुनहु तात कछु मोर सिखावन ॥

४ जब ते तुम्ह सीता हरि आनी ।
असगुन होहिं न जाहिं बखानी ॥
बेद पुरान जासु जसु गायो ।
राम बिमुख काहुँ न सुख पायो ॥

४८क हिरन्याच्छ भ्राता सहित मधु कैटभ बलवान ।
जेहिं मारे सोइ अवतरेउ कृपासिंधु भगवान ॥

४८ख कालरूप खल बन दहन गुनागार घनबोध ।
सिव बिरंचि जेहि सेवहिं तासों कवन बिरोध ॥

104

Knowing night had fallen, the four monkey legions   1
returned to where Kosala's king was camped,
and as soon as Ram's gracious glance fell on them
all those forest creatures shed their fatigue.
Back in Lanka, Ravan yelled for his advisers   2
and told them all of the champions who were slain.
"Those monkeys have massacred half our army!
Tell me, quickly, what strategy to execute."
Malyavant, a most venerable night-stalker,   3
Ravan's maternal grandfather and trusted minister,[13]
spoke up, giving most prudent counsel.
"Now just listen a bit, son, to my advice:
Ever since you stole Sita and brought her here,   4
there have been ill omens, too many to recount.
He whose fame Veda and *purāṇas* declare
is Ram, and no foe of his has ever won happiness.

He who slew the golden-eyed demon and his brother,   48a
and mighty Madhu and Kaitabh, too—
that same supreme Lord, ocean of mercy,
has come down and taken birth once more.[14]

He who is Death himself, incinerating forests of sinners,   48b
the abode of virtues, perfect enlightenment,
and who is worshiped by Shiva and Brahma—
how can he be opposed?

१   परिहरि बयरु देहु बैदेही ।
भजहु कृपानिधि परम सनेही ॥
ताके बचन बान सम लागे ।
करिआ मुह करि जाहि अभागे ॥

२   बूढ़ भएसि न त मरतेउँ तोही ।
अब जनि नयन देखावसि मोही ॥
तेहिं अपने मन अस अनुमाना ।
बध्यो चहत एहि कृपानिधाना ॥

३   सो उठि गयउ कहत दुर्बादा ।
तब सकोप बोलेउ घननादा ॥
कौतुक प्रात देखिअहु मोरा ।
करिहउँ बहुत कहौं का थोरा ॥

४   सुनि सुत बचन भरोसा आवा ।
प्रीति समेत अंक बैठावा ॥
करत बिचार भयउ भिनुसारा ।
लागे कपि पुनि चहूँ दुआरा ॥

५   कोपि कपिन्ह दुर्घट गढ़ु घेरा ।
नगर कोलाहलु भयउ घनेरा ॥
बिबिधायुध धर निसिचर धाए ।
गढ़ ते पर्बत सिखर ढहाए ॥

So give up your hostility, give back Vaidehi,*   1
and give praise to that most loving sea of mercy."
His words stung like arrows, and Ravan said,
"Blacken your face and go away, accursed one!
If you were not so aged, I would kill you—   2
now, don't ever show me your face again."
Hearing this from Ravan, Malyavant surmised
that the treasury of grace was bent on slaying him.
Scolding Ravan, he arose and departed.   3
Then prince Meghnad spoke up in anger:
"Just see what feats I will perform, come morning!
I will do far more than my words could say."
His son's speech brought Ravan confidence,   4
and he affectionately seated him on his lap.
They pondered and conferred till dawn broke
and the monkeys again assailed the four gates.
Enraged simians surrounded that formidable fortress,   5
and within the city there was terrible tumult.
Bearing all sorts of weapons, night-stalkers advanced
and rained down craggy boulders from the ramparts.

---

* Sita.

६ ढाहे महीधर सिखर कोटिन्ह
बिबिध बिधि गोला चले ।
घहरात जिमि पबिपात गर्जत
जनु प्रलय के बादले ॥
मर्कट बिकट भट जुटत कटत
न लटत तन जर्जर भए ।
गहि सैल तेहि गढ़ पर चलावहिं
जहँ सो तहँ निसिचर हए ॥

४९ मेघनाद सुनि श्रवन अस गढ़ु पुनि छेंका आइ ।
उतर्यो बीर दुर्ग तें सन्मुख चल्यो बजाइ ॥

१ कहँ कोसलाधीस द्रौ भ्राता ।
धन्वी सकल लोक बिरख्याता ॥
कहँ नल नील दुबिद सुग्रीवा ।
अंगद हनूमंत बल सींवा ॥

२ कहाँ बिभीषनु भ्राताद्रोही ।
आजु सबहि हठि मारउँ ओही ॥
अस कहि कठिन बान संधाने ।
अतिसय क्रोध श्रवन लगि ताने ॥

३ सर समूह सो छाड़ै लागा ।
जनु सपच्छ धावहिं बहु नागा ॥
जहँ तहँ परत देखिअहिं बानर ।
सन्मुख होइ न सके तेहि अवसर ॥

108

They hurled down millions of mountain peaks   6
and many kinds and sizes of iron balls
that crashed like lightning bolts and thundered
like the clouds that bring on world dissolution.
The furious monkey soldiers fought with ferocity,
despite bodies riddled with wounds, and never faltered.
Seizing summits, they hurled them at the fort,
slaying night-stalkers wherever they stood.

When Meghnad heard the report   49
that the fortress was again surrounded,
that hero descended from the citadel
and came forward, bellowing:

"Where are those two brothers, lords of Kosala,   1
renowned as bowmen in all the worlds?
Where are Nal, Nil, Dvivid, and Sugriva,
and those paragons of might, Angad and Hanuman?
And where is Vibhishan, that disloyal brother?   2
Today I vow to kill you all, and especially him!"
So saying he readied his cruel arrows,
and in fury, drew his bow-string to its full extent.[15]
He released a great volley of arrows   3
that raced off like countless winged serpents.
Everywhere, monkeys were seen being felled
and none, at that moment, could dare face him.

४ जहँ तहँ भागि चले कपि रीछा ।
बिसरी सबहि जुद्ध कै ईछा ॥
सो कपि भालु न रन महँ देखा ।
कीन्हेसि जेहि न प्रान अवसेषा ॥

५० दस दस सर सब मारेसि परे भूमि कपि बीर ।
सिंहनाद करि गर्जा मेघनाद बल धीर ॥

१ देखि पवनसुत कटक बिहाला ।
क्रोधवंत जनु धायउ काला ॥
महासैल एक तुरत उपारा ।
अति रिस मेघनाद पर डारा ॥

२ आवत देखि गयउ नभ सोई ।
रथ सारथी तुरग सब खोई ॥
बार बार पचार हनुमाना ।
निकट न आव मरमु सो जाना ॥

३ रघुपति निकट गयउ घननादा ।
नाना भाँति करेसि दुर्बादा ॥
अस्त्र सस्त्र आयुध सब डारे ।
कौतुकहीं प्रभु काटि निवारे ॥

४ देखि प्रताप मूढ़ खिसिआना ।
करै लाग माया बिधि नाना ॥
जिमि कोउ करै गरुड़ सैं खेला ।
डरपावै गहि स्वल्प सपेला ॥

110

Monkeys and bears began fleeing in all directions,   4
forgetting their determination to give battle.
On the whole field, no monkey or bear could be seen
whom he had not left just barely alive.

He struck each one of them with ten arrows   50
and the monkey heroes tumbled to the ground.
Then Meghnad, mighty and resolute,
roared in triumph like a lion.

Seeing the army in distress, the son of the wind   1
was enraged and charged like Death himself.
He quickly uprooted a huge mountain
and in a fury hurled it at Meghnad,
who, seeing it coming, rose into the sky,   2
sacrificing his chariot, driver, and horses.
Though Hanuman challenged him time and again,
he would not come near, knowing the monkey's might.
Then Meghnad approached the Raghu lord,   3
taunting him with innumerable insults
and showering him with all kinds of weapons.
But the Lord, in mere play, broke and deflected them.
The fool, abashed at seeing such power,   4
began deploying many kinds of illusions,
like one who, taking on great Garuda,
brandishes a baby snake to frighten him.[16]

५१ जासु प्रबल माया बस सिव बिरंचि बड़ छोट।
ताहि दिखावइ निसिचर निज माया मति खोट॥

१ नभ चढ़ि बरष बिपुल अंगारा।
महि ते प्रगट होहिं जलधारा॥
नाना भाँति पिसाच पिसाची।
मारु काटु धुनि बोलहिं नाची॥

२ बिष्टा पूय रुधिर कच हाड़ा।
बरषइ कबहुँ उपल बहु छाड़ा॥
बरषि धूरि कीन्हेसि अँधिआरा।
सूझ न आपन हाथ पसारा॥

३ कपि अकुलाने माया देखें।
सब कर मरन बना एहि लेखें॥
कौतुक देखि राम मुसुकाने।
भए सभीत सकल कपि जाने॥

४ एक बान काटी सब माया।
जिमि दिनकर हर तिमिर निकाया॥
कृपादृष्टि कपि भालु बिलोके।
भए प्रबल रन रहहिं न रोके॥

५२ आयसु मागि राम पहिं अंगदादि कपि साथ।
लछिमन चले क्रुद्ध होइ बान सरासन हाथ॥

Before him—whose maya holds sway over all,   51
great and small, not excepting Shiva and Brahma—
that deluded night-stalker displayed
his own paltry magic.

Soaring into the sky, he rained down burning coals,   1
as great jets of water burst out of the earth
and countless kinds of male and female goblins[17]
danced about shrieking, "Kill! Maim!"
Feces, pus, blood, hair, and bones pelted down,   2
interspersed with torrents of rock and ash.
Then he released dust so thick that darkness fell
and none could see even his own outstretched hand.
When they saw these illusions, the monkeys grew   3
    distraught
and reckoned they all were surely doomed.
Beholding this farce, Ram merely smiled,
yet he knew that all his monkeys were terrified.
With a single arrow, he cut through the demonic maya   4
as the day-bringing sun dispels dense darkness.
Then he cast so gracious a look over monkeys and bears
that, reenergized, they could not be stopped on the field.

Asking Ram's permission, and accompanied   52
by Angad and other monkeys,
Lakshman went forth in anger,
taking up his arrows and bow.

१   छतज नयन उर बाहु बिसाला ।
हिमगिरि निभ तनु कछु एक लाला ॥
इहाँ दसानन सुभट पठाए ।
नाना अस्त्र सस्त्र गहि धाए ॥

२   भूधर नख बिटपायुध धारी ।
धाए कपि जय राम पुकारी ॥
भिरे सकल जोरिहि सन जोरी ।
इत उत जय इच्छा नहिं थोरी ॥

३   मुठिकन्ह लातन्ह दातन्ह काटहिं ।
कपि जयसील मारि पुनि डाटहिं ॥
मारु मारु धरु धरु धरु मारू ।
सीस तोरि गहि भुजा उपारू ॥

४   असि रव पूरि रही नव खंडा ।
धावहिं जहँ तहँ रुंड प्रचंडा ॥
देखहिं कौतुक नभ सुर बृंदा ।
कबहुँक बिसमय कबहुँ अनंदा ॥

५३   रुधिर गाड़ भरि भरि जम्यो ऊपर धूरि उड़ाइ ।
जनु अँगार रासिन्ह पर मृतक धूम रह्यो छाइ ॥

१   घायल बीर बिराजहिं कैसे ।
कुसुमित किंसुक के तरु जैसे ॥
लछिमन मेघनाद द्वौ जोधा ।
भिरहिं परसपर करि अति क्रोधा ॥

His eyes were red, his chest broad, arms thick,   1
and his body, fair as Himalaya's snow, was slightly flushed.
For his part, Ravan dispatched stalwart warriors
who raced forth clutching countless armaments.
With weapons of crags, tree trunks, and their own nails,   2
the monkeys charged, shouting, "Victory to Ram!"
Clashing, they all squared off in single combats,
with both sides equally intent on triumphing.
Pounding with fists and feet, biting with their teeth,   3
the monkeys, sure of victory, pummeled and taunted
    them.
"Strike!" "Kill!" "Seize and destroy!"
"Tear off his head!" "Grab his arms and rip them out!"
—such cries permeated all the nine regions,[18]   4
as headless torsos raced wildly here and there.
Watching the spectacle from the sky, the host of gods
was at times anxious, at times delighted.

Blood collected to fill all pits in the field,   53
and over them, dust blew,
so they looked like beds of glowing embers
shrouded in cremation smoke.[19]

With their streaming wounds, heroes appeared   1
like flame-of-the-forest trees in full bloom.[20]
The two warriors Lakshman and Meghnad
struggled with each other in immense rage,

२ एकहिं एक सकइ नहिं जीती ।
निसिचर छल बल करइ अनीती ॥
क्रोधवंत तब भयउ अनंता ।
भंजेउ रथ सारथी तुरंता ॥

३ नाना बिधि प्रहार कर सेषा ।
राच्छस भयउ प्रान अवसेषा ॥
रावन सुत निज मन अनुमाना ।
संकठ भयउ हरिहि मम प्राना ॥

४ बीरघातिनी छाड़िसि साँगी ।
तेज पुंज लछिमन उर लागी ॥
मुरुछा भई सक्ति के लागें ।
तब चलि गयउ निकट भय त्यागें ॥

५४ मेघनाद सम कोटि सत जोधा रहे उठाइ ।
जगदाधार सेष किमि उठै चले खिसिआइ ॥

१ सुनु गिरिजा क्रोधानल जासू ।
जारइ भुवन चारिदस आसू ॥
सक संग्राम जीति को ताही ।
सेवहिं सुर नर अग जग जाही ॥

२ यह कौतूहल जानइ सोई ।
जा पर कृपा राम कै होई ॥
संध्या भइ फिरि द्वौ बाहनी ।
लगे सँभारन निज निज अनी ॥

yet neither one could triumph.   2
The night-stalker fought wickedly, using deceit,
but then endless Anant* grew enraged[21]
and quickly destroyed his chariot and driver.
Shesh assaulted him in countless ways,   3
so that the demon barely clung to his breath.
That son of Ravan thought to himself,
"This is serious—he looks to take my life!"
Then he hurled the spear called "hero-slayer"—   4
a mass of fiery energy that lodged in Lakshman's chest.
He fainted when that weapon struck,
and his foe grew bold and approached him.

A billion demon warriors equal to Meghnad   54
tried to pick him up,
but how could they lift Shesh, support of the world?[22]
Abashed, they all slunk away.

Shiva said, "Girija, he whose anger is the fire   1
that instantly incinerates the fourteen worlds—
who could truly defeat in battle the one
who is worshiped by gods, mortals, and all beings?[23]
This marvel can be comprehended only   2
by one who has received Ram's grace."
As twilight fell, the two armies retreated
and began accounting for their legions.

---

* Lakshman.

३ ब्यापक ब्रह्म अजित भुवनेस्वर ।
लछिमन कहाँ बूझ करुनाकर ॥
तब लगि लै आयउ हनुमाना ।
अनुज देखि प्रभु अति दुख माना ॥

४ जामवंत कह बैद सुषेना ।
लंकाँ रहइ को पठई लेना ॥
धरि लघु रूप गयउ हनुमंता ।
आनेउ भवन समेत तुरंता ॥

५५ राम पदारबिंद सिर नायउ आइ सुषेन ।
कहा नाम गिरि औषधी जाहु पवनसुत लेन ॥

१ राम चरन सरसिज उर राखी ।
चला प्रभंजनसुत बल भाषी ॥
उहाँ दूत एक मरमु जनावा ।
रावनु कालनेमि गृह आवा ॥

२ दसमुख कहा मरमु तेहिं सुना ।
पुनि पुनि कालनेमि सिरु धुना ॥
देखत तुम्हहि नगरु जेहिं जारा ।
तासु पंथ को रोकन पारा ॥

३ भजि रघुपति करु हित आपना ।
छाँड़हु नाथ मृषा जल्पना ॥
नील कंज तनु सुंदर स्यामा ।
हृदयँ राखु लोचनाभिरामा ॥

The all-pervading God, unassailable Lord of the worlds,   3
and treasury of mercy asked, "Where is Lakshman?"
Then Hanuman brought him in, and at the sight[24]
of his young brother, the Lord felt intense sorrow.
Jambavan said, "The physician Sushen[25]   4
resides in Lanka. Who can be sent to fetch him?"
Assuming tiny form, Hanuman went
and brought him at once, house and all.

Sushen approached and bowed   55
his head at Ram's blessed feet.
Then he named a mountain and healing herb
and said, "Go, son of the wind, and bring it."[26]

Focusing his heart on Ram's holy feet   1
and affirming his own might, the tempest's son left.[27]
But back in Lanka, a spy reported the matter,
and then Ravan came to Kalnemi's abode.
Ten-head told him everything, and, listening,   2
Kalnemi beat his brow in despair and said,
"He who burned the city right before your eyes—
who is going to be able to obstruct his path?
For your own good, worship the Raghu lord   3
and give up your vain boasting, master.
His dark body, lovely as a blue lotus,
enchants the eyes—set it in your heart.

४   मैं तैं मोर मूढ़ता त्यागू ।
महा मोह निसि सूतत जागू ॥
काल ब्याल कर भच्छक जोई ।
सपनेहुँ समर कि जीतिअ सोई ॥

५६   सुनि दसकंठ रिसान अति तेहिं मन कीन्ह बिचार ।
राम दूत कर मरौं बरु यह खल रत मल भार ॥

१   अस कहि चला रचिसि मग माया ।
सर मंदिर बर बाग बनाया ॥
मारुतसुत देखा सुभ आश्रम ।
मुनिहि बूझि जल पियौं जाइ श्रम ॥

२   राच्छस कपट बेष तहँ सोहा ।
मायापति दूतहि चह मोहा ॥
जाइ पवनसुत नायउ माथा ।
लाग सो कहै राम गुन गाथा ॥

३   होत महा रन रावन रामहिं ।
जितिहहिं राम न संसय या महिं ॥
इहाँ भएँ मैं देखउँ भाई ।
ग्यान दृष्टि बल मोहि अधिकाई ॥

४   मागा जल तेहिं दीन्ह कमंडल ।
कह कपि नहिं अघाउँ थोरें जल ॥
सर मज्जन करि आतुर आवहु ।
दिच्छा देउँ ग्यान जेहिं पावहु ॥

Renounce the folly of dualism and greed,[28]   4
and awake from your sleep in delusion's night.
He who devours the serpent of deadly time—
can anyone even dream of defeating him in battle?"

Listening to him, the ten-necked one grew enraged,   56
and Kalnemi thought to himself,
"Better to die at the hand of Ram's messenger;
this villain is mired in a mass of sin."

With this, he went and fabricated an illusion   1
on Hanuman's way—a lake, shrine, and lovely garden.
The son of the wind saw the hermitage and thought,
"I will ask the sage for water to dispel my fatigue."
The demon, in false guise, looked splendid there—   2
trying to trick the messenger of maya's own Lord.
When the son of the wind presented his respects,
that "sage" began singing of Ram's virtues, saying,
"There is now a great battle between Ravan and Ram,   3
in which Ram will triumph—no doubt about that.
Though I stay here, I can see it all, brother,
for I possess immense powers of inner vision."
Hanuman asked for water and the sage offered his pot,[29]   4
but the monkey said, "So little water won't sate my thirst."
"Then go bathe in the lake," the other said, "and return at
    once;
I will initiate you so you acquire knowledge."[30]

५७ सर पैठत कपि पद गहा मकरीं तब अकुलान ।
मारी सो धरि दिब्य तनु चली गगन चढ़ि जान ॥

१ कपि तव दरस भइउँ निष्पापा ।
मिटा तात मुनिबर कर सापा ॥
मुनि न होइ यह निसिचर घोरा ।
मानहु सत्य बचन कपि मोरा ॥

२ अस कहि गई अपछरा जबहीं ।
निसिचर निकट गयउ कपि तबहीं ॥
कह कपि मुनि गुरदछिना लेहू ।
पाछें हमहि मंत्र तुम्ह देहू ॥

३ सिर लंगूर लपेटि पछारा ।
निज तनु प्रगटेसि मरती बारा ॥
राम राम कहि छाड़ेसि प्राना ।
सुनि मन हरषि चलेउ हनुमाना ॥

४ देखा सैल न औषध चीन्हा ।
सहसा कपि उपारि गिरि लीन्हा ॥
गहि गिरि निसि नभ धावत भयऊ ।
अवधपुरी ऊपर कपि गयऊ ॥

५८ देखा भरत बिसाल अति निसिचर मन अनुमानि ।
बिनु फर सायक मारेउ चाप श्रवन लगि तानि ॥

As soon as the monkey stepped into the lake,   57
a frenzied female crocodile seized his foot.
When he killed her, she assumed a divine form
and rose skyward on a celestial chariot,

saying, "Seeing you, monkey, I am freed of sin,   1
and a great sage's curse is removed, brother.[31]
But this one is no sage; he's a cruel night-stalker.
Know my words to be true, monkey."
No sooner had the *apsarā,* saying this, left,   2
than the monkey went to that night-stalker
and said, "Take my guru gift now, sage,[32]
and you can give me your mantra later."
Wrapping his tail around his head, Hanuman felled him,   3
and as he died, the demon showed his true form.
Crying, "Ram, Ram!" he gave up his life—
Hanuman heard this and left, well content.[33]
He saw the peak, but could not recognize the herb,   4
so he impulsively tore out the whole mountain,
and grasping it, was racing back through the night sky
when the monkey passed over Avadh city.

Bharat saw that enormous shape   58
and, guessing it might be a night-stalking demon,
took up a blunt arrow,
drew his bow-string to its full extent, and fired.

123

१ परेउ मुरुछि महि लागत सायक।
सुमिरत राम राम रघुनायक॥
सुनि प्रिय बचन भरत तब धाए।
कपि समीप अति आतुर आए॥

२ बिकल बिलोकि कीस उर लावा।
जागत नहिं बहु भाँति जगावा॥
मुख मलीन मन भए दुखारी।
कहत बचन भरि लोचन बारी॥

३ जेहिं बिधि राम बिमुख मोहि कीन्हा।
तेहिं पुनि यह दारुन दुख दीन्हा॥
जौं मोरें मन बच अरु काया।
प्रीति राम पद कमल अमाया॥

४ तौ कपि होउ बिगत श्रम सूला।
जौं मो पर रघुपति अनुकूला॥
सुनत बचन उठि बैठ कपीसा।
कहि जय जयति कोसलाधीसा॥

५९ लीन्ह कपिहि उर लाइ पुलकित तनु लोचन सजल।
प्रीति न हृदयँ समाइ सुमिरि राम रघुकुल तिलक॥

१ तात कुसल कहु सुखनिधान की।
सहित अनुज अरु मातु जानकी॥
कपि सब चरित समास बखाने।
भए दुखी मन महुँ पछिताने॥

124

At the arrow's impact, Hanuman fell to earth senseless,   1
yet repeating, "Ram, Ram, lord of the Raghus."
Hearing those dear words, Bharat leaped up
and anxiously hurried to where the monkey lay,
saw his distress, and hugged him to his breast,   2
but despite all efforts, he could not be aroused.
With stricken face and a heavy heart,
Bharat spoke, his eyes filling with tears:
"The cruel destiny that turned me against Ram   3
now gives me this further, awful sorrow.
But if, in my mind, speech, and bodily acts
I have only guileless love for Ram's holy feet,
may this monkey be free of distress and pain—   4
yes, if the Raghu lord is pleased with me."
As soon as he heard this, that lord of monkeys sat up
crying, "Victory! Victory to the king of Kosala!"

Then Bharat again held the monkey to his heart,   59
his body thrilling, eyes flooded with tears,
and heart unable to contain the love he felt
in recalling Ram, crown jewel of the Raghu line.[34]

"Tell me, friend," he asked, "how he is—the abode   1
of bliss—with our young brother and Mother Janaki."
As Hanuman narrated all their deeds in brief,
Bharat grew depressed and repentant at heart,

२ अहह दैव मैं कत जग जायउँ ।
प्रभु के एकहु काज न आयउँ ॥
जानि कुअवसरु मन धरि धीरा ।
पुनि कपि सन बोले बलबीरा ॥

३ तात गहरु होइहि तोहि जाता ।
काजु नसाइहि होत प्रभाता ॥
चढ़ु मम सायक सैल समेता ।
पठवौं तोहि जहँ कृपानिकेता ॥

४ सुनि कपि मन उपजा अभिमाना ।
मोरें भार चलिहि किमि बाना ॥
राम प्रभाव बिचारि बहोरी ।
बंदि चरन कह कपि कर जोरी ॥

६०क तव प्रताप उर राखि प्रभु जैहउँ नाथ तुरंत ।
अस कहि आयसु पाइ पद बंदि चलेउ हनुमंत ॥

६०ख भरत बाहुबल सील गुन प्रभु पद प्रीति अपार ।
मन महुँ जात सराहत पुनि पुनि पवनकुमार ॥

१ उहाँ राम लछिमनहि निहारी ।
बोले बचन मनुज अनुसारी ॥
अर्ध राति गइ कपि नहिं आयउ ।
राम उठाइ अनुज उर लायउ ॥

and thought, "Alas, Fate! Why was I born in this world,   2
unable to be of even the least service to the Lord?"
Yet understanding the crisis, he took courage,
and then that mighty hero addressed Hanuman:
"Friend, your arrival will be delayed   3
and your mission will fail if dawn breaks.
So climb, with your mountain, onto my arrow,
and I will propel you there, to the abode of mercy."
Hearing this, a conceit arose in the monkey's heart: 4
"How, with my weight, will an arrow move?"
But then, reflecting on Ram's infinite power,
he bowed at Bharat's feet, and humbly said,

"My lord, keeping your might in my heart,[35]   60a
I will proceed there at once, master."
So saying, and taking Bharat's leave,
Hanuman bowed at his feet and departed.

The strength of Bharat's arms, his nobility, virtue,   60b
and limitless love for the Lord's feet—
inwardly praising all these again and again,
the son of the wind sped on.

Meanwhile Ram, gazing at Lakshman,   1
grieved like an ordinary man, saying,
"Half the night is gone and the monkey is not back."[36]
Ram lifted his young brother to his breast.

२ सकहु न दुखित देखि मोहि काऊ ।
बंधु सदा तव मृदुल सुभाऊ ॥
मम हित लागि तजेहु पितु माता ।
सहेहु बिपिन हिम आतप बाता ॥

३ सो अनुराग कहाँ अब भाई ।
उठहु न सुनि मम बच बिकलाई ॥
जौं जनतेउँ बन बंधु बिछोहू ।
पिता बचन मनतेउँ नहिं ओहू ॥

४ सुत बित नारि भवन परिवारा ।
होहिं जाहिं जग बारहिं बारा ॥
अस बिचारि जियँ जागहु ताता ।
मिलइ न जगत सहोदर भ्राता ॥

५ जथा पंख बिनु खग अति दीना ।
मनि बिनु फनि करिबर कर हीना ॥
अस मम जिवन बंधु बिनु तोही ।
जौं जड़ दैव जिआवै मोही ॥

६ जैहउँ अवध कवन मुहु लाई ।
नारि हेतु प्रिय भाइ गँवाई ॥
बरु अपजस सहतेउँ जग माहीं ।
नारि हानि बिसेष छति नाहीं ॥

७ अब अपलोकु सोकु सुत तोरा ।
सहिहि निठुर कठोर उर मोरा ॥
निज जननी के एक कुमारा ।
तात तासु तुम्ह प्रान अधारा ॥

"You could never bear to see me suffer,   2
brother, and your disposition was always mild.
For my sake, you left your father and mother
to endure cold, heat, and harsh wind in the forest.
But where is that ardor now, dear brother?   3
Why don't you rise, hearing my anguished words?
Had I known that I would lose my brother in exile,
I would not have heeded those orders from father.[37]
Sons, wealth, wife, home, and family   4
come and go, time and again in this world.
Awaken, dear one, reflecting on this:
a blood brother is not easily found on earth![38]
Wretched as a wingless bird, a king cobra   5
without its gem, or a trunkless great elephant,
so will my life be without you, brother,
should senseless fate somehow keep me alive.
How can I show my face, going back to Avadh,   6
having lost, for a woman's sake, a dear brother?
Better that I endure disgrace in the world
for forfeiting a wife, which is no great loss.
Now, dishonor, as well as grief for you, child,   7
this cruel, hard heart of mine will have to bear.
You are your mother's only son,[39]
dear one, and the support of her very life.

८ सौंपेसि मोहि तुम्हहि गहि पानी ।
सब बिधि सुखद परम हित जानी ॥
उतरु काह दैहउँ तेहि जाई ।
उठि किन मोहि सिखावहु भाई ॥

९ बहु बिधि सोचत सोच बिमोचन ।
स्रवत सलिल राजिव दल लोचन ॥
उमा एक अखंड रघुराई ।
नर गति भगत कृपाल देखाई ॥

६१ प्रभु प्रलाप सुनि कान बिकल भए बानर निकर ।
आइ गयउ हनुमान जिमि करुना महँ बीर रस ॥

१ हरषि राम भेंटेउ हनुमाना ।
अति कृतग्य प्रभु परम सुजाना ॥
तुरत बैद तब कीन्हि उपाई ।
उठि बैठे लछिमन हरषाई ॥

२ हृदयँ लाइ प्रभु भेंटेउ भ्राता ।
हरषे सकल भालु कपि ब्राता ॥
कपि पुनि बैद तहाँ पहुँचावा ।
जेहि बिधि तबहिं ताहि लइ आवा ॥

३ यह बृत्तांत दसानन सुनेऊ ।
अति बिषाद पुनि पुनि सिर धुनेऊ ॥
ब्याकुल कुंभकरन पहिं आवा ।
बिबिध जतन करि ताहि जगावा ॥

She took your hand and entrusted you to me,   8
believing I would ensure your welfare and happiness.
Going back to her, how will I answer for myself?
Brother, why do you not rise and instruct me?"
Thus the liberator from grief grieved in many ways,   9
as his eyes, large and lovely as lotus petals, shed tears.
But, Uma, the Raghu king is the one, indivisible reality,
who displays human ways out of mercy for devotees.

Listening to the Lord's lamentations,   61
the army of monkeys grew anguished.
Just then, Hanuman arrived,
like the heroic mood bursting into a scene of pathos.[40]

Ram embraced Hanuman with delight,   1
for the all-knowing Lord was profoundly grateful.
Then the physician quickly applied the remedy
and Lakshman sat up, free of distress.
The Lord hugged his brother to his heart   2
as the legions of bears and monkeys rejoiced.
Then Hanuman returned the physician to Lanka
exactly as he had previously brought him.
When the ten-headed king heard this news,   3
he despaired and repeatedly beat his brow.
Then, greatly upset, he went to Kumbhakaran,
and using all sorts of efforts, woke him up.

४ जागा निसिचर देखिअ कैसा ।
मानहुँ कालु देह धरि बैसा ॥
कुंभकरन बूझा कहु भाई ।
काहे तव मुख रहे सुखाई ॥

५ कथा कही सब तेहिं अभिमानी ।
जेहि प्रकार सीता हरि आनी ॥
तात कपिन्ह सब निसिचर मारे ।
महा महा जोधा संघारे ॥

६ दुर्मुख सुररिपु मनुज अहारी ।
भट अतिकाय अकंपन भारी ॥
अपर महोदर आदिक बीरा ।
परे समर महि सब रनधीरा ॥

६२ सुनि दसकंधर बचन तब कुंभकरन बिलखान ।
जगदंबा हरि आनि अब सठ चाहत कल्यान ॥

१ भल न कीन्ह तैं निसिचर नाहा ।
अब मोहि आइ जगाएहि काहा ॥
अजहूँ तात त्यागि अभिमाना ।
भजहु राम होइहि कल्याना ॥

२ हैं दससीस मनुज रघुनायक ।
जाके हनूमान से पायक ॥
अहह बंधु तैं कीन्हि खोटाई ।
प्रथममहिं मोहि न सुनाएहि आई ॥

Aroused from sleep, that night-stalker   4
looked like the very embodiment of Death.
Kumbhakaran asked, "Tell me, brother,
why has your face become so drawn?"[41]
Then that arrogant one recounted the whole tale   5
of how he kidnapped Sita and brought her there.
"The monkeys have killed all the night-stalkers, brother,
slaughtering even our greatest warriors.
Durmukh, Devantak, man-eating Narantak,[42]   6
the mighty fighters Atikay and Akampan,
and even Mahodar and other heroes,
resolute in combat, have fallen on the field."

On hearing his ten-headed brother's words,   62
Kumbhakaran fell into despair, and said,[43]
"You stole the mother of the universe,
fool, and yet you hope to prosper?

You have not acted rightly, lord of night-stalkers,   1
so why come and awaken me now?
Even today, brother, if you relinquish your pride
and worship Ram, all will be well.
Can that Raghu lord be a mere man, Ten-head,   2
whose foot-soldier was the likes of Hanuman?
Alas, brother! It was your grievous blunder
not to have come and informed me sooner.

३ कीन्हेहु प्रभु बिरोध तेहि देवक ।
सिव बिरंचि सुर जाके सेवक ॥
नारद मुनि मोहि ग्यान जो कहा ।
कहतेउँ तोहि समय निरबहा ॥

४ अब भरि अंक भेंटु मोहि भाई ।
लोचन सुफल करौं मैं जाई ॥
स्याम गात सरसीरुह लोचन ।
देखौं जाइ ताप त्रय मोचन ॥

६३ राम रूप गुन सुमिरत मगन भयउ छन एक ।
रावन मागेउ कोटि घट मद अरु महिष अनेक ॥

१ महिष खाइ करि मदिरा पाना ।
गर्जा बज्राघात समाना ॥
कुंभकरन दुर्मद रन रंगा ।
चला दुर्ग तजि सेन न संगा ॥

२ देखि बिभीषनु आगें आयउ ।
परेउ चरन निज नाम सुनायउ ॥
अनुज उठाइ हृदयँ तेहि लायो ।
रघुपति भक्त जानि मन भायो ॥

३ तात लात रावन मोहि मारा ।
कहत परम हित मंत्र बिचारा ॥
तेहिं गलानि रघुपति पहिं आयउँ ।
देखि दीन प्रभु के मन भायउँ ॥

For, master, you have challenged that God 3
who is worshiped by Shiva, Brahma, and all deities.
The secret knowledge sage Narad imparted to me,
I would have told you, but the time has passed.[44]
Now embrace me lovingly, brother, 4
before I go and reap my eyes' reward,
by beholding that dark, lotus-eyed form
that grants release from the three torments."[45]

Remembering Ram's beauty and virtues, 63
he became, for a moment, immersed in love.
But then Ravan called for millions of jugs of liquor
and countless black buffaloes.

Devouring the buffaloes and quaffing the spirits, 1
Kumbhakaran gave a roar like a thunderclap,
then, drunk with pride and battle frenzy,
went out from the fort, taking no army with him.
When he saw him, Vibhishan came forward 2
and, falling at his feet, identified himself by name.
Kumbhakaran lifted his younger brother into his embrace,
his heart pleased, knowing he was devoted to the Raghu
    lord.
"Ravan kicked me away, brother," Vibhishan said, 3
"after I gave most thoughtful and beneficial counsel.
Pained by that, I came to the Raghu master,
and seeing my misery, the Lord's heart grew tender."

४ सुनु सुत भयउ कालबस रावन ।
सो कि मान अब परम सिखावन ॥
धन्य धन्य तैं धन्य बिभीषन ।
भयहु तात निसिचर कुल भूषन ॥

५ बंधु बंस तैं कीन्ह उजागर ।
भजेहु राम सोभा सुख सागर ॥

६४ बचन कर्म मन कपट तजि भजेहु राम रनधीर ।
जाहु न निज पर सूझ मोहि भयउँ कालबस बीर ॥

१ बंधु बचन सुनि चला बिभीषन ।
आयउ जहँ त्रैलोक बिभूषन ॥
नाथ भूधराकार सरीरा ।
कुंभकरन आवत रनधीरा ॥

२ एतना कपिन्ह सुना जब काना ।
किलकिलाइ धाए बलवाना ॥
लिए उठाइ बिटप अरु भूधर ।
कटकटाइ डारहिं ता ऊपर ॥

३ कोटि कोटि गिरि सिखर प्रहारा ।
करहिं भालु कपि एक एक बारा ॥
मुर्यो न मनु तनु टर्यो न टार्यो ।
जिमि गज अर्क फलनि को मार्यो ॥

"Child," said Kumbhakaran, "Ravan is in death's grip   4
now, so how can he heed exemplary instruction?
You are blessed, Vibhishan, truly blessed,
and have become, dear one, the jewel of our demon clan.
You have illuminated our lineage, brother,   5
by worshiping Ram, ocean of beauty and bliss.

Relinquish hypocrisy in speech, deed, and thought,   64
and adore Ram, who is steadfast in battle.
Now go, as I cannot distinguish family from foe,
for, brother, I have fallen under death's spell."

When he heard his brother's words, Vibhishan left   1
and returned to Ram, ornament of the three worlds.
 "Master, he whose body is like a mountain
and who is resolute in war—Kumbhakaran—approaches."
No sooner had the monkeys heard this   2
than those mighty ones raced forward screeching,
seized great trees and hilltops,
and rained them on him, gnashing their teeth in rage.
Repeated barrages of billions of boulders   3
loosed, in unison, by the bears and monkeys,
no more distracted him or made him flinch
than the floss of milkweed flung at an elephant.[46]

४ तब मारुतसुत मुठिका हन्यो ।
पर्यो धरनि ब्याकुल सिर धुन्यो ॥
पुनि उठि तेहिं मारेउ हनुमंता ।
घुर्मित भूतल परेउ तुरंता ॥

५ पुनि नल नीलहि अवनि पछारेसि ।
जहँ तहँ पटकि पटकि भट डारेसि ॥
चली बलीमुख सेन पराई ।
अति भय त्रसित न कोउ समुहाई ॥

६५ अंगदादि कपि मुरुछित करि समेत सुग्रीव ।
काँख दाबि कपिराज कहुँ चला अमित बल सींव ॥

१ उमा करत रघुपति नरलीला ।
खेल गरुड़ जिमि अहिगन मीला ॥
भृकुटि भंग जो कालहि खाई ।
ताहि कि सोहइ ऐसि लराई ॥

२ जग पावनि कीरति बिस्तरिहहिं ।
गाइ गाइ भवनिधि नर तरिहहिं ॥
मुरुछा गइ मारुतसुत जागा ।
सुग्रीवहि तब खोजन लागा ॥

३ सुग्रीवहु कै मुरुछा बीती ।
निबुकि गयउ तेहि मृतक प्रतीती ॥
काटेसि दसन नासिका काना ।
गरजि अकास चलेउ तेहिं जाना ॥

Then the son of the wind delivered a mighty punch   4
and he fell to earth, confounded and clutching his head.
But Kumbhakaran got up again and struck Hanuman,
who at once grew dizzy and collapsed to the ground.
Next, he threw down both Nal and Nil   5
and other champions, felling them on every side.
The monkey army panicked and fled outright,
utterly terror-stricken, with none able to face him.

He knocked out Angad and the other monkey heroes   65
together with Sugriv, and then,
jamming the monkey king into his armpit,
the incomparably mighty demon strode away.

"But Uma," Shiva said, "the Raghu lord, in human play,   1
is merely sporting, like Garuda in a den of snakes.[47]
Can he, whose merest frown devours deadly Time,
be enhanced by such a skirmish as this?
He will only further his world-sanctifying fame,   2
so people who sing of it will cross rebirth's sea."
His swoon ended, the wind's son became alert
and began looking for King Sugriv.
When Sugriv's faint, too, had passed,   3
he slipped free, and the demon thought him dead.
In a flash, the monkey bit off his nose and ears
and leaped skyward, roaring, before the giant even knew.

४   गहेउ चरन गहि भूमि पछारा ।
अति लाघवँ उठि पुनि तेहि मारा ॥
पुनि आयउ प्रभु पहिं बलवाना ।
जयति जयति जय कृपानिधाना ॥

५   नाक कान काटे जियँ जानी ।
फिरा क्रोध करि भइ मन ग्लानी ॥
सहज भीम पुनि बिनु श्रुति नासा ।
देखत कपि दल उपजी त्रासा ॥

६६   जय जय जय रघुबंस मनि धाए कपि दै हूह ।
एकहि बार तासु पर छाड़ेन्हि गिरि तरु जूह ॥

१   कुंभकरन रन रंग बिरुद्धा ।
सन्मुख चला काल जनु क्रुद्धा ॥
कोटि कोटि कपि धरि धरि खाई ।
जनु टीड़ी गिरि गुहाँ समाई ॥

२   कोटिन्ह गहि सरीर सन मर्दा ।
कोटिन्ह मीजि मिलव महि गर्दा ॥
मुख नासा श्रवनन्हि कीं बाटा ।
निसरि पराहिं भालु कपि ठाटा ॥

३   रन मद मत्त निसाचर दर्पा ।
बिस्व ग्रसिहि जनु एहि बिधि अर्पा ॥
मुरे सुभट सब फिरहिं न फेरे ।
सूझ न नयन सुनहिं नहिं टेरे ॥

Kumbhakaran grabbed his feet and hurled him down,   4
but the monkey instantly rose to strike him again,
and then that mighty hero came before the Lord,
crying, "Victory! Victory to the abode of mercy!"
Realizing that his nose and ears were severed,   5
Kumbhakaran was distressed and came on in a rage.
Awful to begin with, and now without ears and nose,
the sight of him aroused terror in the monkey army.

But screaming, "Victory! Victory! Victory   66
to the jewel of Raghus!" they dashed forward
and let loose at him, all at once,
another great volley of boulders and trees.

Raging in his battle frenzy, Kumbhakaran   1
came on like an embodiment of angry Death.
Seizing millions of monkeys, he swallowed them,
like locust swarms vanishing into a mountain cave.
Myriads he seized and smashed against his body,   2
myriads he crushed by hand and ground into the dust,
while through the vents of his mouth, nose, and ears,
masses of bears and monkeys emerged and escaped.
Drunk with war, the night-stalker was as arrogant   3
as if the creator had offered him the whole world to eat.
All the warriors retreated and could not be made to return,
for their eyes saw nothing and they were deaf to orders.

४ कुंभकरन कपि फौज बिडारी ।
सुनि धाई रजनीचर धारी ॥
देखी राम बिकल कटकाई ।
रिपु अनीक नाना बिधि आई ॥

६७ सुनु सुग्रीव बिभीषन अनुज सँभारेहु सैन ।
मैं देखउँ खल बल दलहि बोले राजिवनैन ॥

१ कर सारंग साजि कटि भाथा ।
अरि दल दलन चले रघुनाथा ॥
प्रथम कीन्हि प्रभु धनुष टँकोरा ।
रिपु दल बधिर भयउ सुनि सोरा ॥

२ सत्यसंध छाँड़े सर लच्छा ।
कालसर्प जनु चले सपच्छा ॥
जहँ तहँ चले बिपुल नाराचा ।
लगे कटन भट बिकट पिसाचा ॥

३ कटहिं चरन उर सिर भुजदंडा ।
बहुतक बीर होहिं सत खंडा ॥
घुर्मि घुर्मि घायल महि परहीं ।
उठि सँभारि सुभट पुनि लरहीं ॥

४ लागत बान जलद जिमि गाजहिं ।
बहुतक देखि कठिन सर भाजहिं ॥
रुंड प्रचंड मुंड बिनु धावहिं ।
धरु धरु मारु मारु धुनि गावहिं ॥

142

Hearing that Kumbhakaran had routed the monkey host, 4
an army of night-stalkers came running.
Ram now beheld his legions in disarray
and many divisions of enemy troops advancing.

"Sugriv, Vibhishan, and brother Lakshman— 67
you all attend to our army.
I will see to this mighty monster and his minions"—
so the lotus-eyed lord declared.

Taking up his Sharnga bow, strapping on his quiver, 1
the Raghu lord went to destroy the enemy horde.
First, the lord twanged the bow-string
and its boom deafened the foe's forces.
Then that truth-avowed one shot a hundred thousand 2
    arrows
that flew like winged and deadly serpents.
Clouds of iron-tipped arrows sped everywhere
and began tearing into dreadful demon warriors,[48]
severing feet, chests, heads, and arms, 3
till many heroes were cut into a hundred pieces.
The wounded staggered about, then fell to earth,
but great champions managed to rise and fight again.
Some, as the arrows struck, bellowed like thunderheads, 4
but many, seeing those awful missiles, simply fled.
Headless trunks ran about furiously,
howling, "Seize him!" "Grab him!" "Strike!" "Kill!"

६८ छन महुँ प्रभु के सायकन्हि काटे बिकट पिसाच ।
पुनि रघुबीर निषंग महुँ प्रबिसे सब नाराच ॥

१ कुंभकरन मन दीख बिचारी ।
हति छन माझ निसाचर धारी ॥
भा अति क्रुद्ध महाबल बीरा ।
कियो मृगनायक नाद गँभीरा ॥

२ कोपि महीधर लेइ उपारी ।
डारइ जहँ मर्कट भट भारी ॥
आवत देखि सैल प्रभु भारे ।
सरन्हि काटि रज सम करि डारे ॥

३ पुनि धनु तानि कोपि रघुनायक ।
छाँड़े अति कराल बहु सायक ॥
तनु महुँ प्रबिसि निसरि सर जाहीं ।
जिमि दामिनि घन माझ समाहीं ॥

४ सोनित स्रवत सोह तन कारे ।
जनु कज्जल गिरि गेरु पनारे ॥
बिकल बिलोकि भालु कपि धाए ।
बिहँसा जबहिं निकट कपि आए ॥

६९ महानाद करि गर्जा कोटि कोटि गहि कीस ।
महि पटकइ गजराज इव सपथ करइ दससीस ॥

In but an instant, the Lord's arrows   68
laid waste the awful demonic horde,
and then all those iron-tipped missiles
came back into the Raghu hero's quiver.

Kumbhakaran marked well how,   1
in a moment, the night-stalker host was slain.
That mighty hero grew extremely enraged
and emitted the deep roar of a lordly lion.
In a fury, he uprooted whole mountains   2
and hurled them at the greatest monkey champions,
but when Lord Ram saw those huge peaks coming,
he fired arrows that shattered them as if into dust.
Then again drawing his bow in fury, the Raghu lord   3
released a swarm of most terrible arrows
that entered the giant's body and shot out again,
like flashes of lightning in a dark thunderhead.
His black body streaming blood looked as awesome   4
as a mountain of lampblack gushing red ochre.
Seeing him in distress, bears and monkeys ran forward,
but as soon as they came near, the giant guffawed,

and then, with a deafening roar,   69
seized tens of millions of monkeys
and, like a bull elephant, slammed them to earth,
proclaiming the might of his ten-headed master.

१ भागे भालु बलीमुख जूथा ।
बृकु बिलोकि जिमि मेष बरूथा ॥
चले भागि कपि भालु भवानी ।
बिकल पुकारत आरत बानी ॥

२ यह निसिचर दुकाल सम अहई ।
कपिकुल देस परन अब चहई ॥
कृपा बारिधर राम खरारी ।
पाहि पाहि प्रनतारति हारी ॥

३ सकरुन बचन सुनत भगवाना ।
चले सुधारि सरासन बाना ॥
राम सेन निज पाछें घाली ।
चले सकोप महा बलसाली ॥

४ खैंचि धनुष सर सत संधाने ।
छूटे तीर सरीर समाने ॥
लागत सर धावा रिस भरा ।
कुधर डगमगत डोलति धरा ॥

५ लीन्ह एक तेहिं सैल उपाटी ।
रघुकुल तिलक भुजा सोइ काटी ॥
धावा बाम बाहु गिरि धारी ।
प्रभु सोउ भुजा काटि महि पारी ॥

६ काटें भुजा सोह खल कैसा ।
पच्छहीन मंदर गिरि जैसा ॥
उग्र बिलोकनि प्रभुहि बिलोका ।
ग्रसन चहत मानहुँ त्रैलोका ॥

146

The army of bears and monkeys ran away,   1
like a flock of sheep who have spied a wolf.
"Those bears and monkeys fled the field, Bhavani,"
Shiva said, "calling out in desperate anguish:
'This night-stalker is like a deadly famine   2
bent on befalling the whole monkey realm.
Ram, raincloud of compassion, killer of Khar,
dispeller of dependents' pain—protect us, protect us!'"
When he heard these pathetic cries, the supreme Lord   3
readied his bow and arrows and went forward.
Placing the army behind him, Ram,
the almighty one, angrily advanced.
Drawing his bow, he readied a hundred arrows,   4
fired, and they penetrated the demon's body.
When they struck, he began running in a rage,
causing mountains to shake and earth to tremble.
He seized and uprooted a mountain to hurl,   5
but the crest-jewel of Raghus cut off his arm.
Clutching the peak in his left hand, he charged,
but the Lord severed that arm too, toppling it to earth.
With his arms cut off, the monster had the majesty   6
of Mount Mandara deprived of its wings.[49]
He stared at the Lord with a look of such awful wrath
that he seemed ready to swallow the three worlds.

७० करि चिक्कार घोर अति धावा बदनु पसारि ।
गगन सिद्ध सुर त्रासित हा हा हेति पुकारि ॥

१ सभय देव करुनानिधि जान्यो ।
श्रवन प्रजंत सरासनु तान्यो ॥
बिसिख निकर निसिचर मुख भरेऊ ।
तदपि महाबल भूमि न परेऊ ॥

२ सरन्हि भरा मुख सन्मुख धावा ।
काल त्रोन सजीव जनु आवा ॥
तब प्रभु कोपि तीब्र सन लीन्हा ।
धर ते भिन्न तासु सिर कीन्हा ॥

३ सो सिर परेउ दसानन आगें ।
बिकल भयउ जिमि फनि मनि त्यागें ॥
धरनि धसइ धर धाव प्रचंडा ।
तब प्रभु काटि कीन्ह दुइ खंडा ॥

४ परे भूमि जिमि नभ तें भूधर ।
हेठ दाबि कपि भालु निसाचर ॥
तासु तेज प्रभु बदन समाना ।
सुर मुनि सबहिं अचंभव माना ॥

५ सुर दुंदुभीं बजावहिं हरषहिं ।
अस्तुति करहिं सुमन बहु बरषहिं ॥
करि बिनती सुर सकल सिधाए ।
तेही समय देवरिषि आए ॥

148

With a terrible roar, he ran forward, 70
spreading wide his immense maw,
while in the sky, gods and perfected beings
cried out in terror, "Woe! Alas!"

The treasury of mercy knew the gods were afraid, 1
so he drew his bow-string to its full extent,
filling the night-stalker's maw with a volley of arrows,
yet even then that mighty one did not fall to earth.
His mouth stuffed with arrows, he still ran forward, 2
like a living, onrushing quiver of Death.
Then the Lord, in anger, took up a sharp arrow
and neatly severed his head from its trunk.
That head landed in front of his ten-headed brother, 3
who grew as distraught as a cobra bereft of its gem.
Yet the awful headless torso ran on, ruining the earth,
and then the Lord sliced it into two segments
that crashed to earth like mountains falling from the sky, 4
crushing monkeys, bears, and demons beneath them.
But his radiant energy merged in the Lord's countenance,
and all the gods and sages, witnessing this, were amazed.[50]
Overjoyed, the gods began sounding kettledrums 5
and raining down blossoms amid hymns of praise.
Entreating Ram, the gods all departed,
and then the divine sage Narad approached.

६   गगनोपरि हरि गुन गन गाए ।
रुचिर बीररस प्रभु मन भाए ॥
बेगि हतहु खल कहि मुनि गए ।
राम समर महि सोभत भए ॥

७   संग्राम भूमि बिराज रघुपति
अतुल बल कोसल धनी ।
श्रम बिंदु मुख राजीव लोचन
अरुन तन सोनित कनी ॥
भुज जुगल फेरत सर सरासन
भालु कपि चहु दिसि बने ।
कह दास तुलसी कहि न सक
छबि सेष जेहि आनन घने ॥

७१   निसिचर अधम मलाकर ताहि दीन्ह निज धाम ।
गिरिजा ते नर मंदमति जे न भजहिं श्रीराम ॥

१   दिन कें अंत फिरीं द्वौ अनी ।
समर भई सुभटन्ह श्रम घनी ॥
राम कृपाँ कपि दल बल बाढ़ा ।
जिमि तृन पाइ लाग अति डाढ़ा ॥

From high in the firmament, he sang of Hari's virtues   6
in a fitting martial mood that pleased the Lord's heart,
and left, declaring, "Now quickly slay the arch villain."
Ram looked splendid on the field of battle.

On the battlefield, the Raghu lord is resplendent—   7
the incomparably mighty sovereign of Kosala.[51]
There are beads of sweat on his face, his lotus-petal eyes
are tinged with red, and drops of blood speckle his limbs.
His two arms brandish bow and arrows,
as bears and monkeys attend him on all sides.
This beauty, says his servant Tulsi, cannot be expressed
even by world-serpent Shesh with his myriad mouths.

"That vile night-stalker was a treasury of sins,"   71
Shiva said, "yet Ram gave him his own eternal abode.
Daughter of the mountain,* how dense and stupid
people are, who do not worship Lord Ram!"

At day's end, both armies retreated,   1
for the battle had greatly strained even champions.
By Ram's grace, the might of the monkey army
grew like a fire that flares when fueled with straw,

---

* Parvati.

२   छीजहिं निसिचर दिनु अरु राती ।
     निज मुख कहें सुकृत जेहि भाँती ॥
     बहु बिलाप दसकंधर करई ।
     बंधु सीस पुनि पुनि उर धरई ॥

३   रोवहिं नारि हृदय हति पानी ।
     तासु तेज बल बिपुल बखानी ॥
     मेघनाद तेहि अवसर आयउ ।
     कहि बहु कथा पिता समुझायउ ॥

४   देखेहु कालि मोरि मनुसाई ।
     अबहिं बहुत का करौं बड़ाई ॥
     इष्टदेव सैं बल रथ पायउँ ।
     सो बल तात न तोहि देखायउँ ॥

५   एहि बिधि जल्पत भयउ बिहाना ।
     चहुँ दुआर लागे कपि नाना ॥
     इत कपि भालु काल सम बीरा ।
     उत रजनीचर अति रनधीरा ॥

६   लरहिं सुभट निज निज जय हेतू ।
     बरनि न जाइ समर खगकेतू ॥

७२   मेघनाद मायामय रथ चढ़ि गयउ अकास ।
     गर्जेउ अट्टहास करि भइ कपि कटकहि त्रास ॥

152

while the night-stalkers waned, day and night,   2
like one who boasts of his own good deeds.
Ten-necked Ravan lamented loud and long,
pressing his brother's head to his heart time and again,
as the women wailed and beat their breasts,   3
lauding his great virility and martial might.
Just then, Meghnad approached
and exhorted his father with many inspiring tales.
"Just see, tomorrow, my manly valor—   4
what need to boast of it at this moment?
The might and the magic chariot I have won
from my patron god, father, I have not shown you."[52]
Such idle boasting went on till morning,   5
when myriad monkeys again assailed the four gates.
On one side were deadly bear and monkey champions,
and on the other, battle-hardened night-stalkers.
The warriors fought fiercely, each craving victory,   6
and their battle, king of birds,* is beyond description.[53]

Mounting his magical chariot   72
Meghnad took to the skies
and roared in mocking challenge,
causing panic in the monkey ranks.

---

* Garuda.

१ सक्ति सूल तरवारि कृपाना ।
अस्त्र सस्त्र कुलिसायुध नाना ॥
डारइ परसु परिघ पाषाना ।
लागेउ बृष्टि करै बहु बाना ॥

२ दस दिसि रहे बान नभ छाई ।
मानहुँ मघा मेघ झरि लाई ॥
धरु धरु मारु सुनिअ धुनि काना ।
जो मारइ तेहि कोउ न जाना ॥

३ गहि गिरि तरु अकास कपि धावहिं ।
देखहिं तेहि न दुखित फिरि आवहिं ॥
अवघट घाट बाट गिरि कंदर ।
माया बल कीन्हेसि सर पंजर ॥

४ जाहिं कहाँ ब्याकुल भए बंदर ।
सुरपति बंदि परे जनु मंदर ॥
मारुतसुत अंगद नल नीला ।
कीन्हेसि बिकल सकल बलसीला ॥

५ पुनि लछिमन सुग्रीव बिभीषन ।
सरन्हि मारि कीन्हेसि जर्जर तन ॥
पुनि रघुपति सैं जूझे लागा ।
सर छाँड़इ होइ लागहिं नागा ॥

६ ब्याल पास बस भए खरारी ।
स्वबस अनंत एक अबिकारी ॥
नट इव कपट चरित कर नाना ।
सदा स्वतंत्र एक भगवाना ॥

Spears, tridents, broadswords, and daggers,   1
and countless kinds of adamantine projectiles,
with hatchets, pikes, and boulders, he hurled down
amid a rain of countless arrows
that covered all ten directions of the sky   2
like torrents released by the clouds of Magha.[54]
Cries of "Seize!" "Bind!" and "Kill!" were heard,
yet none could perceive the attackers.
Seizing boulders and trees, the monkeys leaped skyward,   3
but, unable to see him, returned crestfallen.
Every escape route—ravines, roads, and mountain caves—
he blocked, by his wizardry, with arrow-fences.[55]
Thinking, "Where can we go?" the monkeys panicked,   4
like Mount Mandara when trapped by Indra.[56]
The son of the wind,* Angad, Nal, and Nil—
the demon confounded all these mighty ones,
then turning on Lakshman, Sugriv, and Vibhishan,   5
riddled their bodies with arrows.
At last, he engaged the Raghu lord in combat,
loosing arrows that turned, as they struck, into snakes,
so that Khar's killer† became bound by serpent-snares.   6
Though boundless and almighty, singular and flawless,
he performs, like a showman, many beguiling acts,
yet remains the eternally free and unitary God.

---

* Hanuman.
† Ram.

७ रन सोभा लगि प्रभुहिं बँधायो ।
नागपास देवन्ह भय पायो ॥

७३ गिरिजा जासु नाम जपि मुनि काटहिं भव पास ।
सो कि बंध तर आवइ ब्यापक बिस्व निवास ॥

१ चरित राम के सगुन भवानी ।
तर्कि न जाहिं बुद्धि बल बानी ॥
अस बिचारि जे तग्य बिरागी ।
रामहि भजहिं तर्क सब त्यागी ॥

२ ब्याकुल कटकु कीन्ह घननादा ।
पुनि भा प्रगट कहइ दुर्बादा ॥
जामवंत कह खल रहु ठाढ़ा ।
सुनि करि ताहि क्रोध अति बाढ़ा ॥

३ बूढ़ जानि सठ छाँड़ेउँ तोही ।
लागेसि अधम पचारै मोही ॥
अस कहि तरल त्रिसूल चलायो ।
जामवंत कर गहि सोइ धायो ॥

४ मारिसि मेघनाद कै छाती ।
परा भूमि घुर्मित सुरघाती ॥
पुनि रिसान गहि चरन फिरायो ।
महि पछारि निज बल देखरायो ॥

For the glory of battle, the Lord let himself be bound,   7
but his serpent-snares gave the gods a fright.

"Girija, he—by the repetition of whose name,"   73
Shiva said, "sages sever the snares of rebirth—
could that omnipresent one, ground of cosmic being,
ever come into bondage?

Bhavani, Ram's embodied acts   1
defy analysis by force of intellect or speech.
Realizing this, metaphysicians and ascetics,
abandoning all reason, simply worship Ram."
Having sorely afflicted the army, Meghnad   2
reappeared and began bellowing abuse.
Jambavan cried, "Stay there, scoundrel!"
At this, the demon grew still more enraged and said,
"Considering your old age, I have spared you, fool,   3
but now, wretch, you would dare challenge me?"
With this, he hurled a blazing trident,
but Jambavan caught it in his paw, ran forward,
and rammed it into Meghnad's chest.   4
That scourge of the gods swooned and fell to earth.
Then the angry bear seized his feet, spun him round,
and slammed him to the ground, showing his own might.

५ बर प्रसाद सो मरइ न मारा ।
तब गहि पद लंका पर डारा ॥
इहाँ देवरिषि गरुड़ पठायो ।
राम समीप सपदि सो आयो ॥

७४क खगपति सब धरि खाए माया नाग बरूथ ।
माया बिगत भए सब हरषे बानर जूथ ॥

७४ख गहि गिरि पादप उपल नख धाए कीस रिसाइ ।
चले तमीचर बिकलतर गढ़ पर चढ़े पराइ ॥

१ मेघनाद कै मुरछा जागी ।
पितहि बिलोकि लाज अति लागी ॥
तुरत गयउ गिरिबर कंदरा ।
करौं अजय मख अस मन धरा ॥

२ इहाँ बिभीषन मंत्र बिचारा ।
सुनहु नाथ बल अतुल उदारा ॥
मेघनाद मख करइ अपावन ।
खल मायावी देव सतावन ॥

३ जौं प्रभु सिद्ध होइ सो पाइहि ।
नाथ बेगि पुनि जीति न जाइहि ॥
सुनि रघुपति अतिसय सुख माना ।
बोले अंगदादि कपि नाना ॥

But because of his boon, the wounded demon did not 5
    die,[57]
so Jambavan grabbed his feet and hurled him into Lanka.
Meanwhile, the divine sage Narad dispatched Garuda,
who flew at once to where Ram was lying.

That lord of birds pounced on the swarm 74a
of magical serpents and devoured them,
and, released from this illusion,
all the legions of monkeys rejoiced.

With hilltops, trees, and boulders in their claws 74b
they rushed forward with renewed rage,
as the panicking night-stalkers fled
and scrambled into their fort.

When Meghnad regained consciousness, 1
he saw his father and felt utterly ashamed.
He hastened to a special cave in the mountain,
his mind set on a rite to render him invincible.
Back in camp, Vibhishan gave thoughtful counsel: 2
"Incomparably mighty and benevolent master,
Meghnad is commencing a most unholy rite.
He is a wicked sorcerer who torments the gods,
and if he manages to succeed in it, lord, 3
to defeat him then will not be easy."
Hearing this, the Raghu lord was much pleased
and summoned Angad and many other monkeys.

४ लछिमन संग जाहु सब भाई।
करहु बिधंस जग्य कर जाई॥
तुम्ह लछिमन मारेहु रन ओही।
देखि सभय सुर दुख अति मोही॥

५ मारेहु तेहि बल बुद्धि उपाई।
जेहिं छीजै निसिचर सुनु भाई॥
जामवंत सुग्रीव बिभीषन।
सेन समेत रहेहु तीनिउ जन॥

६ जब रघुबीर दीन्हि अनुसासन।
कटि निषंग कसि साजि सरासन॥
प्रभु प्रताप उर धरि रनधीरा।
बोले घन इव गिरा गँभीरा॥

७ जौं तेहि आजु बधें बिनु आवौं।
तौ रघुपति सेवक न कहावौं॥
जौं सत संकर करहिं सहाई।
तदपि हतउँ रघुबीर दोहाई॥

७५ रघुपति चरन नाइ सिरु चलेउ तुरंत अनंत।
अंगद नील मयंद नल संग सुभट हनुमंत॥

१ जाइ कपिन्ह सो देखा बैसा।
आहुति देत रुधिर अरु भैंसा॥
कीन्ह कपिन्ह सब जग्य बिधंसा।
जब न उठइ तब करहिं प्रसंसा॥

"All of you brothers, go along with Lakshman   4
and wreak havoc on that sacrificial rite.
And you, Lakshman, slay him on the field,
for seeing the gods' terror saddens me greatly.
Strike him down, using your strength and intelligence,   5
so that the power of the night-stalkers will ebb.[58]
Jambavan, Sugriv, and Vibhishan—
you three, with your troops, stay with him."[59]
When the Raghu hero had given this command,   6
Lakshman strapped on his quiver and readied his bow.
Placing the Lord's might in his heart, that resolute one,
in a voice grave as a thundering cloud, declared:
"If, today, I return without having killed him,   7
let me not be called a servant of the Raghu lord.
Though a hundred Shivas should come to his aid,
even then, I swear by the Raghu hero, to slay him."

Bowing his head at the Raghu lord's feet,   75
Anant, the infinite one, quickly departed[60]
accompanied by Angad, Nil, Mayand, Nal,
Hanuman, and other great warriors.

Approaching, the monkeys saw Meghnad seated,   1
making oblations of blood and buffalo flesh.
They all fell to disrupting the rite,
and when he did not rise, taunted him with praise.

२ तदपि न उठइ धरेन्हि कच जाई।
लातन्हि हति हति चले पराई॥
लै त्रिसूल धावा कपि भागे।
आए जहँ रामानुज आगे॥

३ आवा परम क्रोध कर मारा।
गर्ज घोर रव बारहिं बारा॥
कोपि मरुतसुत अंगद धाए।
हति त्रिसूल उर धरनि गिराए॥

४ प्रभु कहँ छाँड़ेसि सूल प्रचंडा।
सर हति कृत अनंत जुग खंडा॥
उठि बहोरि मारुति जुबराजा।
हतहिं कोपि तेहि घाउ न बाजा॥

५ फिरे बीर रिपु मरइ न मारा।
तब धावा करि घोर चिकारा॥
आवत देखि क्रुद्ध जनु काला।
लछिमन छाड़े बिसिख कराला॥

६ देखेसि आवत पबि सम बाना।
तुरत भयउ खल अंतरधाना॥
बिबिध बेष धरि करइ लराई।
कबहुँक प्रगट कबहुँ दुरि जाई॥

७ देखि अजय रिपु डरपे कीसा।
परम क्रुद्ध तब भयउ अहीसा॥
लछिमन मन अस मंत्र दृढ़ावा।
एहि पापिहि मैं बहुत खेलावा॥

When he still would not get up, they seized his hair,   2
kicked him repeatedly, and ran away.
Grabbing a trident, he pursued the fleeing monkeys,
who ran to where Ram's brother was standing.
Driven by immense rage, the demon approached,   3
roaring horribly, time and again.
The wind's son* and Angad angrily raced forth,
but with a trident blow to the chest, he toppled them both.
Then he hurled a terrible spear at Lord Anant,   4
who fired an arrow that broke it in two.
The wind's son and the crown prince† rose again
to wrathfully strike him, but he remained unhurt.
When the foe, though struck, was not killed, the heroes   5
    retreated,
and then he charged with a horrible roar.
Seeing Meghnad approaching like furious Death,
Lakshman fired off a formidable arrow,
but when he saw it coming, thunderbolt-like,   6
the villain instantly became invisible.
Then, assuming diverse forms, he continued fighting,
alternately showing and concealing himself.
Seeing that unbeatable foe, the monkeys were afraid,   7
but Lakshman, lord of serpents, grew fully enraged,
and with firm will mused thus to himself:
"I have let this sinner play long enough."

---

* Hanuman.
† Angad.

८ सुमिरि कोसलाधीस प्रतापा ।
सर संधान कीन्ह करि दापा ॥
छाड़ा बान माझ उर लागा ।
मरती बार कपटु सब त्यागा ॥

७६ रामानुज कहँ रामु कहँ अस कहि छाँड़ेसि प्रान ।
धन्य धन्य तव जननी कह अंगद हनुमान ॥

१ बिनु प्रयास हनुमान उठायो ।
लंका द्वार राखि पुनि आयो ॥
तासु मरन सुनि सुर गंधर्बा ।
चढ़ि बिमान आए नभ सर्बा ॥

२ बरषि सुमन दुंदुभीं बजावहिं ।
श्रीरघुनाथ बिमल जसु गावहिं ॥
जय अनंत जय जगदाधारा ।
तुम्ह प्रभु सब देवन्हि निस्तारा ॥

३ अस्तुति करि सुर सिद्ध सिधाए ।
लछिमन कृपासिंधु पहिं आए ॥
सुत बध सुना दसानन जबहीं ।
मुरुछित भयउ परेउ महि तबहीं ॥

४ मंदोदरी रुदन कर भारी ।
उर ताड़न बहु भाँति पुकारी ॥
नगर लोग सब ब्याकुल सोचा ।
सकल कहहिं दसकंधर पोचा ॥

Recalling the fiery might of Kosala's king,   8
he confidently readied an arrow, took aim,
and shot—and that arrow lodged in Meghnad's breast.
Dying, he abandoned all trickery, and cried,

"Where is Ram's brother, and where is Ram?"   76
and uttering this, gave up his life's breath.
"Fortunate and blessed is the mother who bore you!"
said Angad and Hanuman.[61]

Hanuman effortlessly lifted his body,   1
laid it at the gate of Lanka, and returned.
Hearing of his death, the gods and heavenly musicians
mounted their celestial chariots and came there.
They released a rain of blossoms, beat kettledrums,   2
and sang of the Raghu lord's pure renown:[62]
"Victory to you, endless serpent, support of the world,
for you, lord, have liberated all the gods."[63]
Chanting his praise, gods and perfected beings departed,   3
and Lakshman returned to Ram, ocean of compassion.
As soon as Ravan heard of his son's slaying,
he fainted and fell to the ground.
Queen Mandodari wailed in grief,   4
beating her breast and calling to him repeatedly.
The city's people were all stricken with sorrow
and began demeaning their ten-headed king.

७७ तब दसकंठ बिबिधि बिधि समुझाईं सब नारि ।
नस्वर रूप जगत सब देखहु हृदयँ बिचारि ॥

१ तिन्हहि ग्यान उपदेसा रावन ।
आपुन मंद कथा सुभ पावन ॥
पर उपदेस कुसल बहुतेरे ।
जे आचरहिं ते नर न घनेरे ॥

२ निसा सिरानि भयउ भिनुसारा ।
लगे भालु कपि चारिहुँ द्वारा ॥
सुभट बोलाइ दसानन बोला ।
रन सन्मुख जा कर मन डोला ॥

३ सो अबहीं बरु जाउ पराई ।
संजुग बिमुख भएँ न भलाई ॥
निज भुज बल मैं बयरु बढ़ावा ।
देहउँ उतरु जो रिपु चढ़ि आवा ॥

४ अस कहि मरुत बेग रथ साजा ।
बाजे सकल जुझाऊ बाजा ॥
चले बीर सब अतुलित बली ।
जनु कज्जल कै आँधी चली ॥

५ असगुन अमित होहिं तेहि काला ।
गनइ न भुज बल गर्ब बिसाला ॥

Then ten-necked Ravan tried to console   77
his women in various ways:
"All material creation is ephemeral;
ponder in your hearts and perceive this."

Ravan preached words of wisdom to them,   1
and, though vile himself, spoke holy truths.
Many, indeed, are adept at lecturing others,
but few are they who practice such teachings.
That night passed, dawn broke,   2
and the bears and monkeys besieged the four gates.
Summoning his stalwarts, the ten-faced one said,
"Anyone whose mind wavers in the face of battle—
better that he run away right now,   3
for to turn back from combat is ignoble.
By my arms' might, I have aroused great enmity,
and I myself will answer any foe who dares approach."
So he declared, then readied his wind-swift chariot   4
as all the martial instruments began to blare,
and those heroes, matchlessly mighty, went forth
like an onrushing storm of soot.
Countless evil omens appeared at that time,   5
but Ravan ignored them in the great pride of his might.[64]

६ अति गर्ब गनइ न सगुन असगुन
सत्रवहिं आयधु हाथ ते ।
भट गिरत रथ ते बाजि गज
चिक्करत भाजहिं साथ ते ॥
गोमाय गीध कराल खर रव
स्वान बोलहिं अति घने ।
जनु कालदूत उलूक बोलहिं
बचन परम भयावने ॥

७८ ताहि कि संपति सगुन सुभ सपनेहुँ मन बिश्राम ।
भूत द्रोह रत मोहबस राम बिमुख रति काम ॥

१ चलेउ निसाचर कटकु अपारा ।
चतुरंगिनी अनी बहु धारा ॥
बिबिधि भाँति बाहन रथ जाना ।
बिपुल बरन पताक ध्वज नाना ॥

२ चले मत्त गज जूथ घनेरे ।
प्राबिट जलद मरुत जनु प्रेरे ॥
बरन बरन बिरदैत निकाया ।
समर सूर जानहिं बहु माया ॥

३ अति बिचित्र बाहिनी बिराजी ।
बीर बसंत सेन जनु साजी ॥
चलत कटक दिगसिंधुर डगहीं ।
छुभित पयोधि कुधर डगमगहीं ॥

In his excessive pride, he marked neither good omens   6
nor bad—as when weapons slipped from heroes' hands,
warriors tumbled from their chariots, and horses
and elephants shrieked and fled formation.
Jackals, vultures, crows, and donkeys were heard
amid a great chorus of howling dogs,
and owls, like Death's own emissaries,
hooted most menacingly.

But could he enjoy secure wealth   78
and good auguries, or even dream of inner peace,
who was bent on oppressing beings, gripped by delusion,
addicted to lust, and hostile to Ram?

The vast army of night-stalkers advanced,   1
with its four divisions and many columns,[65]
its countless kinds of vehicles, wagons, chariots,
and array of multicolored pennants and banners.
Phalanxes of rutting elephants pressed forward   2
like monsoon clouds driven by a stiff wind,
with legions of famed warriors, colorfully attired,
all battle-hardened and adept in sorcery.
That extraordinary and splendid army   3
seemed decked out by audacious Spring himself,
and on its advance, the cosmic elephants faltered,
the sea grew agitated, and mountains quaked.

४ उठी रेनु रबि गयउ छपाई ।
मरुत थकित बसुधा अकुलाई ॥
पनव निसान घोर रव बाजहिं ।
प्रलय समय के घन जनु गाजहिं ॥

५ भेरि नफीरि बाज सहनाई ।
मारू राग सुभट सुखदाई ॥
केहरि नाद बीर सब करहीं ।
निज निज बल पौरुष उच्चरहीं ॥

६ कहइ दसानन सुनहु सुभट्टा ।
मर्दहु भालु कपिन्ह के ठट्टा ॥
हौं मारिहउँ भूप द्वौ भाई ।
अस कहि सन्मुख फौज रेंगाई ॥

७ यह सुधि सकल कपिन्ह जब पाई ।
धाए करि रघुबीर दोहाई ॥

८ धाए बिसाल कराल मर्कट
भालु काल समान ते ।
मानहुँ सपच्छ उड़ाहिं भूधर
बृंद नाना बान ते ॥
नख दसन सैल महाद्रुमायुध
सबल संक न मानहीं ।
जय राम रावन मत्त गज
मृगराज सुजसु बखानहीं ॥

It raised so much dust that the sun was hidden,   4
the wind stopped blowing, and the earth grew anxious.
Drums great and small sounded in awful cacophony,
like the rumble of clouds that augur apocalypse.[66]
Kettledrums, clarinets, and oboes blared forth   5
martial ragas that made true warriors rejoice.
All those heroes roared like mighty lions,
each extolling his own manliness and might.
Their ten-headed king said, "Listen, champions: 6
slaughter that horde of bears and monkeys,
and I will finish off the two princely brothers."
So saying, he sent his army forward.
When the monkey host got word of this,   7
they too ran forth, shouting the Raghu hero's praise.

They raced forward, huge and fearsome monkeys   8
and bears, who were all like Death himself,
as if ranges of mountains, endowed with wings,
and of many colors and shapes, flew along.
Armed with their nails and teeth, with boulders
and great tree trunks, they were potent and fearless,
and shouting, "Victory to Ram, lion-king to the crazed
elephant of Ravan!" they extolled their lord's fame.

७९ दुहु दिसि जय जयकार करि निज निज जोरी जानि ।
भिरे बीर इत रामहि उत रावनहि बखानि ॥

१ रावनु रथी बिरथ रघुबीरा ।
देखि बिभीषन भयउ अधीरा ॥
अधिक प्रीति मन भा संदेहा ।
बंदि चरन कह सहित सनेहा ॥

२ नाथ न रथ नहिं तन पद त्राना ।
केहि बिधि जितब बीर बलवाना ॥
सुनहु सखा कह कृपानिधाना ।
जेहिं जय होइ सो स्यंदन आना ॥

३ सौरज धीरज तेहि रथ चाका ।
सत्य सील दृढ़ ध्वजा पताका ॥
बल बिबेक दम परहित घोरे ।
छमा कृपा समता रजु जोरे ॥

४ ईस भजनु सारथी सुजाना ।
बिरति चर्म संतोष कृपाना ॥
दान परसु बुधि सक्ति प्रचंडा ।
बर बिग्यान कठिन कोदंडा ॥

५ अमल अचल मन त्रोन समाना ।
सम जम नियम सिलीमुख नाना ॥
कवच अभेद बिप्र गुर पूजा ।
एहि सम बिजय उपाय न दूजा ॥

With cries of "Victory!" on both sides,   79
each hero sought out his equal,
and here praising Ram, there Ravan,
they began to clash.

Ravan had a chariot and the Raghu hero did not;   1
observing this, Vibhishan grew anxious,
and out of his great love, began to doubt.[67]
Saluting Ram's feet, he said with affection:
"Master, with no chariot, shield, or even footwear,   2
how will you triumph over that mighty hero?"
The ocean of mercy replied, "Listen, friend:
the chariot of victory is of a different sort.
Valor and fortitude are that vehicle's wheels,   3
truth and virtuous conduct, its upright standards.
Its horses—strength, discernment, restraint, and
     altruism—
are harnessed by forgiveness, mercy, and equanimity,
and devotion to God is their skilled driver.   4
Detachment is its hero's shield, contentment his sword,
charity his battle ax, knowledge his keen spear,
and true wisdom is his mighty bow.
A firm and flawless heart is his quiver;   5
self-control, penance, and discipline his many arrows;
reverence for Brahmans and guru his impenetrable armor.
No other means of victory can compare to this,

६   सखा धर्ममय अस रथ जाकें ।
जीतन कहँ न कतहुँ रिपु ताकें ॥

८क   महा अजय संसार रिपु जीति सकइ सो बीर ।
जाकें अस रथ होइ दृढ़ सुनहु सखा मतिधीर ॥

८ख   सुनि प्रभु बचन बिभीषन हरषि गहे पद कंज ।
एहि मिस मोहि उपदेसेहु राम कृपा सुख पुंज ॥

८ग   उत पचार दसकंधर इत अंगद हनुमान ।
लरत निसाचर भालु कपि करि निज निज प्रभु आन ॥

१   सुर ब्रह्मादि सिद्ध मुनि नाना ।
देखत रन नभ चढ़े बिमाना ॥
हमहू उमा रहे तेहिं संगा ।
देखत राम चरित रन रंगा ॥

२   सुभट समर रस दुहु दिसि माते ।
कपि जयसील राम बल ताते ॥
एक एक सन भिरहिं पचारहिं ।
एकन्ह एक मर्दि महि पारहिं ॥

friend; one who has such a dharma-chariot 6
can nowhere be defeated by any foe.

Even that awful enemy—invincible samsara— 80a
can be bested by the hero
who possesses this infallible chariot.
Know this, my friend of firm wisdom."

When he had heard the Lord's speech, 80b
Vibhishan joyfully clasped his spotless feet.
"You use this pretext to instruct me, Ram,
for you are the treasury of mercy and bliss."

Meanwhile, Ravan bellowed in challenge, 80c
as did, on this side, Angad and Hanuman.
Night-stalkers, bears, and monkeys fought fiercely,
each invoking his respective lord.

Brahma and the gods, with many perfected ones and sages 1
observed the battle from celestial chariots.
I too was among them, Uma,
watching Ram's noble deeds in his martial play.
Fighters on both sides were delirious with the zeal of war, 2
but the monkeys had the advantage of Ram's might.
They grappled singly, shouting challenges,
each pummeling his opponent and hurling him to earth.

३ मारहिं काटहिं धरहिं पछारहिं ।
सीस तोरि सीसन्ह सन मारहिं ॥
उदर बिदारहिं भुजा उपारहिं ।
गहि पद अवनि पटकि भट डारहिं ॥

४ निसिचर भट महि गाड़हिं भालू ।
ऊपर ढारि देहिं बहु बालू ॥
बीर बलीमुख जुद्ध बिरुद्धे ।
देखिअत बिपुल काल जनु क्रुद्धे ॥

५ क्रुद्धे कृतांत समान कपि तन
स्रवत सोनित राजहीं ।
मर्दहिं निसाचर कटक भट
बलवंत घन जिमि गाजहीं ॥
मारहिं चपेटन्हि डाटि दातन्ह
काटि लातन्ह मीजहीं ।
चिक्करहिं मर्कट भालु छल बल
करहिं जेहिं खल छीजहीं ॥

They struck, bit, seized, and toppled their foes, 3
and severing heads, used them as weapons.
They ripped open bellies, tore out arms,
and, seizing warriors by the feet, slammed them to the
    ground.
Bear soldiers buried their night-stalker foes 4
and threw piles of sand over them.[68]
In their battle offensive, the heroic monkeys
looked like countless embodiments of angry Death.

Like enraged embodiments of the annihilator of all, 5
the monkeys, their limbs streaming blood, looked
    glorious.
Those mighty warriors decimated the night-stalker army,
all the while roaring like thunderheads.
Taunting them, they delivered powerful slaps,
savaged them with teeth, and pounded them with kicks.
Bellowing fiercely, monkeys and bears deployed
every stratagem so that those evildoers perished.

६ धरि गाल फारहिं उर बिदारहिं
गल अँतावरि मेलहीं ।
प्रह्लादपति जनु बिबिध तनु धरि
समर अंगन खेलहीं ॥
धरु मारु काटु पछारु घोर
गिरा गगन महि भरि रही ।
जय राम जो तृन ते कुलिस कर
कुलिस ते कर तृन सही ॥

८१ निज दल बिचलत देखेसि बीस भुजाँ दस चाप ।
रथ चढ़ि चलेउ दसानन फिरहु फिरहु करि दाप ॥

१ धायउ परम क्रुद्ध दसकंधर ।
सन्मुख चले हूह दै बंदर ॥
गहि कर पादप उपल पहारा ।
डारेन्हि ता पर एकहिं बारा ॥

२ लागहिं सैल बज्र तन तासू ।
खंड खंड होइ फूटहिं आसू ॥
चला न अचल रहा रथ रोपी ।
रन दुर्मद रावन अति कोपी ॥

३ इत उत झपटि दपटि कपि जोधा ।
मर्दै लाग भयउ अति क्रोधा ॥
चले पराइ भालु कपि नाना ।
त्राहि त्राहि अंगद हनुमाना ॥

178

They ripped into jowls, and splitting open bellies,   6
pulled out the guts to drape around their necks—
as if Prahlad's lord, assuming countless forms,
was sporting on the field of war.[69]
Awful cries of "Seize!" "Strike!" "Bite!"
and "Throw down!" filled earth and sky.
Victory to Ram, who makes a blade of straw a thunderbolt,
and reduces a thunderbolt to a blade of straw.

When Ravan beheld his army in disarray,   81
he seized ten bows in his twenty arms,
and, mounted on his chariot, rode forth,
brazenly bellowing, "Back! Back to battle!"

The ten-headed one raced on in great fury,   1
and before him came monkeys, screeching excitedly,[70]
their paws gripping trees, boulders, and whole hills,
which they all hurled at him in unison.
But when those summits struck his adamantine frame,   2
they quickly broke into bits and fell away.
He halted his chariot and stood there immovable—
Ravan, intoxicated with battle and in utter rage.
Laying about him, cursing, he seized monkey warriors   3
and began to crush them in a frenzy of wrath.
Bears and monkeys fled him en masse,
crying, "Angad, Hanuman—save us, save us!

४ पाहि पाहि रघुबीर गोसाईं।
यह खल खाइ काल की नाईं॥
तेहिं देखे कपि सकल पराने।
दसहुँ चाप सायक संधाने॥

५ संधानि धनु सर निकर छाड़ेसि
उरग जिमि उड़ि लागहीं।
रहे पूरि सर धरनी गगन दिसि
बिदिसि कहँ कपि भागहीं॥
भयो अति कोलाहल बिकल कपि
दल भालु बोलहिं आतुरे।
रघुबीर करुना सिंधु आरत
बंधु जन रच्छक हरे॥

८२ निज दल बिकल देखि कटि कसि निषंग धनु हाथ।
लछिमन चले क्रुद्ध होइ नाइ राम पद माथ॥

१ रे खल का मारसि कपि भालू।
मोहि बिलोकु तोर मैं कालू॥
खोजत रहेउँ तोहि सुतघाती।
आजु निपाति जुड़ावउँ छाती॥

Protect us, protect us, great lord, Raghu hero,   4
for this villain devours us like almighty Death!"
When Ravan saw the monkeys fleeing wholesale,
he set arrows on all ten of his bows.

Setting arrows on his bows, he discharged a volley of them   5
and they flew like serpents and struck hard.
The earth, the firmament, and all the ten directions
were filled with arrows—where could the monkeys
    escape?
Seized with utter panic, the distraught army
of monkeys and bears cried out piteously,
"Hero of the Raghus, ocean of mercy, brother
of the afflicted, protector of your people, Lord Hari!"

When he saw their army in anguish,   82
Lakshman strapped on his quiver, took bow in hand,
and, having bowed his head at Ram's feet,
went forth in a fury, crying,

"Scoundrel, why assault these monkeys and bears?   1
See me now before you, for I am your death!"
Ravan replied, "It's you I've been after, slayer of my son.
Killing you today, I will get some consolation."

२ अस कहि छाड़ेसि बान प्रचंडा ।
लछिमन किए सकल सत खंडा ॥
कोटिन्ह आयुध रावन डारे ।
तिल प्रवान करि काटि निवारे ॥

३ पुनि निज बानन्ह कीन्ह प्रहारा ।
स्यंदनु भंजि सारथी मारा ॥
सत सत सर मारे दस भाला ।
गिरि सृंगन्ह जनु प्रबिसहिं ब्याला ॥

४ पुनि सत सर मारा उर माहीं ।
परेउ धरनि तल सुधि कछु नाहीं ॥
उठा प्रबल पुनि मुरुछा जागी ।
छाड़िसि ब्रह्म दीन्हि जो साँगी ॥

५ सो ब्रह्म दत्त प्रचंड सक्ति
अनंत उर लागी सही ।
पर्यो बीर बिकल उठाव दसमुख
अतुल बल महिमा रही ॥
ब्रह्मांड भवन बिराज जाकें
एक सिर जिमि रज कनी ।
तेहि चह उठावन मूढ़ रावन
जान नहिं त्रिभुअन धनी ॥

८३ देखि पवनसुत धायउ बोलत बचन कठोर ।
आवत कपिहि हन्यो तेहिं मुष्टि प्रहार प्रघोर ॥

Then he discharged a volley of deadly arrows   2
but Lakshman reduced them to hundreds of fragments.
Ravan hurled billions of weapons at him
but he pulverized and deflected all of them.[71]
Then Lakshman released a torrent of arrows,   3
smashing Ravan's chariot and killing its driver.
He sank a hundred into each of his ten foreheads,
like snakes diving into a many-peaked mountain,
then discharged a hundred into Ravan's breast   4
so that he lost all consciousness and fell to earth.
But when his faint passed, that mighty one rose
and hurled the fatal spear given him by Brahma.

That all-powerful spear, gifted by Brahma,   5
flew unerringly to lodge in Anant's* breast,
and the hero collapsed senseless, but when Ten-head tried
to lift him with his own matchless strength, he failed.[72]
That cosmic serpent—on just one of whose hoods
the universe of worlds glimmers like a dust mote—
foolish Ravan sought to lift, not knowing him
as master of the three worlds.

When the son of the wind saw this,   83
he raced over, shouting angrily.
As soon as the monkey arrived, Ravan
assaulted him with a rain of deadly blows.

* Lakshman's.

183

१   जानु टेकि कपि भूमि न गिरा ।
उठा सँभारि बहुत रिस भरा ॥
मुठिका एक ताहि कपि मारा ।
परेउ सैल जनु बज्र प्रहारा ॥

२   मुरुछा गै बहोरि सो जागा ।
कपि बल बिपुल सराहन लागा ॥
धिग धिग मम पौरुष धिग मोही ।
जौं तैं जिअत रहेसि सुरद्रोही ॥

३   अस कहि लछिमन कहुँ कपि ल्यायो ।
देखि दसानन बिसमय पायो ॥
कह रघुबीर समुझु जियँ भ्राता ।
तुम्ह कृतांत भच्छक सुर त्राता ॥

४   सुनत बचन उठि बैठ कृपाला ।
गई गगन सो सकति कराला ॥
पुनि कोदंड बान गहि धाए ।
रिपु सन्मुख अति आतुर आए ॥

Though knocked to his knees, the monkey did not fall,   1
but soon recovered and rose, filled with rage.
Hanuman hit Ravan with one mighty punch
and he crumpled like a lightning-struck summit,
but alert again, once his dizziness passed,   2
he began to laud the monkey's great strength.
"Shame on my virility," said Hanuman, "and on me, too,
since you, foe of the gods, are still alive!"
Saying this, the monkey carried Lakshman away,   3
leaving his ten-faced foe wonderstruck.
The Raghu hero said, "Brother, know in your heart
that you devour even Death, and are savior of the gods."
As soon as he heard this, merciful Lakshman sat up   4
and that awful weapon flew off into the skies.
Then, seizing his great bow and arrows, he ran
and quickly returned to face their foe.

५ आतुर बहोरि बिभंजि स्यंदन
सूत हति ब्याकुल कियो ।
गिर्यो धरनि दसकंधर बिकलतर
बान सत बेध्यो हियो ॥
सारथी दूसर घालि रथ तेहि
तुरत लंका लै गयो ।
रघुबीर बंधु प्रताप पुंज
बहोरि प्रभु चरनन्हि नयो ॥

८४ उहाँ दसानन जागि करि करै लाग कछु जग्य ।
राम बिरोध बिजय चह सठ हठ बस अति अग्य ॥

१ इहाँ बिभीषन सब सुधि पाई ।
सपदि जाइ रघुपतिहि सुनाई ॥
नाथ करइ रावन एक जागा ।
सिद्ध भएँ नहिं मरिहि अभागा ॥

२ पठवहु नाथ बेगि भट बंदर ।
करहिं बिधंस आव दसकंधर ॥
प्रात होत प्रभु सुभट पठाए ।
हनुमदादि अंगद सब धाए ॥

३ कौतुक कूदि चढ़े कपि लंका ।
पैठे रावन भवन असंका ॥
जग्य करत जबहीं सो देखा ।
सकल कपिन्ह भा क्रोध बिसेषा ॥

186

He came quickly and again smashed his chariot,   5
slew its driver, and left Ravan in dismay.
That ten-necked one toppled to earth in utter confusion,
his breast pierced by a hundred arrows,
but another charioteer thrust him in his vehicle
and rushed him back to Lanka.
Then the Raghu hero's brother, treasury of fiery might,
bowed once more at his lord's feet.

Meanwhile Ravan had again revived   84
and now began performing certain rites,
for that fool of a foe of Ram, impelled by obstinacy
and dense ignorance, yet craved victory.

In the camp, Vibhishan got word of all this   1
and went at once to tell the Raghu lord.
"Master, Ravan is performing a fire rite,
and should it succeed, the wretch will not die.
Quickly dispatch your monkey champions, lord,   2
to wreck it and bring him back to the field."
At daybreak, lord Ram sent his best warriors—
Hanuman, Angad, and others—who raced forth.
Leaping playfully, the monkeys clambered into Lanka   3
and fearlessly entered Ravan's own palace.
Catching sight of him engaged in his ritual,
they all became furious and cried,

४ रन ते निलज भाजि गृह आवा ।
इहाँ आइ बक ध्यान लगावा ॥
अस कहि अंगद मारा लाता ।
चितव न सठ स्वारथ मन राता ॥

५ नहिं चितव जब करि कोप कपि गहि
दसन लातन्ह मारहीं ।
धरि केस नारि निकारि बाहेर
तेऽतिदीन पुकारहीं ॥
तब उठेउ क्रुद्ध कृतांत सम गहि
चरन बानर डारई ।
एहि बीच कपिन्ह बिधंस कृत मख
देखि मन महुँ हारई ॥

८५ जग्य बिधंसि कुसल कपि आए रघुपति पास ।
चलेउ निसाचर क्रुद्ध होइ त्यागि जिवन कै आस ॥

१ चलत होहिं अति असुभ भयंकर ।
बैठहिं गीध उड़ाइ सिरन्ह पर ॥
भयउ कालबस काहु न माना ।
कहेसि बजावहु जुद्ध निसाना ॥

"Shameless one! You fled the field to run home,   4
and here flaunt false piety, like a crafty heron."[73]
So Angad declared and gave him a mighty kick,
but the villain, bent on his own end, took no notice.

When he took no notice, the monkeys grew enraged   5
and attacked him with their teeth while delivering kicks.
Seizing his women by the hair, they dragged them
from the house as they wailed most piteously.
At that, he leaped up like an angry god of death,
seizing monkeys by their feet and hurling them down.
But meanwhile they had trashed his fire altar,
and when he saw that, his heart sank.

Having ruined the rite, those clever monkeys   85
returned to their Raghu lord,
and the night-stalker king came forth in fury,
abandoning all hope of survival.

As he went, there were most frightful ill omens—   1
vultures flocked to perch on his many heads—
but in imminent death's grip, he heeded nothing.
"Sound the war drums!" he shouted,

२ चली तमीचर अनी अपारा ।
बहु गज रथ पदाति असवारा ॥
प्रभु सन्मुख धाए खल कैसें ।
सलभ समूह अनल कहँ जैसें ॥

३ इहाँ देवतन्ह अस्तुति कीन्ही ।
दारुन बिपति हमहि एहिं दीन्ही ॥
अब जनि राम खेलावहु एही ।
अतिसय दुखित होति बैदेही ॥

४ देव बचन सुनि प्रभु मुसुकाना ।
उठि रघुबीर सुधारे बाना ॥
जटा जूट दृढ़ बाँधें माथे ।
सोहहिं सुमन बीच बिच गाथे ॥

५ अरुन नयन बारिद तनु स्यामा ।
अखिल लोक लोचनाभिरामा ॥
कटितट परिकर कस्यो निषंगा ।
कर कोदंड कठिन सारंगा ॥

and the vast demon army advanced 2
with many elephants, chariots, foot soldiers, and cavalry.
They raced forward to face the Lord
like a cloud of locusts rushing to a flame.
For their part, the gods made prayerful petition: 3
"This demon has brought us awful affliction.
Now, don't play with him anymore, Ram,
for your Vaidehi is suffering terribly."
The Lord smiled at the gods' speech;[74] 4
then the Raghu hero rose and readied his arrows.
He tied his matted plaits firmly above his forehead—
how lovely they looked, all braided with blossoms.
His eyes reddish, body dark as a thundercloud, 5
he delighted the eyes of all the worlds
as he fastened his waistband, securing his quiver,
and took his mighty bow, Sharnga, in hand.

६ सारंग कर सुंदर निषंग
सिलीमुखाकर कटि कस्यो ।
भुजदंड पीन मनोहरायत
उर धरासुर पद लस्यो ॥
कह दास तुलसी जबहिं प्रभु सर
चाप कर फेरन लगे ।
ब्रह्मांड दिग्गज कमठ अहि महि
सिंधु भूधर डगमगे ॥

८६ सोभा देखि हरषि सुर बरषहिं सुमन अपार ।
जय जय जय करुनानिधि छबि बल गुन आगार ॥

१ एहीं बीच निसाचर अनी ।
कसमसात आई अति घनी ॥
देखि चले सन्मुख कपि भट्टा ।
प्रलयकाल के जनु घन घट्टा ॥

२ बहु कृपान तरवारि चमंकहिं ।
जनु दहँ दिसि दामिनीं दमंकहिं ॥
गज रथ तुरग चिकार कठोरा ।
गर्जहिं मनहुँ बलाहक घोरा ॥

३ कपि लंगूर बिपुल नभ छाए ।
मनहुँ इंद्रधनु उए सुहाए ॥
उठइ धूरि मानहुँ जलधारा ।
बान बुंद भै बृष्टि अपारा ॥

The Sharnga bow was in his lovely hand, 6
an inexhaustible quiver fastened at his waist.
His arms were thick and strong, and on his broad,
beguiling chest the Brahman's foot-mark gleamed.[75]
His servant Tulsi says: As soon as the Lord took up
arrows and bow and brandished them threateningly,
the cosmos, its supporting elephants, tortoise, and
    serpent,
and the earth, sea, and mountains all trembled.

Rejoicing at his loveliness, the gods 86
showered down countless blossoms,
crying, "Victory! Victory to the all-merciful
treasury of beauty, strength, and virtue!"

Meanwhile, the night-stalker legions, 1
dense and clamorous, had approached.
Seeing this, monkey warriors advanced to face them
like the massed thunderheads of doomsday.[76]
Countless scimitars and long swords glittered 2
like lightning flashes in the ten directions,
and the tumult of elephants, chariots, and horses
was like the frightful rumbling of rain clouds.
The long tails of the monkey host curved skyward 3
like ascending rainbows—lovely emblems of Indra.[77]
Vast clouds of dust, like distant storms,
soon became a downpour of countless arrow-drops.[78]

४ दुहुँ दिसि पर्बत करहिं प्रहारा ।
बज्रपात जनु बारहिं बारा ॥
रघुपति कोपि बान झरि लाइ ।
घायल भै निसिचर समुदाई ॥

५ लागत बान बीर चिक्करहीं ।
घुर्मि घुर्मि जहँ तहँ महि परहीं ॥
स्त्रवहिं सैल जनु निर्झर भारी ।
सोनित सरि कादर भयकारी ॥

६ कादर भयंकर रुधिर सरिता
चली परम अपावनी ।
दोउ कूल दल रथ रेत चक्र
अबर्त बहति भयावनी ॥
जलजंतु गज पदचर तुरग खर
बिबिध बाहन को गने ।
सर सक्ति तोमर सर्प चाप
तरंग चर्म कमठ घने ॥

८७ बीर परहिं जनु तीर तरु मज्जा बहु बह फेन ।
कादर देखि डरहिं तहँ सुभटन्ह के मन चेन ॥

Mountains, hurled from both directions, struck 4
like continual claps of thunder.
Roused to anger, Lord Raghu released a rain of arrows
that badly wounded the night-stalker legions.
As his arrows struck, warriors shrieked in pain, 5
staggered about, then fell to earth on all sides,
their wounds gushing like mountain cascades
to form a torrent of blood, terrifying to the timid.

Causing terror in cowards, that river of blood 6
surged along in supreme unholiness.
The two armies were its banks, smashed chariots
its gravel, their wheels, eddies in its horrific flow.
Its aquatic creatures were slain elephants, infantry,
horses, mules, and diverse vehicles, too many to count.
Arrows, lances, and spears were its water snakes,
longbows its waves, and shields its packs of tortoises.

Great heroes toppled like trees on its banks, 87
and bobbing bone marrow was its plentiful foam.
But though cowards were frightened on seeing it,
the minds of stalwart warriors stayed calm.

१ मज्झहिं भूत पिसाच बेताला ।
प्रमथ महा झोटिंग कराला ।
काक कंक लै भुजा उड़ाहीं ।
एक ते छीनि एक लै खाहीं ॥

२ एक कहहिं ऐसिउ सौंघाई ।
सठहु तुम्हार दरिद्र न जाई ॥
कहँरत भट घायल तट गिरे ।
जहँ तहँ मनहुँ अर्धजल परे ॥

३ खैंचहिं गीध आँत तट भए ।
जनु बंसी खेलत चित दए ॥
बहु भट बहहिं चढ़े खग जाहीं ।
जनु नाविर खेलहिं सरि माहीं ॥

४ जोगिनि भरि भरि खप्पर संचहिं ।
भूत पिसाच बधू नभ नंचहिं ॥
भट कपाल करताल बजावहिं ।
चामुंडा नाना बिधि गावहिं ॥

५ जंबुक निकर कटक्कट कट्टहिं ।
खाहिं हुआहिं अघाहिं दपट्टहिं ॥
कोटिन्ह रुंड मुंड बिनु डोल्लहिं ।
सीस परे महि जय जय बोल्लहिं ॥

For bathers, it had ghosts, goblins, vampires,[79]   1
and awful minions of Rudra, bristling with stiff hair.
Crows and buzzards flew off with severed arms,
snatching them from each other and devouring them.
One of them said, "There's such plenty here,   2
and you fools act as though you are needy."
Moaning, wounded warriors lay fallen on the bank
on all sides, like half-immersed corpses on a ghat.[80]
Vultures drew out entrails, then stood on the shore   3
like attentive fishermen angling for a catch.
Birds perched on the many drifting corpses,
as if enjoying a boating party in midriver.
Yoginis filled cranial cups brimful with blood,   4
and ghost and goblin women danced in the air,
while, to the cymbal-clash of heroes' skulls,
fierce battlefield goddesses sang raucously.[81]
Packs of jackals noisily gnawed, jaws chattering,   5
as they ate their fill, howled, and barked at one another.
Headless trunks by the millions wandered about,
as heads, just fallen to earth, still shouted, "Victory!"

६ बोल्लहिं जो जय जय मुंड रुंड
प्रचंड सिर बिनु धावहीं ।
खप्परिन्ह खग्ग अलुज्झि जुज्झहिं
सुभट भटन्ह ढहावहीं ॥
बानर निसाचर निकर मर्दहिं
राम बल दर्पित भए ।
संग्राम अंगन सुभट सोवहिं
राम सर निकरन्हि हए ॥

८८ रावन हृदयँ बिचारा भा निसिचर संघार ।
मैं अकेल कपि भालु बहु माया करौं अपार ॥

१ देवन्ह प्रभुहि पयादें देखा ।
उपजा उर अति छोभ बिसेषा ॥
सुरपति निज रथ तुरत पठावा ।
हरष सहित मातलि लै आवा ॥

२ तेज पुंज रथ दिब्य अनूपा ।
हरषि चढ़े कोसलपुर भूपा ॥
चंचल तुरग मनोहर चारी ।
अजर अमर मन सम गतिकारी ॥

३ रथारूढ़ रघुनाथहि देखी ।
धाए कपि बलु पाइ बिसेषी ॥
सही न जाइ कपिन्ह कै मारी ।
तब रावन माया बिस्तारी ॥

Severed heads cried, "Victory! Victory!"   6
even as their headless trunks dashed madly about.
Trapped in skulls, carrion birds fought wildly,
while stalwart warriors went on felling others.
The monkeys slaughtered the demonic horde,
emboldened by Ram's own might,
and in that courtyard of carnage, great champions slept,
slain by Ram's relentless arrows.

Ravan knew in his heart   88
that his night-stalkers were finished.
"I am alone, the monkeys and bears, many,
so let me fabricate a powerful illusion."

The gods saw the Lord fighting on foot   1
and became inwardly depressed.
Their king quickly sent his own chariot
and Matali* happily brought it to Ram—
a matchless divine vehicle, ablaze with splendor—   2
and Kosala's monarch gladly mounted it.
Its four frisky horses were enchanting,
forever young, and swift as thought.
Seeing their Raghu master on this chariot,   3
the monkeys charged with renewed vigor,
and when their onslaught grew unbearable,
Ravan generated a vast deception.

* Indra's charioteer.

४   सो माया रघुबीरहि बाँची ।
लछिमन कपिन्ह सो मानी साँची ॥
देखी कपिन्ह निसाचर अनी ।
अनुज सहित बहु कोसलधनी ॥

५   बहु राम लछिमन देखि मर्कट
भालु मन अति अपडरे ।
जनु चित्र लिखित समेत लछिमन
जहँ सो तहँ चितवहिं खरे ॥
निज सेन चकित बिलोकि हँसि
सर चाप सजि कोसलधनी ।
माया हरी हरि निमिष महुँ
हरषी सकल मर्कट अनी ॥

८९   बहुरि राम सब तन चितइ बोले बचन गँभीर ।
द्वंदजुद्ध देखहु सकल श्रमित भए अति बीर ॥

१   अस कहि रथ रघुनाथ चलावा ।
बिप्र चरन पंकज सिरु नावा ॥
तब लंकेस क्रोध उर छावा ।
गर्जत तर्जत सन्मुख धावा ॥

The Raghu hero alone saw through that maya,[82]   4
but Lakshman and the monkeys took it as real,
and beheld, amid the night-stalker army,
countless kings of Kosala along with his brother.

Seeing countless pairs of Ram and Lakshman,   5
the monkeys and bears were dumbstruck with fear.
Frozen as if in a painting, along with Lakshman,
they all just stood there, staring in disbelief.
Marking his soldiers' stupefaction, Kosala's lord
laughed and placed an arrow on his bow.
In one instant Lord Hari lifted that illusion[83]
to the great joy of the whole monkey host.

Then Ram looked toward them all   89
and solemnly declared,
"Now witness our single combat,
for all you heroes are much fatigued."

Saying this, the Raghu lord advanced his chariot,   1
after bowing his head to the seers' holy feet.
Then rage filled the Lankan king's heart
and he raced forward to face him, roaring challenges.

२ जीतेहु जे भट संजुग माहीं ।
सुनु तापस मैं तिन्ह सम नाहीं ॥
रावन नाम जगत जस जाना ।
लोकप जाकें बंदीखाना ॥

३ खर दूषन बिराध तुम्ह मारा ।
बधेहु ब्याध इव बालि बिचारा ॥
निसिचर निकर सुभट संघारेहु ।
कुंभकरन घननादहि मारेहु ॥

४ आजु बयरु सबु लेउँ निबाही ।
जौं रन भूप भाजि नहिं जाही ॥
आजु करउँ खलु काल हवाले ।
परेहु कठिन रावन के पाले ॥

५ सुनि दुर्बचन कालबस जाना ।
बिहँसि बचन कह कृपानिधाना ॥
सत्य सत्य सब तव प्रभुताई ।
जल्पसि जनि देखाउ मनुसाई ॥

६ जनि जल्पना करि सुजसु नासहि
नीति सुनहि करहि छमा ।
संसार महँ पूरुष त्रिबिध
पाटल रसाल पनस समा ॥

"Those warriors whom you've beaten in battle—   2
listen well, ascetic—I am not like them.
Ravan is my name, the world knows my fame—
how I locked up the very lords of the cosmos.[84]
True, you slew Khar, Dushan, and Viradh,   3
and killed poor Bali on the sly, like a poacher.
You slaughtered legions of night-stalker warriors,
and even Kumbhakaran and Meghnad.
But today I will settle all these scores,   4
unless, earthly king, you flee the field.
Today, scoundrel, I will hand you over to Death,
for you have fallen into Ravan's fatal grip."[85]
At these harsh words, and knowing him to be doomed,   5
the sea of mercy merely smiled and said:
"Your greatness is truly as you say,
but now, don't babble. Show your manhood.

Do not, by babbling on, destroy your great renown,   6
and pardon me, but heed this prudent counsel:
in this world, there are three kinds of men,
akin to trumpet flower, mango, and jackfruit trees.

एक सुमनप्रद एक सुमन फल
एक फलइ केवल लागहीं ।
एक कहहिं कहहिं करहिं अपर
एक करहिं कहत न बागहीं ॥

९० राम बचन सुनि बिहँसा मोहि सिखावत ग्यान ।
बयरु करत नहिं तब डरे अब लागे प्रिय प्रान ॥

१ कहि दुर्बचन क्रुद्ध दसकंधर ।
कुलिस समान लाग छाँड़ै सर ॥
नानाकार सिलीमुख धाए ।
दिसि अरु बिदिसि गगन महि छाए ॥

२ पावक सर छाँड़ेउ रघुबीरा ।
छन महुँ जरे निसाचर तीरा ॥
छाड़िसि तीब्र सक्ति खिसिआई ।
बान संग प्रभु फेरि चलाई ॥

३ कोटिन्ह चक्र त्रिसूल पबारै ।
बिनु प्रयास प्रभु काटि निवारै ॥
निफल होहिं रावन सर कैसें ।
खल के सकल मनोरथ जैसें ॥

४ तब सत बान सारथी मारेसि ।
परेउ भूमि जय राम पुकारेसि ॥
राम कृपा करि सूत उठावा ।
तब प्रभु परम क्रोध कहुँ पावा ॥

One yields flowers, one both flowers and fruit,
and one bears fruit alone. Just so, among men,
one merely talks, another both talks and acts,
and the third decisively acts, without glib talk."

He heard Ram's speech and guffawed: 90
"So, would you teach me wisdom?
You were not afraid to take me on,
but now you seem to value your life."

Spewing insults, the ten-necked one, enraged,   1
began releasing arrows like thunderbolts.
Projectiles of countless shapes shot forth
to cover all ten directions of earth and sky.
But the Raghu hero discharged a flaming arrow   2
that instantly incinerated those of the night-stalker.
Abashed, Ravan released another powerful weapon,
but with an arrow the Lord reversed its course.
Discuses and tridents he hurled by the millions,   3
yet the Lord effortlessly broke and deflected them.
Ravan's arrows proved as unsuccessful
as all the desires of a wicked man.
Then he fired a hundred arrows at the charioteer,   4
who tumbled to earth crying, "Victory to Ram!"
With compassion, Ram lifted up his driver,
and then the Lord became truly wrathful.

५ भए क्रुद्ध जुद्ध बिरुद्ध रघुपति
त्रोन सायक कसमसे ।
कोदंड धुनि अति चंड सुनि
मनुजाद सब मारुत ग्रसे ॥
मंदोदरी उर कंप कंपति
कमठ भू भूधर त्रसे ।
चिक्करहिं दिग्गज दसन गहि महि
देखि कौतुक सुर हँसे ॥

११ तानेउ चाप श्रवन लगि छाँड़े बिसिख कराल ।
राम मारगन गन चले लहलहात जनु ब्याल ॥

१ चले बान सपच्छ जनु उरगा ।
प्रथमहिं हतेउ सारथी तुरगा ॥
रथ बिभंजि हति केतु पताका ।
गर्जा अति अंतर बल थाका ॥

२ तुरत आन रथ चढ़ि खिसिआना ।
अस्त्र सस्त्र छाँड़ेसि बिधि नाना ॥
बिफल होहिं सब उद्यम ताके ।
जिमि परद्रोह निरत मनसा के ॥

३ तब रावन दस सूल चलावा ।
बाजि चारि महि मारि गिरावा ॥
तुरग उठाइ कोपि रघुनायक ।
खैंचि सरासन छाँड़े सायक ॥

When he grew wrathful in the enmity of battle,   5
the Raghu lord's arrows rattled restlessly in their quiver,
and at the deep twang of his bow's string,
all the man-eating demons were seized by panic.[86]
Mandodari's heart quavered, and the ocean,
cosmic tortoise, earth, and mountains grew afraid.
The elephants of the quadrants trumpeted and sank their
    tusks in the ground,
as the watching gods smiled at the spectacle.[87]

Drawing his bow-string to its full extent,   91
he discharged his dreadful arrows,
and that mass of Ram's missiles
streaked along like sinuous serpents.

Flying like winged vipers, those arrows   1
first slew Ravan's driver and horses,
then shattered his chariot, felling its standards.
The demon, though inwardly spent, roared much.
Abashed, he quickly mounted another chariot   2
and discharged many sorts of weapons,
but all his exertions bore no fruit,
like the scheming of an ever-malicious person.
Next Ravan hurled ten mighty spears   3
that struck and toppled Ram's four horses.[88]
Making them rise, the Raghu lord wrathfully
drew his bow and discharged arrows.

४ रावन सिर सरोज बनचारी ।
   चलि रघुबीर सिलीमुख धारी ॥
   दस दस बान भाल दस मारे ।
   निसरि गए चले रुधिर पनारे ॥

५ स्रवत रुधिर धायउ बलवाना ।
   प्रभु पुनि कृत धनु सर संधाना ॥
   तीस तीर रघुबीर पबारे ।
   भुजन्हि समेत सीस महि पारे ॥

६ काटतहीं पुनि भए नबीने ।
   राम बहोरि भुजा सिर छीने ॥
   प्रभु बहु बार बाहु सिर हए ।
   कटत झटिति पुनि नूतन भए ॥

७ पुनि पुनि प्रभु काटत भुज सीसा ।
   अति कौतुकी कोसलाधीसा ॥
   रहे छाइ नभ सिर अरु बाहू ।
   मानहुँ अमित केतु अरु राहू ॥

To Ravan's heads, like a cluster of lotuses,   4
the Raghu's arrows flew like a line of eager bees.
Ten of them, striking each of his ten foreheads,
went right through, releasing ruddy rivulets.
Streaming blood, that mighty one still charged,   5
as the Lord once more readied arrows on his bow.
The Raghu hero fired thirty at once, which made
Ravan's heads as well as arms tumble to earth.
But even as they were cut off, new ones appeared   6
and Ram once more severed them all.
The Lord repeatedly sliced off those heads and arms,
yet, though cut off, they instantly appeared anew.
Time and again, the Lord severed arms and heads,   7
for Kosala's king is supremely sportive.
Heads and arms spread across the sky
like countless forms of Ketu and Rahu.[89]

८ जनु राहु केतु अनेक नभ पथ
सखत सोनित धावहीं ।
रघुबीर तीर प्रचंड लागहिं
भूमि गिरन न पावहीं ॥
एक एक सर सिर निकर छेदे
नभ उड़त इमि सोहहीं ।
जनु कोपि दिनकर कर निकर
जहँ तहँ बिधुंतुद पोहहीं ॥

१२ जिमि जिमि प्रभु हर तासु सिर तिमि तिमि होहिं अपार ।
सेवत बिषय बिबर्ध जिमि नित नित नूतन मार ॥

१ दसमुख देखि सिरन्ह कै बाढ़ी ।
बिसरा मरन भई रिस गाढ़ी ॥
गर्जेउ मूढ़ महा अभिमानी ।
धायउ दसहु सरासन तानी ॥

२ समर भूमि दसकंधर कोप्यो ।
बरषि बान रघुपति रथ तोप्यो ॥
दंड एक रथ देखि न परेऊ ।
जनु निहार महुँ दिनकर दुरेऊ ॥

३ हाहाकार सुरन्ह जब कीन्हा ।
तब प्रभु कोपि कारमुक लीन्हा ॥
सर निवारि रिपु के सिर काटे ।
ते दिसि बिदिसि गगन महि पाटे ॥

It was as if countless Rahus and Ketus, streaming blood,   8
were racing along the celestial track,
for the impact of the Raghu hero's furious arrows
would not let them fall to earth.
Each arrow pierced multiple heads
and, coursing across the sky, they were as splendid
as if an enraged sun had released myriad rays
on every side to skewer the moon's oppressor.*

However many of Ravan's heads the Lord removed,   92
they kept reappearing endlessly,
just as sensual urges, once indulged, multiply
with ever renewed desire.[90]

When he witnessed the regrowth of his heads,   1
Ravan forgot about death and became enraged.
Bellowing in his immense arrogance, the fool
charged forward, clutching ten fully nocked bows.
Raging on the battlefield, the many-necked one   2
showered arrows that covered the Raghu's chariot,
so that, for some time, his vehicle could not be seen,[91]
as when the sun is hidden by mist.
But when cries of woe arose from the gods,   3
the Lord grew angry and took up his bow.
Dispelling those arrows, he severed his foe's heads
till they blanketed the sky and earth in all directions.

---

* Rahu, the eclipse-causing demon.

४	काटे सिर नभ मारग धावहिं ।
	जय जय धुनि करि भय उपजावहिं ॥
	कहँ लछिमन सुग्रीव कपीसा ।
	कहँ रघुबीर कोसलाधीसा ॥

५	कहँ रामु कहि सिर निकर धाए
	देखि मर्कट भजि चले ।
	संधानि धनु रघुबंसमनि हँसि
	सरन्हि सिर बेधे भले ॥
	सिर मालिका कर कालिका गहि
	बृंद बृंदन्हि बहु मिलीं ।
	करि रुधिर सरि मज्जनु मनहुँ
	संग्राम बट पूजन चलीं ॥

९३	पुनि दसकंठ क्रुद्ध होइ छाँड़ी सक्ति प्रचंड ।
	चली बिभीषन सन्मुख मनहुँ काल कर दंड ॥

१	आवत देखि सक्ति अति घोरा ।
	प्रनतारति भंजन पन मोरा ॥
	तुरत बिभीषन पाछें मेला ।
	सन्मुख राम सहेउ सोइ सेला ॥

The severed heads hurtled through the heavens,   4
still bellowing in challenge and arousing terror—
"Where is Lakshman?" "Where is Sugriv, monkey lord?"
"Where is Kosala's king, hero of the Raghus?"

Roaring, "Where is Ram?" that flock of heads flew by,   5
and the monkeys saw this and fled in panic.
But, with a smile, the jewel of Raghus discharged his bow
and neatly threaded the heads on myriad arrows.
Taking those garlands of heads in hand,
multitudes of little Kalis assembled there, as though,
fresh from their holy bath in the river of blood,
they were off to worship the battlefield's sacred tree.[92]

Then the ten-necked one, further enraged,   93
hurled a terrible spear
that flew straight at Vibhishan
like the staff of the god of death.

Seeing the awful weapon's approach, Ram thought,   1
"I have vowed to end the pain of refuge seekers"
and, quickly setting Vibhishan behind him,
came forward to face the full force of that spear.

२ लागि सक्ति मुरुछा कछु भई।
प्रभु कृत खेल सुरन्ह बिकलई॥
देखि बिभीषन प्रभु श्रम पायो।
गहि कर गदा क्रुद्ध होइ धायो॥

३ रे कुभाग्य सठ मंद कुबुद्धे।
तैं सुर नर मुनि नाग बिरुद्धे॥
सादर सिव कहुँ सीस चढ़ाए।
एक एक के कोटिन्ह पाए॥

४ तेहि कारन खल अब लगि बाँच्यो।
अब तव कालु सीस पर नाच्यो॥
राम बिमुख सठ चहसि संपदा।
अस कहि हनेसि माझ उर गदा॥

५ उर माझ गदा प्रहार घोर
कठोर लागत महि पर्यो।
दस बदन सोनित स्रवत पुनि
संभारि धायो रिस भर्यो॥
द्वौ भिरे अतिबल मल्लजुद्ध
बिरुद्ध एकु एकहि हनै।
रघुबीर बल दर्पित बिभीषनु
घाली नहिं ता कहुँ गनै॥

Upon its impact, he grew a little faint—   2
the Lord was just playing, though the gods panicked—
and when he saw his master under strain,
Vibhishan seized a mace and ran forward in a rage,
screaming, "Ill-fated scoundrel! Vile fool,   3
enemy of gods, humans, sages, and serpent lords!
You reverently offered up your skulls to Shiva,
and for each and every one, gained millions.
That is why, villain, you have been spared so far,   4
but now your death dances on your head.
Hostile to Ram, fool, you yet expect to flourish."
With this, he struck Ravan in the chest with his mace.

At the awful blow to his chest of that dreadful mace,   5
Ravan at once fell sprawling on the earth,
blood streaming from all his ten mouths.
Regaining his senses, he rose and advanced, furious.
Those two surpassingly strong ones wrestled,
and clashing angrily, rained blows on each other,
yet Vibhishan, emboldened by the Raghu hero's might,
reckoned his foe to be of no account.[93]

९४ उमा बिभीषनु रावनहि सन्मुख चितव कि काउ ।
सो अब भिरत काल ज्यों श्रीरघुबीर प्रभाउ ॥

१ देखा श्रमित बिभीषनु भारी ।
धायउ हनूमान गिरि धारी ॥
रथ तुरंग सारथी निपाता ।
हृदय माझ तेहि मारेसि लाता ॥

२ ठाढ़ रहा अति कंपित गाता ।
गयउ बिभीषनु जहँ जनत्राता ॥
पुनि रावन कपि हतेउ पचारी ।
चलेउ गगन कपि पूँछ पसारी ॥

३ गहिसि पूँछ कपि सहित उड़ाना ।
पुनि फिरि भिरेउ प्रबल हनुमाना ॥
लरत अकास जुगल सम जोधा ।
एकहि एकु हनत करि क्रोधा ॥

४ सोहहिं नभ छल बल बहु करहीं ।
कज्जल गिरि सुमेरु जनु लरहीं ॥
बुधि बल निसिचर परइ न पार्यो ।
तब मारुत सुत प्रभु संभार्यो ॥

"But Uma," Shiva remarked, "would Vibhishan   94
ever have dared even to look Ravan in the eye?
Yet now he grapples with him like Death himself,
through the majesty of the great Raghu hero!"

When he saw Vibhishan becoming much fatigued,   1
Hanuman sped forward bearing a mountain.
He smashed Ravan's chariot, with horses and driver,
and landed a kick squarely in the demon's chest.
Though he stayed upright, Ravan shook uncontrollably,   2
and Vibhishan returned to Ram, who protects his own.
Then Ravan, roaring a challenge, struck the monkey,
but he just expanded his tail and took to the air.
Ravan seized the tail and the monkey flew with him,   3
whereupon mighty Hanuman turned and fought him.
Well matched, the two warriors battled in the sky,
striking one another in their rage.
With many agile feints, their glorious celestial combat   4
resembled golden Meru grappling with a mountain of
    soot.
But when he could not, by wit or might, fell the night-
    stalker,
the son of the wind inwardly invoked the Lord.

५   संभारि श्रीरघुबीर धीर
पचारि कपि रावनु हन्यो ।
महि परत पुनि उठि लरत देवन्ह
जुगल कहुँ जय जय भन्यो ॥
हनुमंत संकट देखि मर्कट
भालु क्रोधातुर चले ।
रन मत्त रावन सकल सुभट
प्रचंड भुज बल दलमले ॥

९५   तब रघुबीर पचारे धाए कीस प्रचंड ।
कपि बल प्रबल देखि तेहिं कीन्ह प्रगट पाषंड ॥

१   अंतरधान भयउ छन एका ।
पुनि प्रगटे खल रूप अनेका ॥
रघुपति कटक भालु कपि जेते ।
जहँ तहँ प्रगट दसानन तेते ॥

२   देखे कपिन्ह अमित दससीसा ।
जहँ तहँ भजे भालु अरु कीसा ॥
भागे बानर धरहिं न धीरा ।
त्राहि त्राहि लछिमन रघुबीरा ॥

३   दहँ दिसि धावहिं कोटिन्ह रावन ।
गर्जहिं घोर कठोर भयावन ॥
डरे सकल सुर चले पराई ।
जय कै आस तजहु अब भाई ॥

Inwardly recalling the resolute Raghu hero,[94]   5
the monkey challenged Ravan and struck him,
and both toppled to earth, then rose again, fighting,
as the gods cheered them on with cries of "Victory!"
Seeing that Hanuman was hard-pressed,
monkeys and bears charged forward, enraged,
but war-crazed Ravan seized all those stalwarts
and crushed them in his mighty arms.

Then, urged on by the Raghu hero,   95
the mightiest monkeys ran toward him,
and seeing the strength of their force,
the demon foe fabricated a deception.

For just an instant, the villain vanished,   1
and then he manifested in myriad forms.
For every bear and monkey in the Raghu's army
there appeared, on all sides, a ten-headed foe!
When they beheld that endless array of Ravans,   2
the bears and monkeys ran in all directions,
put to flight, unable to muster courage, crying,
"Save us, Lakshman; rescue us, Raghu hero!"
Millions of Ravans raced in the ten directions,   3
emitting harsh and terrifying roars.
The frightened gods all fled the scene, lamenting,
"Abandon any hope of victory now, brothers.

४ सब सुर जिते एक दसकंधर ।
अब बहु भए तकहु गिरि कंदर ॥
रहे बिरंचि संभु मुनि ग्यानी ।
जिन्ह जिन्ह प्रभु महिमा कछु जानी ॥

५ जाना प्रताप ते रहे निर्भय
कपिन्ह रिपु माने फुरे ।
चले बिचलि मर्कट भालु सकल
कृपाल पाहि भयातुरे ॥
हनुमंत अंगद नील नल
अतिबल लरत रन बाँकुरे ।
मर्दहिं दसानन कोटि कोटिन्ह
कपट भू भट अंकुरे ॥

९६ सुर बानर देखे बिकल हँस्यो कोसलाधीस ।
सजि सारंग एक सर हते सकल दससीस ॥

१ प्रभु छन महुँ माया सब काटी ।
जिमि रबि उएँ जाहिं तम फाटी ॥
रावनु एकु देखि सुर हरषे ।
फिरे सुमन बहु प्रभु पर बरषे ॥

A single Ravan defeated all of us celestials;   4
now he's so many—just hide in some mountain cave!"
Only Brahma, Shiva, and great sages stood fast—
those who grasped a little of the Lord's majesty.

Those who understood his might stood unafraid,   5
but the monkeys took those enemies to be real
and, greatly agitated, fled with the bears,
all crying in terror, "Save us, merciful one!"
Hanuman, Angad, Nil, and Nal—
these stalwart warriors fought on ferociously,
crushing millions of illusory ten-faced troops
who seemed to have sprouted from the earth.

Beholding the anguish of the gods and monkeys,   96
the lord of Kosala laughed,
and fixing a single arrow on his divine bow,
annihilated all those ten-headed demons.

In an instant, the Lord cut through all the sorcery,   1
as darkness is dispelled at the sun's rising.
Seeing a single Ravan, the gods rejoiced
and, returning, showered the Lord with blossoms.

२   भुज उठाइ रघुपति कपि फेरे ।
फिरे एक एकन्ह तब टेरे ॥
प्रभु बलु पाइ भालु कपि धाए ।
तरल तमकि संजुग महि आए ॥

३   अस्तुति करत देवतन्हि देखें ।
भयउँ एक मैं इन्ह के लेखें ॥
सठहु सदा तुम्ह मोर मरायल ।
अस कहि कोपि गगन पर धायल ॥

४   हाहाकार करत सुर भागे ।
खलहु जाहु कहँ मोरें आगे ॥
देखि बिकल सुर अंगद धायो ।
कूदि चरन गहि भूमि गिरायो ॥

५   गहि भूमि पार्यो लात मार्यो
बालिसुत प्रभु पहिं गयो ।
संभारि उठि दसकंठ घोर
कठोर रव गर्जत भयो ॥
करि दाप चाप चढ़ाइ दस
संधानि सर बहु बरषई ।
किए सकल भट घायल भयाकुल
देखि निज बल हरषई ॥

१७   तब रघुपति रावन के सीस भुजा सर चाप ।
काटे बहुत बढ़े पुनि जिमि तीरथ कर पाप ॥

Raising his arms, the Raghu master rallied his troops,   2
and they came back then, calling to one another.
Drawing strength from the Lord, bears and monkeys
bounded, enraged, onto the field of war.
When he saw the gods praising Ram, Ravan thought,   3
"They dare suppose that I am reduced to one."[95]
Saying, "You fools are forever beaten by me!"
he angrily leaped into the heavens,
putting the gods to flight amid many cries of woe.   4
"Scoundrels," said Ravan, "where will you escape me?"
At the sight of the gods' distress, Angad raced forward,
leaped and, seizing his feet, hurled Ravan back to earth.

He seized him, threw him to the ground, kicked him,   5
and then Bali's son returned to his lord.
But ten-headed Ravan collected his wits, rose,
and began to roar loudly and menacingly.
In great anger, he took up ten bows, fitted them,
and unleashed a deluge of arrows
that wounded and terrified all Ram's champions—
and Ravan rejoiced at seeing his own strength.

Then the Raghu lord severed Ravan's heads   97
and arms, with all their arrows and bows.
But they only grew still more,
like sins committed in a holy place.[96]

१ सिर भुज बाढ़ि देखि रिपु केरी ।
भालु कपिन्ह रिस भई घनेरी ॥
मरत न मूढ़ कटेहुँ भुज सीसा ।
धाए कोपि भालु भट कीसा ॥

२ बालितनय मारुति नल नीला ।
बानरराज दुबिद बलसीला ॥
बिटप महीधर करहिं प्रहारा ।
सोइ गिरि तरु गहि कपिन्ह सो मारा ॥

३ एक नखन्हि रिपु बपुष बिदारी ।
भागि चलहिं एक लातन्ह मारी ॥
तब नल नील सिरन्हि चढ़ि गयऊ ।
नखन्हि लिलार बिदारत भयऊ ॥

४ रुधिर देखि बिषाद उर भारी ।
तिन्हहि धरन कहुँ भुजा पसारी ॥
गहे न जाहिं करन्हि पर फिरहीं ।
जनु जुग मधुप कमल बन चरहीं ॥

५ कोपि कूदि द्वौ धरेसि बहोरी ।
महि पटकत भजे भुजा मरोरी ॥
पुनि सकोप दस धनु कर लीन्हे ।
सरन्हि मारि घायल कपि कीन्हे ॥

६ हनुमदादि मुरुछित करि बंदर ।
पाइ प्रदोष हरष दसकंधर ॥
मुरुछित देखि सकल कपि बीरा ।
जामवंत धायउ रनधीरा ॥

Seeing the enemy's heads and arms grow back,   1
the bears and monkeys became furious.
"Even with arms and heads severed, the dolt won't die,"
they cried, and those feral troops charged in a rage.
Bali's son and the son of the wind, Nal and Nil,   2
the monkey king, and Dvivid—all these mighty ones
loosed a barrage of tree trunks and mountaintops,
but he caught them and struck the monkeys with them.
One hero rent the enemy's body with his nails   3
while another delivered kicks, then quickly fled.
Then Nal and Nil climbed onto his heads
and, with their nails, began ripping into his brow.
Seeing his own blood, he was much disheartened   4
and reached up with his arms to seize them,
but could not, for they flitted over his hands
like two bees roaming on a cluster of lotuses.
Then, leaping in rage, he caught hold of the two   5
to slam them to earth, but they twisted his arms and fled.
With renewed anger, he took ten bows in his hands
and, firing arrows, wounded all the monkeys.
Rendering Hanuman and many others senseless,   6
ten-headed Ravan rejoiced as evening fell.
But when he saw all the monkey heroes unconscious,
Jambavan, steadfast in battle, came charging,

७   संग भालु भूधर तरु धारी ।
मारन लगे पचारि पचारी ॥
भयउ क्रुद्ध रावन बलवाना ।
गहि पद महि पटकइ भट नाना ॥

८   देखि भालुपति निज दल घाता ।
कोपि माझ उर मारेसि लाता ॥

९   उर लात घात प्रचंड लागत
बिकल रथ ते महि परा ।
गहि भालु बीसहुँ कर मनहुँ
कमलन्हि बसे निसि मधुकरा ॥
मुरुछित बिलोकि बहोरि पद हति
भालुपति प्रभु पहिं गयो ।
निसि जानि स्यंदन घालि तेहि तब
सूत जतनु करत भयो ॥

१८   मुरुछा बिगत भालु कपि सब आए प्रभु पास ।
निसिचर सकल रावनहि घेरि रहे अति त्रास ॥

१   तेही निसि सीता पहिं जाई ।
त्रिजटा कहि सब कथा सुनाई ॥
सिर भुज बाढ़ि सुनत रिपु केरी ।
सीता उर भइ त्रास घनेरी ॥

together with bears clutching peaks and trees,   7
to strike the demon, taunting him repeatedly.
Mighty Ravan grew even angrier
and, seizing their feet, threw down many champions.
Seeing his legions bested, the king of bears   8
was enraged and planted a kick in the demon's chest.

At the impact of that powerful blow to the chest,   9
Ravan fell from his chariot to earth, unconscious.
In the grip of his twenty hands, bears were lodged
like bees in lotuses that had closed for the night.
Seeing Ravan senseless, the bear king kicked him
once more, and then went back to the Lord.[97]
Knowing night had fallen, Ravan's driver thrust him
into his chariot and attempted to revive him.

The bears and monkeys regained their senses   98
and all returned to the Lord's side,
while the night-stalkers gathered around Ravan
in a mood of deepest dread.

That very night, Sita was visited   1
by Trijata, who told her all the news.
Hearing that the foe's heads and arms regrew,
Sita's heart became terror stricken,

२ मुख मलीन उपजी मन चिंता ।
त्रिजटा सन बोली तब सीता ॥
होइहि कहा कहसि किन माता ।
केहि बिधि मरिहि बिस्व दुखदाता ॥

३ रघुपति सर सिर कटेहुँ न मरई ।
बिधि बिपरीत चरित सब करई ॥
मोर अभाग्य जिआवत ओही ।
जेहिं हौं हरि पद कमल बिछोही ॥

४ जेहिं कृत कपट कनक मृग झूठा ।
अजहुँ सो दैव मोहि पर रूठा ॥
जेहिं बिधि मोहि दुख दुसह सहाए ।
लछिमन कहुँ कटु बचन कहाए ॥

५ रघुपति बिरह सबिष सर भारी ।
तकि तकि मार बार बहु मारी ॥
ऐसेहुँ दुख जो राख मम प्राना ।
सोइ बिधि ताहि जिआव न आना ॥

६ बहु बिधि कर बिलाप जानकी ।
करि करि सुरति कृपानिधान की ॥
कह त्रिजटा सुनु राजकुमारी ।
उर सर लागत मरइ सुरारी ॥

७ प्रभु ताते उर हतइ न तेही ।
एहि के हृदयँ बसति बैदेही ॥

her face, downcast, her mind anxious.   2
Then Sita said to Trijata,
"Won't you tell me what will happen, mother?
How will this scourge of the world meet his end?
Decapitated by the Raghu's arrows, he does not die—   3
surely hostile fate must be doing all this.
Yes, my own ill fortune is keeping him alive,
which separated me from Hari's lovely feet
and fabricated the false, illusory deer of gold—   4
even now, that same destiny is displeased with me.
The fate that forced me to bear insufferable sorrow,
that made me speak harsh words to Lakshman,
that made desire, armed with the poisoned arrows   5
of Ram's absence, stalk and strike me again and again,
and that, even in such agony, restrains my life's breath—
that fate, and no other, is keeping him alive."
Thus Janak's daughter lamented in many ways,   6
constantly recalling Ram, treasury of mercy.
But Trijata said, "Princess, listen to me:
once an arrow enters his heart, the gods' foe will die,
yet the Lord does not strike him there, because   7
there, in Ravan's heart, Vaidehi dwells.

८   एहि के हृदयँ बस जानकी
जानकी उर मम बास है।
मम उदर भुअन अनेक लागत
बान सब कर नास है॥
सुनि बचन हरष बिषाद मन अति
देखि पुनि त्रिजटाँ कहा।
अब मरिहि रिपु एहि बिधि सुनहि
सुंदरि तजहि संसय महा॥

९९   काटत सिर होइहि बिकल छुटि जाइहि तव ध्यान।
तब रावनहि हृदय महुँ मरिहहिं रामु सुजान॥

१   अस कहि बहुत भाँति समुझाई।
पुनि त्रिजटा निज भवन सिधाई॥
राम सुभाउ सुमिरि बैदेही।
उपजी बिरह बिथा अति तेही॥

२   निसिहि ससिहि निंदति बहु भाँती।
जुग सम भई सिराति न राती॥
करति बिलाप मनहिं मन भारी।
राम बिरहँ जानकी दुखारी॥

३   जब अति भयउ बिरह उर दाहू।
फरकेउ बाम नयन अरु बाहू॥
सगुन बिचारि धरी मन धीरा।
अब मिलिहहिं कृपाल रघुबीरा॥

'Janaki dwells in his heart'—so Ram muses—   8
'and Janaki's heart is my own abode.
And within me are countless worlds, and so,
one arrow's impact would annihilate them all.'"
At this speech, Sita's heart both rejoiced and despaired,
and marking this, Trijata spoke again:
"But now your foe will truly die, and in this way—
listen, lovely one, and relinquish your grave doubt:

Distracted by the severing of his heads,   99
he will lose his focus on you.
Then Ravan's heart will be fatally struck
by all-knowing Ram."

After saying this and further instructing Sita,   1
Trijata left for her own abode.
Recalling Ram's tender nature, Vaidehi
suffered the intense pain of separation.
She poured scorn on the night and moon—   2
"The night's become an aeon and will not pass"—
and with profound inner lamentation
Janaki agonized in separation from Ram.
But as its fire arose to consume her heart,   3
her left eye and arm began to throb.
Considering it a good omen, she took courage—
"Now I will surely meet the merciful Raghu hero."

४ इहाँ अर्धनिसि रावनु जागा ।
  निज सारथि सन खीझन लागा ॥
  सठ रनभूमि छड़ाइसि मोही ।
  धिग धिग अधम मंदमति तोही ॥

५ तेहिं पद गहि बहु बिधि समुझावा ।
  भोरु भएँ रथ चढ़ि पुनि धावा ॥
  सुनि आगवनु दसानन केरा ।
  कपिदल खरभर भयउ घनेरा ॥

६ जहँ तहँ भूधर बिटप उपारी ।
  धाए कटकटाइ भट भारी ॥

७ धाए जो मर्कट बिकट भालु
  कराल कर भूधर धरा ।
  अति कोप करहिं प्रहार मारत
  भजि चले रजनीचरा ॥
  बिचलाइ दल बलवंत कीसन्ह
  घेरि पुनि रावनु लियो ।
  चहुँ दिसि चपेटन्हि मारि नखन्हि
  बिदारि तनु ब्याकुल कियो ॥

१०० देखि महा मर्कट प्रबल रावन कीन्ह बिचार ।
  अंतरहित होइ निमिष महुँ कृत माया बिस्तार ॥

Meanwhile, when night was half over, Ravan regained   4
his wits and began reviling his charioteer—
"Fool, you snatched me from the battlefield.
Shame on your contemptible stupidity, shame!"—
as the driver clasped his feet and pleaded with him.   5
At dawn, Ravan mounted his chariot and rode out again,
and when they heard of the ten-headed one's approach
there was great commotion in the monkey army.
Uprooting hills and mighty trees on every side,   6
those champions charged, gnashing their teeth.

Those massive monkeys and fierce bears   7
ran forward, clutching mountains in their paws.
Enraged, they struck with them,
and at their impact the night-stalkers fled.
Having broken the foe's ranks, the mighty monkeys
surrounded Ravan once more,
pummeling him from all sides, tearing his flesh
with their nails, and driving him to distraction.

Seeing the strength of those great monkeys,   100
Ravan pondered momentarily,
then vanished, and in an instant
generated a vast illusion.

·

१ जब कीन्ह तेहिं पाषंड ।
भए प्रगट जंतु प्रचंड ॥
बेताल भूत पिसाच ।
कर धरें धनु नाराच ॥

२ जोगिनि गहें करबाल ।
एक हाथ मनुज कपाल ॥
करि सद्य सोनित पान ।
नाचहिं करहिं बहु गान ॥

३ धरु मारु बोलहिं घोर ।
रहि पूरि धुनि चहुँ ओर ॥
मुख बाइ धावहिं खान ।
तब लगे कीस परान ॥

४ जहँ जाहिं मर्कट भागि ।
तहँ बरत देखहिं आगि ॥
भए बिकल बानर भालु ।
पुनि लाग बरषै बालु ॥

५ जहँ तहँ थकित करि कीस ।
गर्जेउ बहुरि दससीस ॥
लछिमन कपीस समेत ।
भए सकल बीर अचेत ॥

६ हा राम हा रघुनाथ ।
कहि सुभट मीजहिं हाथ ॥
एहि बिधि सकल बल तोरि ।
तेहिं कीन्ह कपट बहोरि ॥

When he worked his sorcery,[98]   1
ferocious beings instantly appeared—
ghouls, ghosts, and goblins,[99]
all bearing bows and arrows,
and yoginis clutching scimitars,   2
a human head in their other hand,
furiously lapping fresh blood
while dancing and singing lustily.
Their horrid cries—"Grab him!" "Kill him!"—   3
filled the four directions
as they advanced with hungry open maws.
Then the monkeys began to flee,
but wherever they ran   4
they beheld searing flames.
The monkeys and bears grew distraught,
and he began pelting them with sand.
Harassing the monkeys wherever they were,   5
the ten-headed one roared time and again,
until Lakshman, together with Sugriv
and all those heroes, grew insensible.
"Oh Ram! Alas, Raghu master!"   6
the warriors cried, wringing their hands.
In this way, having crippled their might,
Ravan deployed yet another deception.

७ प्रगटेसि बिपुल हनुमान ।
धाए गहे पाषान ॥
तिन्ह रामु घेरे जाइ ।
चहँ दिसि बरूथ बनाइ ॥

८ मारहु धरहु जनि जाइ ।
कटकटहिं पूँछ उठाइ ॥
दहँ दिसि लँगूर बिराज ।
तेहिं मध्य कोसलराज ॥

९ तेहिं मध्य कोसलराज सुंदर
स्याम तन सोभा लही ।
जनु इंद्रधनुष अनेक की
बर बारि तुंग तमालही ॥
प्रभु देखि हरष बिषाद उर सुर
बदत जय जय जय करी ।
रघुबीर एकहिं तीर कोपि
निमेष महुँ माया हरी ॥

He generated countless Hanumans,   7
charging forward, each bearing a boulder
and racing to surround Ram
in massed ranks on every side, crying,
"Strike and bind him!" "Don't let him escape!"   8
They gnashed their teeth and raised their tails—
those glorious tails were uplifted on every side
and in their midst shone Kosala's lord.

In their midst, the handsome lord of Kosala[100]   9
with his dark body, looked as lovely
as a lofty evergreen bay tree, ringed
by a splendid fence of countless rainbows.
Beholding the Lord, the gods were both pleased
and anxious at heart, and kept cheering for his victory.
Then the Raghu hero, moved to anger, instantly
and with a single arrow banished the illusion.

१०	माया बिगत कपि भालु हरषे
	बिटप गिरि गहि सब फिरे ।
	सर निकर छाड़े राम रावन
	बाहु सिर पुनि महि गिरे ॥
	श्रीराम रावन समर चरित
	अनेक कल्प जो गावहीं ।
	सत सेष सारद निगम कबि
	तेउ तदपि पार न पावहीं ॥

१०१क	ताके गुन गन कछु कहे जड़मति तुलसीदास ।
	निज पौरुस अनुसार जिमि मसक उड़ाहिं अकास ॥

१०१ख	काटे सिर भुज बार बहु मरत न भट लंकेस ।
	प्रभु क्रीड़त सुर सिद्ध मुनि ब्याकुल देखि कलेस ॥

१	काटत बढ़हिं सीस समुदाई ।
	जिमि प्रति लाभ लोभ अधिकाई ॥
	मरइ न रिपु श्रम भयउ बिसेषा ।
	राम बिभीषन तन तब देखा ॥

२	उमा काल मर जाकीं ईछा ।
	सो प्रभु जन कर प्रीति परीछा ॥
	सुनु सरबग्य चराचर नायक ।
	प्रनतपाल सुर मुनि सुखदायक ॥

The illusion dispelled, monkeys and bears rejoiced,   10
and seizing trees and summits, they all returned.
Ram released a volley of arrows that made
Ravan's arms and heads again plummet to earth.
Even if, for endless aeons, the battlefield exploits
of Lord Ram and Ravan were to be sung
by hundreds of Sheshas, Sharads, Vedas, and poets,
even they could never encompass their glory.[101]

Dull-witted Tulsidas   101a
has told just a fraction of their many feats—
like a gnat mustering the courage
to soar into the firmament.[102]

Though his heads and arms were severed many times,   101b
the stalwart king of Lanka did not die.
Seeing the Lord playing, gods, perfected ones, and sages
grew anxious at his apparent distress.

No sooner cut, than the mass of heads grew anew,   1
just as greed grows with every acquisition.
When despite his great efforts the foe did not die,
Ram turned to look at Vibhishan.
Uma, he at whose whim Death himself dies,   2
that Lord was just testing his servant's love.
Vibhishan said, "Omniscient master of all beings,
protector of the meek, delighter of gods and sages—listen:

३ . नाभिकुंड पियूष बस याकें ।
नाथ जिअत रावनु बल ताकें ॥
सुनत बिभीषन बचन कृपाला ।
हरषि गहे कर बान कराला ॥

४ असुभ होन लागे तब नाना ।
रोवहिं खर सृकाल बहु स्वाना ॥
बोलहिं खग जग आरति हेतू ।
प्रगट भए नभ जहँ तहँ केतू ॥

५ दस दिसि दाह होन अति लागा ।
भयउ परब बिनु रबि उपरागा ॥
मंदोदरि उर कंपति भारी ।
प्रतिमा स्रवहिं नयन मग बारी ॥

६ प्रतिमा रुदहिं पबिपात नभ अति
बात बह डोलति मही ।
बरषहिं बलाहक रुधिर कच रज
असुभ अति सक को कही ॥
उतपात अमित बिलोकि नभ सुर
बिकल बोलहिं जय जए ।
सुर सभय जानि कृपाल रघुपति
चाप सर जोरत भए ॥

a pool of ambrosia is lodged in his navel,   3
lord, and by its power Ravan lives on."
When the merciful one heard Vibhishan's words,
he was pleased and took mighty arrows in hand.
Then numerous ill omens became manifest—   4
asses brayed, packs of jackals and dogs howled,
birds screeched, portending worldly woe,[103]
and comets appeared, dotting the heavens.
Fires broke out in the ten directions,   5
there was an untimely eclipse of the sun,
Queen Mandodari's heart began to throb,
and tears coursed from the eyes of statues.

Statues started weeping, lightning rent the sky,   6
mighty winds blew, the very earth shook,
clouds began raining blood, hair, and dust—
who can describe so many evil portents?
Beholding the countless ill omens, the gods
in heaven anxiously cried, "Victory! Victory!"
Aware of their fear, the merciful Raghu lord
began fixing arrows to his bow.

१०२ खैंचि सरासन श्रवन लगि छाड़े सर एकतीस ।
रघुनायक सायक चले मानहुँ काल फनीस ॥

१ सायक एक नाभि सर सोषा ।
अपर लगे भुज सिर करि रोषा ॥
लै सिर बाहु चले नाराचा ।
सिर भुज हीन रुंड महि नाचा ॥

२ धरनि धसइ धर धाव प्रचंडा ।
तब सर हति प्रभु कृत दुइ खंडा ॥
गर्जेउ मरत घोर रव भारी ।
कहाँ रामु रन हतौं पचारी ॥

३ डोली भूमि गिरत दसकंधर ।
छुभित सिंधु सरि दिग्गज भूधर ॥
धरनि परेउ द्वौ खंड बढ़ाई ।
चापि भालु मर्कट समुदाई ॥

४ मंदोदरि आगें भुज सीसा ।
धरि सर चले जहाँ जगदीसा ॥
प्रबिसे सब निषंग महु जाई ।
देखि सुरन्ह दुंदुभीं बजाई ॥

५ तासु तेज समान प्रभु आनन ।
हरषे देखि संभु चतुरानन ॥
जय जय धुनि पूरी ब्रह्मंडा ।
जय रघुबीर प्रबल भुजदंडा ॥

Drawing his bow-string to its fullest extent,   102
he released thirty-one arrows,
and those missiles of the Raghu master
sped forth like deadly serpent kings.

One arrow parched the nectar pool in Ravan's navel,   1
the others struck furiously in his arms and heads
and flew on, carrying them all away.
His headless, limbless trunk tottered on the field,
but when it began to run madly, ravaging the earth,   2
the Lord cut it in two with a single arrow.
Dying, Ravan unleashed a thunderous roar:
"Where is Ram, that I may challenge and slay him?"
At the fall of the ten-necked one, earth quaked,   3
seas, rivers, mountains, and cosmic elephants swayed.
As they toppled to earth, the two halves of his body
    swelled
to crush hordes of bears and monkeys.
Laying his arms and heads before Mandodari,   4
the fatal arrows returned to the Lord of the world,
where they all reentered his quiver—
seeing this, the gods sounded their kettledrums.
Ravan's radiance merged in the Lord's countenance;[104]   5
witnessing this, Shambhu and Brahma rejoiced.
Shouts of "Victory! Victory!" echoed through the cosmos:
"Hail the mighty-armed hero of the Raghus!"

६   बरषहिं सुमन देव मुनि बृंदा ।
    जय कृपाल जय जयति मुकुंदा ॥

७   जय कृपा कंद मुकुंद द्वंद
    हरन सरन सुखप्रद प्रभो ।
    खल दल बिदारन परम कारन
    कारुनीक सदा बिभो ॥
    सुर सुमन बरषहिं हरष संकुल
    बाज दुंदुभि गहगही ।
    संग्राम अंगन राम अंग
    अनंग बहु सोभा लही ॥

८   सिर जटा मुकुट प्रसून बिच बिच
    अति मनोहर राजहीं ।
    जनु नीलगिरि पर तड़ित पटल
    समेत उडुगन भ्राजहीं ॥
    भुजदंड सर कोदंड फेरत
    रुधिर कन तन अति बने ।
    जनु रायमुनीं तमाल पर
    बैठीं बिपुल सुख आपने ॥

१०३ कृपादृष्टि करि बृष्टि प्रभु अभय किए सुर बृंद ।
     भालु कीस सब हरषे जय सुख धाम मुकुंद ॥

Showering blossoms, hosts of gods and sages cried, 6
"Victory to the compassionate one, to Mukunda![105]

Victory to the bounteous cloud of mercy, to Mukunda, 7
liberator from duality, Lord who delights refuge seekers,
who rends the army of evil ones—the first cause,
both utterly kind and eternally glorious!"
Raining down blossoms, delirious with joy,
crowds of deities sounded their booming drums,
while there, on the field of war, Ram's limbs
stole the comeliness from countless Kamas.*
The matted locks that crowned his head, dotted 8
with flowers, were glorious and enchanting,
like a blue mountaintop sheathed in lightning streaks[106]
interspersed with shimmering constellations.
His strong arms toyed with arrows and his great bow,
and the tiny drops of blood that adorned his form
were like countless little ruddy birds, resting[107]
in pure delight on the dark trunk of a *tamāl* tree.

Showering his gracious glances on all, 103
the Lord made the divine host free of fear,
while all the bears and monkeys exulted, crying,
"Victory to Mukunda, abode of bliss!"

* God of love.

The Aftermath

१ पति सिर देखत मंदोदरी ।
मुरुछित बिकल धरनि खसि परी ॥
जुबति बृंद रोवत उठि धाईं ।
तेहि उठाइ रावन पहिं आईं ॥

२ पति गति देखि ते करहिं पुकारा ।
छूटे कच नहिं बपु सँभारा ॥
उर ताड़ना करहिं बिधि नाना ।
रोवत करहिं प्रताप बखाना ॥

३ तव बल नाथ डोल नित धरनी ।
तेज हीन पावक ससि तरनी ॥
सेष कमठ सहि सकहिं न भारा ।
सो तनु भूमि परेउ भरि छारा ॥

४ बरुन कुबेर सुरेस समीरा ।
रन सन्मुख धरि काहुँ न धीरा ॥
भुजबल जितेहु काल जम साईं ।
आजु परेहु अनाथ की नाईं ॥

५ जगत बिदित तुम्हारि प्रभुताई ।
सुत परिजन बल बरनि न जाई ॥
राम बिमुख अस हाल तुम्हारा ।
रहा न कोउ कुल रोवनिहारा ॥

६ तव बस बिधि प्रपंच सब नाथा ।
सभय दिसिप नित नावहिं माथा ॥
अब तव सिर भुज जंबुक खाहीं ।
राम बिमुख यह अनुचित नाहीं ॥

When Mandodari saw her husband's head   1
she fainted in anguish and fell to the ground.
A crowd of women ran to her, weeping,
then lifted her up and brought her to Ravan.
Beholding her lord's state, she wailed   2
and untied her hair, indifferent to comportment,
and beat her breast time and again,
sobbing, as she recounted his daring exploits.
"Before your might, lord, earth always trembled,   3
and fire, moon, and sun lost their luster.
Your form, whose weight the cosmic serpent and tortoise
could not bear, now sprawls on the ground, dust covered.
Varun and Kuber,* the king of gods, the wind—   4
none could muster courage to face you in battle.
Your mighty arms defeated Time and Yama,† lord,
yet today you lie here like a helpless, unprotected one.[1]
Your sovereignty was famed throughout the world,   5
the might of your sons and kinsmen, indescribable.
But enmity to Ram has reduced you to this state
in which none remains in our clan to mourn you.
Brahma's whole creation was under your sway, master,   6
and the lords of space always bowed to you in fear.
Now your heads and arms are gnawed by jackals,
but this is not unfitting for one who defied Ram.

* Gods of the waters and of wealth.
† God of death.

७ काल बिबस पति कहा न माना ।
अग जग नाथु मनुज करि जाना ॥

८ जान्यो मनुज करि दनुज कानन
दहन पावक हरि स्वयं ।
जेहि नमत सिव ब्रह्मादि सुर पिय
भजेहु नहिं करुनामयं ॥
आजन्म ते परद्रोह रत
पापौघमय तव तनु अयं ।
तुम्हहू दियो निज धाम राम
नमामि ब्रह्म निरामयं ॥

१०४ अहह नाथ रघुनाथ सम कृपासिंधु नहिं आन ।
जोगि बृंद दुर्लभ गति तोहि दीन्हि भगवान ॥

१ मंदोदरी बचन सुनि काना ।
सुर मुनि सिद्ध सबन्हि सुख माना ॥
अज महेस नारद सनकादी ।
जे मुनिबर परमारथबादी ॥

२ भरि लोचन रघुपतिहि निहारी ।
प्रेम मगन सब भए सुखारी ॥
रुदन करत देखीं सब नारी ।
गयउ बिभीषनु मन दुख भारी ॥

Under death's spell, husband, you heeded no one,　　　7
and took the Lord of all beings for a mere man.

You considered him but a man—who is blazing fire　　　8
to destroy the demon forest, Lord Hari himself,
worshiped by Shiva, Brahma, and all gods—
dearest, that all-merciful one you would not worship.
This body of yours, bent from birth on oppression
of others, was suffused with countless sins,
yet Ram has given you his own eternal abode,
and I bow to him—flawless *brahma*—in homage.

Ah, my lord! The lord of Raghus　　　104
is a sea of mercy without compeer,
for the state that eludes even hosts of yogis,
he, God himself, has bestowed on you."

Listening to Mandodari's speech　　　1
brought joy to gods, sages, and perfected ones.
Brahma, Mahesh,* Narad, Sanak and his brothers,[2]
and all great sages who expound ultimate truth
drank in the sight of the Raghu lord　　　2
and, lost in love, became utterly blissful.
At the sight of all the women weeping there,
Vibhishan sadly approached, his heart heavy,

* Shiva.

३ बंधु दसा बिलोकि दुख कीन्हा ।
तब प्रभु अनुजहि आयसु दीन्हा ॥
लछिमन तेहि बहु बिधि समुझायो ।
बहुरि बिभीषन प्रभु पहिं आयो ॥

४ कृपादृष्टि प्रभु ताहि बिलोका ।
करहु क्रिया परिहरि सब सोका ॥
कीन्हि क्रिया प्रभु आयसु मानी ।
बिधिवत देस काल जियँ जानी ॥

१०५ मंदोदरी आदि सब देइ तिलांजलि ताहि ।
भवन गई रघुपति गुन गन बरनत मन माहि ॥

१ आइ बिभीषन पुनि सिरु नायो ।
कृपासिंधु तब अनुज बोलायो ॥
तुम्ह कपीस अंगद नल नीला ।
जामवंत मारुति नयसीला ॥

२ सब मिलि जाहु बिभीषन साथा ।
सारेहु तिलक कहेउ रघुनाथा ॥
पिता बचन मैं नगर न आवउँ ।
आपु सरिस कपि अनुज पठावउँ ॥

३ तुरत चले कपि सुनि प्रभु बचना ।
कीन्ही जाइ तिलक की रचना ॥
सादर सिंहासन बैठारी ।
तिलक सारि अस्तुति अनुसारी ॥

and lamented, beholding his brother's state. 3
Then the Lord gave an order to his young brother,
and Lakshman much consoled and instructed Vibhishan,
who then came once more before Lord Ram.
Looking at him with compassion, the Lord said, 4
"Put aside your sorrow and perform his last rites."
Obedient to the Lord's command, he did the rituals
punctiliously, yet mindful of the place and time.[3]

Mandodari and all the other women 105
offered Ravan handfuls of sesame seeds,[4]
and then turned homeward, inwardly
reflecting on Ram's innumerable virtues.

Vibhishan returned and bowed once more, 1
and the sea of mercy summoned his own brother.
"Take with you the monkey king, Angad, Nal, Nil,
Jambavan, and Hanuman—those prudent ones—
and all go with Vibhishan and perform 2
his royal consecration," said the Raghu master.
"By my father's order, I will not enter a city,
so I send as proxies these monkeys and you, brother."
Heeding the Lord's words, the monkeys went at once 3
and made preparations for the ceremony.
Reverently seating Vibhishan on a lion throne,
they put the *tilak* on his forehead to a litany of praise.[5]

४ जोरि पानि सबहीं सिर नाए ।
　　सहित बिभीषन प्रभु पहिं आए ॥
　　तब रघुबीर बोलि कपि लीन्हे ।
　　कहि प्रिय बचन सुखी सब कीन्हे ॥

५ किए सुखी कहि बानी सुधा सम
　　बल तुम्हारें रिपु हयो ।
　　पायो बिभीषन राज तिहुँ पुर
　　जसु तुम्हारो नित नयो ।
　　मोहि सहित सुभ कीरति तुम्हारी
　　परम प्रीति जो गाइहैं ।
　　संसार सिंधु अपार पार
　　प्रयास बिनु नर पाइहैं ॥

१०६ प्रभु के बचन श्रवन सुनि नहिं अघाहिं कपि पुंज ।
　　बार बार सिर नावहिं गहहिं सकल पद कंज ॥

१ पुनि प्रभु बोलि लियउ हनुमाना ।
　　लंका जाहु कहेउ भगवाना ॥
　　समाचार जानकिहि सुनावहु ।
　　तासु कुसल लै तुम्ह चलि आवहु ॥

254

All bowed to him, palms joined in reverence,   4
and then, with Vibhishan, returned to the Lord.
The Raghu hero called the monkeys to his side
and delighted them all with words of endearment.

He delighted them with speech that was like nectar: 5
"It was due to your might that our enemy was slain
and Vibhishan obtained sovereignty, and your fame
will forever resound through the three worlds.
People who sing, with profound love,
of your blessed fame together with my own,
will effortlessly gain safe passage across
the shoreless sea of illusory existence."

Listening to the Lord's lovely words,   106
the monkeys' ears could never be sated.
Again and again they bowed before him
and held firmly to his lotus-like feet.

Then the Lord called for Hanuman   1
and the holy one said, "Go to Lanka,
convey all the news to Janaki,
and return to report on her well-being."

२ तब हनुमंत नगर महुँ आए ।
सुनि निसिचरी निसाचर धाए ॥
बहु प्रकार तिन्ह पूजा कीन्ही ।
जनकसुता देखाइ पुनि दीन्ही ॥

३ दूरिहि ते प्रनाम कपि कीन्हा ।
रघुपति दूत जानकी चीन्हा ॥
कहहु तात प्रभु कृपानिकेता ।
कुसल अनुज कपि सेन समेता ॥

४ सब बिधि कुसल कोसलाधीसा ।
मातु समर जीत्यो दससीसा ॥
अबिचल राजु बिभीषन पायो ।
सुनि कपि बचन हरष उर छायो ॥

५ अति हरष मन तन पुलक लोचन
सजल कह पुनि पुनि रमा ।
का देउँ तोहि त्रैलोक महुँ कपि
किमपि नहिं बानी समा ॥
सुनु मातु मैं पायो अखिल जग
राजु आजु न संसयं ।
रन जीति रिपुदल बंधु जुत
पस्यामि राममनामयं ॥

Hanuman entered the city, and when they heard,   2
the night-stalker women and men came running
to honor him in every way,
and then showed him Janak's daughter.
The monkey saluted her from a respectful distance,   3
but Janaki recognized the Raghu lord's messenger
and said, "Tell me, son, is my Lord, abode of grace,
well, along with his young brother and monkey host?"
Hanuman said, "Kosala's king fares well in every way,   4
mother, for he has defeated his ten-headed foe in battle,
and Vibhishan has won secure sovereignty."
The monkey's speech filled her heart with joy.

Her heart was overjoyed, her body shivered with bliss,   5
tears filled her eyes, and Ram's consort repeatedly said,
"What can I give you, monkey? For in all three worlds
there is nothing to equal the import of your words."
"Mother," Hanuman replied, "today I won sovereignty
over all of creation, beyond doubt, when I saw
on the field—his enemy's army beaten
and his brother at his side—faultless Lord Ram."

१०७ सुनु सुत सदगुन सकल तव हृदयँ बसहुँ हनुमंत ।
सानुकूल कोसलपति रहहुँ समेत अनंत ॥

१ अब सोइ जतन करहु तुम्ह ताता ।
देखौं नयन स्याम मुदु गाता ॥
तब हनुमान राम पहिं जाई ।
जनकसुता कै कुसल सुनाई ॥

२ सुनि संदेसु भानुकुलभूषन ।
बोलि लिए जुबराज बिभीषन ॥
मारुतसुत के संग सिधावहु ।
सादर जनकसुतहि लै आवहु ॥

३ तुरतहिं सकल गए जहँ सीता ।
सेवहिं सब निसिचरीं बिनीता ॥
बेगि बिभीषन तिन्हहि सिखायो ।
तिन्ह बहु बिधि मज्जन करवायो ॥

४ बहु प्रकार भूषन पहिराए ।
सिबिका रुचिर साजि पुनि ल्याए ॥
ता पर हरषि चढ़ी बैदेही ।
सुमिरि राम सुखधाम सनेही ॥

५ बेतपानि रच्छक चहु पासा ।
चले सकल मन परम हुलासा ॥
देखन भालु कीस सब आए ।
रच्छक कोपि निवारन धाए ॥

Sita said, "Hanuman, my son, hear my boon: 107
may every virtue abide in your heart,
and may the lord of Kosala, along with Anant,*
forever favor you.

And now, son, do whatever is necessary 1
that my eyes may see his dear, dark form."
Then Hanuman returned to Ram
and reported that Janak's daughter was well.
At this message, the ornament of the solar line 2
sent for Prince Angad and Vibhishan, and said,
"Go forth with the son of the wind
and respectfully bring back Janak's daughter."
They went at once to where Sita was, 3
now reverently attended by all demon women.
Vibhishan quickly instructed them
so that they thoroughly bathed the princess,
then richly adorned her with jewels, 4
and brought a beautiful, decorated palanquin.
Vaidehi climbed joyously into it,
contemplating her beloved Ram, abode of bliss.
Surrounded by staff-bearing guards, 5
the company set forth, hearts overjoyed.
But when the bears and monkeys all came to see her,
the guards angrily advanced to halt them.

---

* The cosmic serpent, incarnate as Lakshman.

६ कह रघुबीर कहा मम मानहु ।
सीतहि सखा पयादें आनहु ॥
देखहुँ कपि जननी की नाईं ।
बिहसि कहा रघुनाथ गोसाईं ॥

७ सुनि प्रभु बचन भालु कपि हरषे ।
नभ ते सुरन्ह सुमन बहु बरषे ॥
सीता प्रथम अनल महुँ राखी ।
प्रगट कीन्हि चह अंतर साखी ॥

१०८ तेहि कारन करुनानिधि कहे कछुक दुर्बाद ।
सुनत जातुधानीं सब लागीं करै बिषाद ॥

१ प्रभु के बचन सीस धरि सीता ।
बोली मन क्रम बचन पुनीता ॥
लछिमन होहु धरम के नेगी ।
पावक प्रगट करहु तुम्ह बेगी ॥

२ सुनि लछिमन सीता कै बानी ।
बिरह बिबेक धरम निति सानी ॥
लोचन सजल जोरि कर दोऊ ।
प्रभु सन कछु कहि सकत न ओऊ ॥

३ देखि राम रुख लछिमन धाए ।
पावक प्रगटि काठ बहु लाए ॥
पावक प्रबल देखि बैदेही ।
हृदयँ हरष नहिं भय कछु तेही ॥

260

Then the hero of the Raghus said, "Hear me,   6
friends—bring Sita here on foot, and let
the monkeys see her, who is like their mother"—
so the great Raghu master said with a laugh.
At the Lord's words, the bears and monkeys rejoiced   7
and the gods rained blossoms from the sky.
Sita had earlier been concealed in fire,
and the inner witness now wished to reveal her.[6]

For this reason alone, the treasury of mercy   108
uttered some harsh words,
and when they heard them,
all the demon women were dismayed.

Humbly accepting the Lord's order, Sita,   1
who was pure in mind, deed, and word, spoke:
"Lakshman, be my faithful helper in dharma[7]
and quickly prepare a great fire."
When Lakshman heard Sita's words, imbued   2
with longing, discernment, duty, and virtue,
his eyes filled with tears and he stood with palms joined,
yet he could not say anything to the Lord.
Reading Ram's countenance, Lakshman hurried   3
to bring ample wood and build a fire.
As Vaidehi looked at that roaring blaze,
her heart was happy and free of fear.

४ जौं मन बच क्रम मम उर माहीं ।
तजि रघुबीर आन गति नाहीं ॥
तौ कृसानु सब कै गति जाना ।
मो कहुँ होउ श्रीखंड समाना ॥

५ श्रीखंड सम पावक प्रबेस
कियो सुमिरि प्रभु मैथिली ।
जय कोसलेस महेस बंदित
चरन रति अति निर्मली ॥
प्रतिबिंब अरु लौकिक कलंक
प्रचंड पावक महुँ जरे ।
प्रभु चरित काहुँ न लखे नभ सुर
सिद्ध मुनि देखहिं खरे ॥

६ धरि रूप पावक पानि गहि
श्री सत्य श्रुति जग बिदित जो ।
जिमि छीरसागर इंदिरा
रामहि समर्पी आनि सो ॥
सो राम बाम बिभाग राजति
रुचिर अति सोभा भली ।
नव नील नीरज निकट मानहुँ
कनक पंकज की कली ॥

१०९क बरषहिं सुमन हरषि सुर बाजहिं गगन निसान ।
गावहिं किंनर सुरबधू नाचहिं चढ़ीं बिमान ॥

"If, in my heart, in thought, word, and act,   4
I have recourse to none but the Raghu hero,
may Fire—who knows the inner state of all—
be for me as cool as sandalwood."

Into that fire, cool as sandalwood, entered   5
Maithili,* contemplating her lord, and saying,
"Victory to Kosala's king, whose feet are adored
with utterly pure love by the great god, Shiva."[8]
Sita's shadow image, along with all worldly taint,
was consumed in that raging inferno.
No one perceived this play of the Lord, though gods,
sages, and perfected ones stood in the sky looking on.
The fire god assumed form and took her by the hand—   6
the true one, Shri, famed in the Veda and the world—
and as the cosmic sea of nectar had once done
with Lakshmi, brought and presented her to Ram.[9]
She shone there, at Ram's left side,
the epitome of perfect beauty and splendor,
as if, close by a newly opened deep-blue lotus,
the bud of a golden one had arisen.

The delighted gods showered flowers   109a
as great drums resounded in the heavens,
and *kinnaras* sang while, atop aerial cars,
divine women danced.

---

* Sita.

१०९ख जनकसुता समेत प्रभु सोभा अमित अपार ।
देखि भालु कपि हरषे जय रघुपति सुख सार ॥

१   तब रघुपति अनुसासन पाई ।
मातलि चलेउ चरन सिरु नाई ॥
आए देव सदा स्वारथी ।
बचन कहहिं जनु परमारथी ॥

२   दीन बंधु दयाल रघुराया ।
देव कीन्हि देवन्ह पर दाया ॥
बिस्व द्रोह रत यह खल कामी ।
निज अघ गयउ कुमारगगामी ॥

३   तुम्ह समरूप ब्रह्म अबिनासी ।
सदा एकरस सहज उदासी ॥
अकल अगुन अज अनघ अनामय ।
अजित अमोघसक्ति करुनामय ॥

४   मीन कमठ सूकर नरहरी ।
बामन परसुराम बपु धरी ॥
जब जब नाथ सुरन्ह दुखु पायो ।
नाना तनु धरि तुम्हइँ नसायो ॥

५   यह खल मलिन सदा सुरद्रोही ।
काम लोभ मद रत अति कोही ॥
अधम सिरोमनि तव पद पावा ।
यह हमरें मन बिसमय आवा ॥

The Lord, joined with Janak's daughter,   109b
was the epitome of boundless beauty,
and seeing this, the bears and monkeys exulted
as they hailed the Raghu master, essence of bliss.

Then, with the Raghu lord's leave, the charioteer   1
Matali bowed at his feet and departed,
and now the gods approached—ever self-interested,
yet holding forth as if set on the supreme goal:
"Friend of the meek, compassionate Raghu sovereign,   2
and God—to the gods, you have shown mercy.
This wicked, lustful scourge of the world, Ravan
the wrongdoer, has been done in by his own sins.
For you are impartial, imperishable *brahma,*   3
eternally changeless, innately dispassionate,
without divisions or attributes, unborn, sinless, perfect,
unconquerable, of irresistible might, yet all-merciful.
You took form as fish, tortoise, boar, man-lion,   4
dwarf, and the ax-wielding Parashuram;
whenever the gods were in distress, master,
you alone, taking many forms, ended their woes.
This tainted villain—forever inimical to the gods,   5
bent on lust, greed, arrogance, and utterly choleric,
the diadem of the despicable—has won your state,
and at this our minds are astonished.

६ हम देवता परम अधिकारी ।
स्वारथ रत प्रभु भगति बिसारी ॥
भव प्रबाहँ संतत हम परे ।
अब प्रभु पाहि सरन अनुसरे ॥

११० करि बिनती सुर सिद्ध सब रहे जहँ तहँ कर जोरि ।
अति सप्रेम तन पुलकि बिधि अस्तुति करत बहोरि ॥

१ जय राम सदा सुखधाम हरे ।
रघुनायक सायक चाप धरे ॥
भव बारन दारन सिंह प्रभो ।
गुन सागर नागर नाथ बिभो ॥

२ तन काम अनेक अनूप छबी ।
गुन गावत सिद्ध मुनींद्र कबी ॥
जसु पावन रावन नाग महा ।
खगनाथ जथा करि कोप गहा ॥

३ जन रंजन भंजन सोक भयं ।
गतक्रोध सदा प्रभु बोधमयं ॥
अवतार उदार अपार गुनं ।
महि भार बिभंजन ग्यानघनं ॥

४ अज ब्यापकमेकमनादि सदा ।
करुनाकर राम नमामि मुदा ॥
रघुबंस बिभूषन दूषन हा ।
कृत भूप बिभीषन दीन रहा ॥

We gods, though supremely entitled to salvation,   6
are bent on self-interest and oblivious of devotion to God,
hence we forever fall into rebirth's maelstrom.
But now, Lord, we take refuge in you—rescue us!"

Having made their petition, gods and perfected ones   110
remained where they were, in attitudes of reverence,
and then Brahma the creator, his body thrilling
with intense love, began a hymn of praise.[10]

"Victory to Ram, eternal abode of joy, divine Hari,[11]   1
lord of the Raghu line, bearing arrows and bow.
You are a lion, Lord, to rip apart rebirth's elephant,
an ocean of virtues, urbane and magnanimous master
embodied with the matchless beauty of countless Kamas.   2
Your merits are sung by perfected ones, great sages, and
      poets.
Of pure renown, you pounced on the great serpent
that was Ravan like an enraged king of birds.*
Succor of humble devotees, destroyer of sorrow and fear,   3
ever beyond anger, Lord, you are omniscience itself.
Bountiful avatar, of boundless noble attributes,
you destroy earth's burden and are a mass of wisdom.
Unborn, all-pervading, unitary, beginningless, eternal,   4
and most merciful Ram—I joyfully bow to you.
Crown jewel of the Raghu clan, killer of Dushan,
you made a king of wretched Vibhishan.[12]

---

* Garuda, the enemy of snakes.

५ गुन ग्यान निधान अमान अजं ।
नित राम नमामि बिभुं बिरजं ॥
भुजदंड प्रचंड प्रताप बलं ।
खल बृंद निकंद महा कुसलं ॥

६ बिनु कारन दीन दयाल हितं ।
छबि धाम नमामि रमा सहितं ॥
भव तारन कारन काज परं ।
मन संभव दारुन दोष हरं ॥

७ सर चाप मनोहर त्रोन धरं ।
जलजारुन लोचन भूपबरं ॥
सुख मंदिर सुंदर श्रीरमनं ।
मद मार मुधा ममता समनं ॥

८ अनवद्य अखंड न गोचर गो ।
सब रूप सदा सब होइ न सो ॥
इति बेद बदंति न दंतकथा ।
रबि आतप भिन्नमभिन्न जथा ॥

९ कृतकृत्य बिभो सब बानर ए ।
निरखंति तवानन सादर ए ॥
धिग जीवन देव सरीर हरे ।
तव भक्ति बिना भव भूलि परे ॥

१० अब दीनदयाल दया करिऐ ।
मति मोरि बिभेदकरी हरिऐ ॥
जेहि ते बिपरीत क्रिया करिऐ ।
दुख सो सुख मानि सुखी चरिऐ ॥

Treasury of virtues and wisdom, free of pride, unborn—   5
I forever bow to you, Ram, stainless and omnipresent.
With the fierce might of your powerful arms
you are most deft in destroying legions of villains.
Spontaneous and merciful benefactor of the lowly,   6
abode of beauty—to you, together with Ramā,* I bow.
Taking us across rebirth's sea, you transcend cause and
    effect[13]
and remove ruinous sins born of the mind.
Bearing beautiful arrows, bow, and quiver,   7
your eyes tinged with lotus-red, you are best of kings,
abode of bliss, handsome lover of Shri,[14]
and queller of arrogance, lust, and false pride.
Flawless, indivisible, imperceptible by the senses,   8
ever imminent in all forms, and yet beyond them—
so the Veda declares; it is not mere imagination—
as the sun and its radiance are different yet nondifferent.[15]
All these monkeys, mighty one, have reached their goal,   9
for they can gaze in reverence at your face,
but alas, Hari, for our long-living divine bodies,
without devotion to you, lost in rebirth's cycle.
Now, kindly helper of the wretched, be kind;   10
remove my false awareness that creates duality,
on account of which I do adverse acts
and, taking sorrow for joy, roam in blithe delusion.

---

* The feminine form of Ram's name, connoting Sita.

११	खल खंडन मंडन रम्य छमा ।
	पद पंकज सेवित संभु उमा ॥
	नृप नायक दे बरदानमिदं ।
	चरनांबुज प्रेम सदा सुभदं ॥

१११	बिनय कीन्हि चतुरानन प्रेम पुलक अति गात ।
	सोभासिंधु बिलोकत लोचन नहीं अघात ॥

१	तेही अवसर दसरथ तहँ आए ।
	तनय बिलोकि नयन जल छाए ॥
	अनुज सहित प्रभु बंदन कीन्हा ।
	आसिरबाद पिताँ तब दीन्हा ॥

२	तात सकल तव पुन्य प्रभाऊ ।
	जीत्यों अजय निसाचर राऊ ॥
	सुनि सुत बचन प्रीति अति बाढ़ी ।
	नयन सलिल रोमावलि ठाढ़ी ॥

३	रघुपति प्रथम प्रेम अनुमाना ।
	चितइ पितहि दीन्हेउ दृढ़ ग्याना ॥
	ताते उमा मोच्छ नहिं पायो ।
	दसरथ भेद भगति मन लायो ॥

४	सगुनोपासक मोच्छ न लेहीं ।
	तिन्ह कहुँ राम भगति निज देहीं ॥
	बार बार करि प्रभुहि प्रनामा ।
	दसरथ हरषि गए सुरधामा ॥

Destroyer of evildoers, earth's enchanting ornament, 11
whose holy feet are worshiped by Shambhu and Uma,*
king of kings—grant me this boon:
constant, blessed love for your lotus-like feet."

Thus four-faced Brahma made humble petition, 111
his body thrilling with intense love,
and as he gazed at that ocean of beauty,
his eyes were never sated.

Then King Dasarath came there,[16] 1
his eyes tearful at the sight of his son.
With his younger brother, the Lord saluted him,
and their father bestowed his blessing on them.
Ram said, "Father, it was all by your merit's power 2
that I defeated the undefeatable demon king."
At his son's words, he was overwhelmed with love;
his eyes shed tears and his whole body thrilled.
Reflecting on his father's prior love, the Raghu lord 3
gave him, with one glance, unshakable insight.[17]
Shiva said, "He did not gain liberation, Uma,
for Dasarath had set his heart on dualist devotion,
and votaries of God-with-attributes do not get release; 4
rather, Ram grants them intimate devotion to himself."
Saluting the Lord again and again,
Dasarath went joyfully to the gods' realm.

―――――

* Shiva and Parvati.

११२ अनुज जानकी सहित प्रभु कुसल कोसलाधीस ।
सोभा देखि हरषि मन अस्तुति कर सुर ईस ॥

१ जय राम सोभा धाम ।
दायक प्रनत बिश्राम ॥
धृत त्रोन बर सर चाप ।
भुजदंड प्रबल प्रताप ॥

२ जय दूषनारि खरारि ।
मर्दन निसाचर धारि ॥
यह दुष्ट मारेउ नाथ ।
भए देव सकल सनाथ ॥

३ जय हरन धरनी भार ।
महिमा उदार अपार ॥
जय रावनारि कृपाल ।
किए जातुधान बिहाल ॥

४ लंकेस अति बल गर्ब ।
किए बस्य सुर गंधर्ब ॥
मुनि सिद्ध नर खग नाग ।
हठि पंथ सब कें लाग ॥

५ परद्रोह रत अति दुष्ट ।
पायो सो फलु पापिष्ठ ॥
अब सुनहु दीन दयाल ।
राजीव नयन बिसाल ॥

Together with his younger brother and Janaki,   112
the Lord, ruler of Kosala, rested content,
and seeing his beauty, the sovereign of celestials*
rejoiced inwardly and began a paean of praise.

"Hail to you, Ram, abode of splendor,[18]   1
you who give relief to petitioners,
who bear glorious quiver, arrows, and bow
with the strength of your mighty arms.
Hail to you, foe of Dushan and Khar,   2
annihilator of legions of night-stalkers,
and when you slew this scoundrel, too,
all gods gained a benevolent protector.
Hail to the lifter of earth's burden,   3
of lofty and limitless grandeur.
Hail to the merciful one, foe of Ravan,
who confounded the demon race.
Lanka's lord was so proud of his might   4
and subjugated gods, *gandharvas,*† sages,
perfect ones, humans, great birds, and serpents;
he was relentless in pursuit of them all.
Utterly wicked, bent on enmity to others,   5
he gained the rightful fruit of his sins.
Now, hear me—merciful to the meek,
Lord with large, lotus-like eyes—

---

* Indra.
† Celestial musicians.

६ मोहि रहा अति अभिमान ।
नहिं कोउ मोहि समान ॥
अब देखि प्रभु पद कंज ।
गत मान प्रद दुख पुंज ॥

७ कोउ ब्रह्म निर्गुन ध्याव ।
अब्यक्त जेहि श्रुति गाव ॥
मोहि भाव कोसल भूप ।
श्रीराम सगुन सरूप ॥

८ बैदेहि अनुज समेत ।
मम हृदयँ करहु निकेत ॥
मोहि जानिऐ निज दास ।
दे भक्ति रमानिवास ॥

९ दे भक्ति रमानिवास त्रास
हरन सरन सुखदायकं ।
सुख धाम राम नमामि काम
अनेक छबि रघुनायकं ॥
सुर बृंद रंजन द्वंद भंजन
मनुज तनु अतुलितबलं ।
ब्रह्मादि संकर सेब्य राम
नमामि करुना कोमलं ॥

११३ अब करि कृपा बिलोकि मोहि आयसु देहु कृपाल ।
काह करौं सुनि प्रिय बचन बोले दीनदयाल ॥

I have been exceedingly arrogant, 6
thinking no one my equal.
But now, Lord, beholding your holy feet,
that pride, source of myriad sorrows, has fled.
Some may meditate on formless *brahma,* 7
whom the Veda hails as indescribable,
but I delight in the king of Kosala, embodied
as Lord Ram and endowed with attributes.
Together with Vaidehi and your brother, 8
make your home in my heart,
and considering me your faithful servant,
grant me devotion to you, husband of Ramā.[19]

Grant me devotion, Ramā's lord, remover of fear 9
and giver of joy to those who take refuge in you.
I bow to you, Ram, as the abode of delight,
Raghu king with the comeliness of countless Kamas,
gladdener of the gods, destroyer of dualities,
embodied as a man of incomparable might,
fit to be worshiped by Brahma, Shankar, and all deities—
I bow to you, Ram, of most tender compassion.

Now, looking on me with mercy, 113
give me an order, gracious one.
What may I do for you?" Hearing Indra's
loving words, the comforter of the lowly said—

१ सुनु सुरपति कपि भालु हमारे ।
परे भूमि निसिचरन्हि जे मारे ॥
मम हित लागि तजे इन्ह प्राना ।
सकल जिआउ सुरेस सुजाना ॥

२ सुनु खगेस प्रभु कै यह बानी ।
अति अगाध जानहिं मुनि ग्यानी ॥
प्रभु सक त्रिभुअन मारि जिआई ।
केवल सक्रहि दीन्हि बड़ाई ॥

३ सुधा बरषि कपि भालु जिआए ।
हरषि उठे सब प्रभु पहिं आए ॥
सुधाबृष्टि भै दुहु दल ऊपर ।
जिए भालु कपि नहिं रजनीचर ॥

४ रामाकार भए तिन्ह के मन ।
मुक्त भए छूटे भव बंधन ॥
सुर अंसिक सब कपि अरु रीछा ।
जिए सकल रघुपति कीं ईछा ॥

५ राम सरिस को दीन हितकारी ।
कीन्हे मुकुत निसाचर झारी ॥
खल मल धाम कामरत रावन ।
गति पाई जो मुनिबर पाव न ॥

११४क सुमन बरषि सब सुर चले चढ़ि चढ़ि रुचिर बिमान ।
देखि सुअवसर प्रभु पहिं आयउ संभु सुजान ॥

"Listen, lord of gods: my monkeys and bears,   1
slain by night-stalkers, are lying on the field.
For my sake, they sacrificed their lives,
so revive them all, wise ruler of celestials."
Bhushundi said, "King of birds, the Lord's words 2
were unfathomable, except to enlightened sages.[20]
Our Lord, who can slay and revivify all three worlds,
merely deigned to honor Indra with this task."
Raining nectar, Indra revived the monkeys and bears, 3
who arose happily and all hurried to the Lord.
Though the shower of ambrosia fell on both armies,
it revived bears and monkeys, but not night-stalkers—
for their minds had been focused on Ram's form 4
and they were liberated, freed of rebirth's bonds,
whereas monkeys and bears had been born of the gods,[21]
and it was the Raghu lord's wish that they live on.
Ram is the incomparable benefactor of the wretched 5
who gave liberation to legions of night-stalkers,
and that archvillain—most vile and lustful Ravan—
attained a state even great sages do not win.

Showering blossoms, all the gods departed,   114a
mounted on their respective vehicles.
But discerning a propitious moment,
wise Shiva approached the Lord.

११४ख परम प्रीति कर जोरि जुग नलिन नयन भरि बारि ।
पुलकित तन गदगद गिराँ बिनय करत त्रिपुरारि ॥

१ मामभिरक्षय रघुकुल नायक ।
धृत बर चाप रुचिर कर सायक ॥
मोह महा घन पटल प्रभंजन ।
संसय बिपिन अनल सुर रंजन ॥

२ अगुन सगुन गुन मंदिर सुंदर ।
भ्रम तम प्रबल प्रताप दिवाकर ॥
काम क्रोध मद गज पंचानन ।
बसहु निरंतर जन मन कानन ॥

३ बिषय मनोरथ पुंज कंज बन ।
प्रबल तुषार उदार पार मन ॥
भव बारिधि मंदर परमं दर ।
बारय तारय संसृति दुस्तर ॥

४ स्याम गात राजीव बिलोचन ।
दीन बंधु प्रनतारति मोचन ॥
अनुज जानकी सहित निरंतर ।
बसहु राम नृप मम उर अंतर ॥

५ मुनि रंजन महि मंडल मंडन ।
तुलसिदास प्रभु त्रास बिखंडन ॥

११५ नाथ जबहिं कोसलपुरीं होइहि तिलक तुम्हार ।
कृपासिंधु मैं आउब देखन चरित उदार ॥

With supreme love, palms reverently joined,   114b
and tears filling his lotus-like eyes,
his body shivering with joy and voice trembling,
the triple cities' foe began his entreaty.[22]

"Protect me, master of the Raghus,   1
bow-bearer, with arrows in your lovely hands—
tempest to disperse delusion's dense clouds,
fire to consume forests of doubt, gladdener of gods.
Formless and with form, beautiful abode of attributes,   2
fiery sun that banishes delusion's darkness,
lion to slay the elephants of lust, anger, and pride—
abide forever in the forest of your devotee's heart.[23]
For the lotus lake of amassed sensual desires   3
you are a deadly frost. Bountiful and beyond mind,
Mount Mandara to churn rebirth's ocean—remove
our terror and take us across illusion's impassable sea.
With your dark body and large, lotus-like eyes—   4
brother to the lowly, liberator of the distressed—
along with Lakshman and Janaki, eternally
deign to dwell, King Ram, within my heart.
You are the delight of sages, ornament of earth,   5
lord of Tulsidas, and destroyer of dread.[24]

Master, to the city of Kosala, when   115
you will be consecrated as its king,
I will assuredly come, sea of mercy,
to see your munificent deeds."

१   करि बिनती जब संभु सिधाए ।
तब प्रभु निकट बिभीषनु आए ॥
नाइ चरन सिरु कह मृदु बानी ।
बिनय सुनहु प्रभु सारँगपानी ॥

२   सकुल सदल प्रभु रावन मार्यो ।
पावन जस त्रिभुवन बिस्तार्यो ॥
दीन मलीन हीन मति जाती ।
मो पर कृपा कीन्हि बहु भाँती ॥

३   अब जन गृह पुनीत प्रभु कीजे ।
मज्जनु करिअ समर श्रम छीजे ॥
देखि कोस मंदिर संपदा ।
देहु कृपाल कपिन्ह कहुँ मुदा ॥

४   सब बिधि नाथ मोहि अपनाइअ ।
पुनि मोहि सहित अवधपुर जाइअ ॥
सुनत बचन मृदु दीनदयाला ।
सजल भए द्वौ नयन बिसाला ॥

११६क   तोर कोस गृह मोर सब सत्य बचन सुनु भ्रात ।
भरत दसा सुमिरत मोहि निमिष कल्प सम जात ॥

११६ख   तापस बेष गात कृस जपत निरंतर मोहि ।
देखौं बेगि सो जतनु करु सखा निहोरउँ तोहि ॥

After Shambhu had paid homage and left,   1
Vibhishan then approached the Lord,
bowed at his feet, and gently said,
"Lord with the Sharnga bow, hear my request:
you have slain Ravan with his kinsmen and army,   2
spread your pure fame through the three worlds,
and to me—wretched, sinful, ignorant, and lowborn—
you have been abundantly gracious.
Now, lord, please purify this servant's abode,   3
and bathe there, to lessen the fatigue of battle.
Then inspect the treasury, palace, and properties,
and joyfully disburse them, kind one, to the monkeys.
Deign to make me your own, master, in all ways,   4
and then, taking me along, go to Avadh city."
When the merciful one heard these sweet words,
tears welled up in his large eyes, and he said,

"Your treasuries and mansions are all mine—   116a
that is indeed true, brother; but listen:
whenever I recall Bharat's plight,
each instant passes like an aeon.

In ascetic garb, his body emaciated,   116b
he constantly repeats my name.
Devise a means so I may see him quickly,
friend; this is my heartfelt entreaty.

११६ग बीतें अवधि जाउँ जौं जिअत न पावउँ बीर ।
सुमिरत अनुज प्रीति प्रभु पुनि पुनि पुलक सरीर ॥

११६घ करेहु कल्प भरि राजु तुम्ह मोहि सुमिरेहु मन माहिं ।
पुनि मम धाम पाइहहु जहाँ संत सब जाहिं ॥

१ सुनत बिभीषन बचन राम के ।
हरषि गहे पद कृपाधाम के ॥
बानर भालु सकल हरषाने ।
गहि प्रभु पद गुन बिमल बखाने ॥

२ बहुरि बिभीषन भवन सिधायो ।
मनि गन बसन बिमान भरायो ॥
लै पुष्पक प्रभु आगें राखा ।
हँसि करि कृपासिंधु तब भाषा ॥

३ चढ़ि बिमान सुनु सखा बिभीषन ।
गगन जाइ बरषहु पट भूषन ॥
नभ पर जाइ बिभीषन तबही ।
बरषि दिए मनि अंबर सबही ॥

४ जोइ जोइ मन भावइ सोइ लेहीं ।
मनि मुख मेलि डारि कपि देहीं ॥
हँसे रामु श्री अनुज समेता ।
परम कौतुकी कृपा निकेता ॥

If I should return past my exile's term,   116c
I would not find that hero alive."
As the Lord recalled his young brother's love,
his body thrilled with rapture, again and again.

Then Ram said, "Reign for a full aeon,[25]   116d
remembering me in your heart,
and then you will reach my own abode
to which all saintly ones go."

When he heard Ram's words, Vibhishan   1
joyfully clasped the feet of the abode of mercy.
All the bears and monkeys rejoiced, too,
and touching the Lord's feet, extolled his pure virtues.
Afterward, Vibhishan proceeded to his palace   2
and filled a magic vehicle with gems and garments.
He brought it—the Pushpak—and set it before Ram,[26]
and then the sea of compassion smilingly said:
"Vibhishan, my friend, mount this vehicle,   3
go into the sky, and rain down these clothes and gems."
At once, Vibhishan soared heavenward
and showered down all the jewels and rich cloth.
Each monkey soldier took whatever appealed to him;   4
they tried to eat the gems, but spit them out.[27]
Ram, with his wife and brother, laughed heartily,
for the treasury of mercy is most playful.

११७क मुनि जेहि ध्यान न पावहिं नेति नेति कह बेद।
कृपासिंधु सोइ कपिन्ह सन करत अनेक बिनोद॥

११७ख उमा जोग जप दान तप नाना मख ब्रत नेम।
राम कृपा नहिं करहिं तसि जसि निष्केवल प्रेम॥

१ भालु कपिन्ह पट भूषन पाए।
पहिरि पहिरि रघुपति पहिं आए॥
नाना जिनस देखि सब कीसा।
पुनि पुनि हँसत कोसलाधीसा॥

१ चितइ सबन्हि पर कीन्ही दाया।
बोले मृदुल बचन रघुराया॥
तुम्हरें बल मैं रावनु मार्यो।
तिलक बिभीषन कहँ पुनि सार्यो॥

३ निज निज गृह अब तुम्ह सब जाहू।
सुमिरेहु मोहि डरपहु जनि काहू॥
सुनत बचन प्रेमाकुल बानर।
जोरि पानि बोले सब सादर॥

४ प्रभु जोइ कहहु तुम्हहि सब सोहा।
हमरें होत बचन सुनि मोहा॥
दीन जानि कपि किए सनाथा।
तुम्ह त्रैलोक ईस रघुनाथा॥

He whom even sages, deep in meditation, cannot reach,   117a
and whom Veda declares to be "not this, not this,"
that very one, the ocean of compassion,
much amused himself with his monkeys.

Shiva said, "Uma—every sort of yoga, mantra repetition,   117b
charity, austerity, sacrifice, fast, and discipline
does not cause Ram to bestow his grace
so much as does sincere and unwavering love."

Bears and monkeys, getting clothing and jewelry,   1
donned them every which way and came before Ram.
At the sight of all those simian species,[28]
the ruler of Kosala laughed again and again.
Gazing indulgently upon them all,   2
the Raghu master gently said,
"It was by your might alone that I slew Ravan
and placed the royal mark on Vibhishan's brow.
Now go, all of you, to your respective homes,   3
remembering me and fearing no one."
At this, the monkeys grew restless with love
and, with palms joined, all reverently said,
"Whatever you say surely befits you, master,   4
but hearing your words, we are bewildered.
Knowing we are lowly monkeys, you became our
    benefactor—
you, Lord of the three worlds and Raghu king.

५ सुनि प्रभु बचन लाज हम मरहीं ।
मसक कहूँ खगपति हित करहीं ॥
देखि राम रुख बानर रीछा ।
प्रेम मगन नहिं गृह कै ईछा ॥

११८क प्रभु प्रेरित कपि भालु सब राम रूप उर राखि ।
हरष बिषाद सहित चले बिनय बिबिध बिधि भाषि ॥

११८ख कपिपति नील रीछपति अंगद नल हनुमान ।
सहित बिभीषन अपर जे जूथप कपि बलवान ॥

११८ग कहि न सकहिं कछु प्रेम बस भरि भरि लोचन बारि ।
सन्मुख चितवहिं राम तन नयन निमेष निवारि ॥

१ अतिसय प्रीति देखि रघुराई ।
लीन्हे सकल बिमान चढ़ाई ॥
मन महुँ बिप्र चरन सिरु नायो ।
उत्तर दिसिहि बिमान चलायो ॥

२ चलत बिमानु कोलाहल होई ।
जय रघुबीर कहइ सबु कोई ॥
सिंहासन अति उच्च मनोहर ।
श्री समेत प्रभु बैठे ता पर ॥

286

But hearing your words, Lord, we could die of shame—   5
for can mosquitoes give aid to the monarch of birds?" *
Discerning Ram's intent, those monkeys and bears
became lost in love, with no wish to return home.[29]

Yet, impelled by Lord Ram, all the monkeys and bears   118a
placed his lovely form in their hearts
and departed with mingled joy and sorrow,
voicing countless expressions of humility.

But the monkey and bear kings, and Nil,   118b
Angad, Nal, and Hanuman,
together with Vibhishan
and the mighty monkey generals,

overcome by love, were unable to speak.   118c
Their eyes overflowing with tears,
they gazed at Ram's form before them,
not allowing their eyes to blink.

When the Raghu king saw their overwhelming love,   1
he let them all board the vehicle.
Then he bowed inwardly to the Brahman seers' feet,
and the vehicle departed northward.
When the Pushpak left, there arose great tumult   2
as everyone cried, "Victory to the Raghu hero!"
On that craft's lofty and captivating royal dais
the Lord was seated with radiant Sita,

---

* Garuda.

287

३   राजत रामु सहित भामिनी ।
मेरु सृंग जनु घन दामिनी ॥
रुचिर बिमान चलेउ अति आतुर ।
कीन्ही सुमन बृष्टि हरषे सुर ॥

४   परम सुखद चलि त्रिबिध बयारी ।
सागर सर सरि निर्मल बारी ॥
सगुन होहिं सुंदर चहुँ पासा ।
मन प्रसन्न निर्मल नभ आसा ॥

५   कह रघुबीर देखु रन सीता ।
लछिमन इहाँ हत्यो इँद्रजीता ॥
हनूमान अंगद के मारे ।
रन महि परे निसाचर भारे ॥

६   कुंभकरन रावन द्रौ भाई ।
इहाँ हते सुर मुनि दुखदाई ॥

११९क इहाँ सेतु बाँध्यों अरु थापेउँ सिव सुख धाम ।
सीता सहित कृपानिधि संभुहि कीन्ह प्रनाम ॥

११९ख जहँ जहँ कृपासिंधु बन कीन्ह बास बिश्राम ।
सकल देखाए जानकिहि कहे सबन्हि के नाम ॥

and with his wife, Ram looked as splendid there   3
as a raincloud streaked with lightning on Meru's summit.
The wonderful vehicle moved at great speed
as the exultant gods released showers of blossoms.
A cool, fragrant breeze began to blow, giving delight,   4
the water of sea, lakes, and rivers became clear,
auspicious omens appeared on all sides,
hearts rejoiced, and the sky and directions grew bright.
The Raghu hero said, "Behold the battlefield, Sita;   5
here Lakshman killed Indra's conqueror, Meghnad,
and see, slain at the hands of Hanuman and Angad,
all those huge night-stalkers lying on the field.
The two brothers, Kumbhakaran and Ravan,   6
tormenters of gods and sages, were killed here.

Here we constructed the causeway over the sea   119a
and ritually installed Shiva, abode of bliss"—
and together with Sita, the treasury of mercy
bowed in homage to Lord Shambhu.[30]

Wherever Ram, ocean of compassion,   119b
had camped or taken rest in the forest—
all these places he showed to Janaki,
identifying each by name.

१ तुरत बिमान तहाँ चलि आवा ।
दंडक बन जहँ परम सुहावा ॥
कुंभजादि मुनिनायक नाना ।
गए रामु सब कें अस्थाना ॥

२ सकल रिषिन्ह सन पाइ असीसा ।
चित्रकूट आए जगदीसा ॥
तहँ करि मुनिन्ह केर संतोषा ।
चला बिमानु तहाँ ते चोखा ॥

३ बहुरि राम जानकिहि देखाई ।
जमुना कलि मल हरनि सुहाई ॥
पुनि देखी सुरसरी पुनीता ।
राम कहा प्रनाम करु सीता ॥

४ तीरथपति पुनि देखु प्रयागा ।
निरखत जन्म कोटि अघ भागा ॥
देखु परम पावनि पुनि बेनी ।
हरनि सोक हरि लोक निसेनी ॥

५ पुनि देखु अवधपुरी अति पावनि ।
त्रिबिध ताप भव रोग नसावनि ॥

१२०क सीता सहित अवध कहुँ कीन्ह कृपाल प्रनाम ।
सजल नयन तन पुलकित पुनि पुनि हरषित राम ॥

१२०ख पुनि प्रभु आइ त्रिबेनीं हरषित मज्जनु कीन्ह ।
कपिन्ह सहित बिप्रन्ह कहुँ दान बिबिध बिधि दीन्ह ॥

The flying vehicle swiftly arrived   1
at the beautiful forest of Dandak,
where pot-born Agastya and many great sages
resided, and Ram went to each of their abodes.
Obtaining the blessings of all these seers,   2
the Lord of the world came to Chitrakut
to give satisfaction to its resident sages
before his vehicle went rapidly onward.
Before long, Ram pointed out to Janaki   3
lovely Yamuna, remover of the dark age's filth,
and then they saw Ganga, river of the gods,
and Ram said, "Salute her, Sita,
then behold Prayag, king of pilgrimage places,   4
the mere sight of which dispels sins of myriad births.
Now see the triple confluence, supremely holy,
remover of sorrow, and ladder to Lord Hari's world.
And then, look to the most sacred city of Avadh,   5
destroyer of the three torments and rebirth's plague."

Together with Sita, that merciful one   120a
bowed his head in reverence to Avadh.
Ram's eyes filled with tears and his body,
again and again, flushed with joy.

Then the Lord came to Triveni, confluence   120b
of the three rivers, and joyously bathed there,
together with the monkeys, bestowing
abundant gifts on Brahman seers.[31]

१ प्रभु हनुमंतहि कहा बुझाई ।
   धरि बटु रूप अवधपुर जाई ॥
   भरतहि कुसल हमारि सुनाएहु ।
   समाचार लै तुम्ह चलि आएहु ॥

२ तुरत पवनसुत गवनत भयऊ ।
   तब प्रभु भरद्वाज पहिं गयऊ ॥
   नाना बिधि मुनि पूजा कीन्ही ।
   अस्तुति करि पुनि आसिष दीन्ही ॥

३ मुनि पद बंदि जुगल कर जोरी ।
   चढ़ि बिमान प्रभु चले बहोरी ॥
   इहाँ निषाद सुना प्रभु आए ।
   नाव नाव कहँ लोग बोलाए ॥

४ सुरसरि नाघि जान तब आयो ।
   उतरेउ तट प्रभु आयसु पायो ॥
   तब सीताँ पूजी सुरसरी ।
   बहु प्रकार पुनि चरनन्हि परी ॥

५ दीन्हि असीस हरषि मन गंगा ।
   सुंदरि तव अहिवात अभंगा ॥
   सुनत गुहा धायउ प्रेमाकुल ।
   आयउ निकट परम सुख संकुल ॥

६ प्रभुहि सहित बिलोकि बैदेही ।
   परेउ अवनि तन सुधि नहिं तेही ॥
   प्रीति परम बिलोकि रघुराई ।
   हरषि उठाइ लियो उर लाई ॥

The Lord then gave instructions to Hanuman: 1
"Take the guise of a Vedic student and go to Avadh.[32]
Tell Bharat of my well-being,
and return quickly with news of him."
The son of the wind departed at once,   2
while the Lord went to Bharadvaj's ashram,
where the sage worshiped him with many rites,
delivered a litany of praise, and blessed him.
Saluting the sage's feet with palms reverently joined,   3
the Lord reentered the aerial car and went on.
When the Nishad chief heard of the Lord's approach,
he called his folk, crying "Boats! Where are the boats?"[33]
Then that wondrous craft soared over the holy stream   4
and landed, at the Lord's command, on its shore.
There, Sita worshiped the divine river
with many rites, and fell at the goddess's feet.[34]
Ganga, with heartfelt joy, bestowed her blessing—   5
"Lovely one, may your marital felicity be unbroken."[35]
Hearing of all this, Guha rushed there, excited by love,
and approached Ram, overcome with bliss.
When he saw the Lord together with Vaidehi,   6
he fell prostrate and lost all bodily awareness.
Seeing his supreme love, the Raghu lord
joyfully lifted him and drew him to his breast.

७ लियो हृदयँ लाइ कृपा निधान
सुजान रायँ रमापती ।
बैठारि परम समीप बूझी
कुसल सो कर बीनती ॥
अब कुसल पद पंकज बिलोकि
बिरंचि संकर सेब्य जे ।
सुख धाम पूरनकाम राम
नमामि राम नमामि ते ॥

८ सब भाँति अधम निषाद सो
हरि भरत ज्यों उर लाइयो ।
मतिमंद तुलसीदास सो प्रभु
मोह बस बिसराइयो ॥
यह रावनारि चरित्र पावन
राम पद रतिप्रद सदा ।
कामादिहर बिग्यानकर सुर
सिद्ध मुनि गावहिं मुदा ॥

१२१क समर बिजय रघुबीर के चरित जे सुनहिं सुजान ।
बिजय बिबेक बिभूति नित तिन्हहि देहिं भगवान ॥

१२१ख यह कलिकाल मलायतन मन करि देखु बिचार ।
श्रीरघुनाथ नाम तजि नाहिन आन अधार ॥

The treasury of mercy lifted him and took him to his   7
    heart,[36]
Ram, king of discerning ones, husband of Ramā.
Then seating him very close to himself, he inquired
of his welfare, and Guha gave a humble reply—
"I am well, now that I behold your holy feet
that are worshiped by Brahma and Lord Shankar,
Ram—abode of bliss, triumphant in your mission—
and I bow to you, Ram, again and again."
That Nishad was debased in every way, yet Hari   8
hugged him to his breast like his own Bharat.
Dull-witted Tulsidas—under the sway[37]
of worldly delusion, you have forgotten such a Lord!
This purifying saga of the deeds of Ravan's foe
eternally grants fervent love for Ram's feet,
removes lust and other sins, and bestows wisdom.
Gods, perfected ones, and sages sing it with delight.

Wise people who listen to the saga   121a
of the Raghu hero's triumph in battle,
attain victory, discernment, and glory,
eternally bestowed on them by God.[38]

This Kali Age is a mire of sin;   121b
reflect on this, mind, and observe
that apart from the noble Raghu lord's name,
nothing else can support you.[39]

इति श्रीमद्रामचरितमानसे
सकलकलिकलुषविध्वंसने षष्ठः सोपानः समाप्तः।

[The end of the sixth stair of the *Rāmcaritmānas,*
which annihilates all impurities of the Kali Age.][40]

NOTES TO THE TRANSLATION

Prelude to War

1   Like the other sub-books, this one opens with a series of Sanskrit verses, here three, known as the *maṅgalācaraṇa* ("auspicious invocation"). The reference to Ram as the "one God" (*ekadevaṃ*) of Brahmans is glossed by many commentators as "primary" or "principal" deity.

2   This *dohā*—seemingly standing apart from the narrative, which begins with the two succeeding *soraṭhās*—offers a list of traditional time units that has generated much commentary. It comprises (though not strictly in order of increased duration) *lava* or "instant," *nimeṣa* (the "blink of an eye"), *paramānu* (which the *Mānaspīyūṣ* defines as "the experiential span of an atomic particle"), *juga* (one of the four "epochs" that make up a cosmic time cycle, or *kalpa*), *baraṣa* or "year," and *kalpa* itself (see *Mānaspīyūṣ* 6.2.1–4). The word *kāla*, with which Ram's bow is identified, means both "time" and "death." There is disagreement among traditional scholars over the placement of this *dohā*. The Gita Press and most other popular editions precede it with the three Sanskrit invocatory verses, as is done at the commencement of the other six sub-books of the *Mānas*. However, the *Mānaspīyūṣ* follows the precedent of several respected eighteenth- and nineteenth-century commentators and places this couplet first, before the Sanskrit ones (traditionally no number is assigned the couplet, though I have numbered it "0a" in my translation). Albeit this decision is supported by some interesting interpretations and by Vijayanand Tripathi's charming observation that "it was also a practice of Gosvamiji [Tulsidas] to not allow any practice to be absolute," no compelling early manuscript evidence is offered for this transposition, hence I have retained the more usual order. For discussion, see *Mānaspīyūṣ* 6.2.4–5.

3   "Submarine fire," *baṛavānala;* the world-destroying conflagration that is held in check by the gods in the body of a mare at the ocean's floor, until the end of a cosmic aeon.

4   "Ram's lord," *rāmesvara;* the name of both the sacred site (now identified with a place on the coast of Tamil Nadu, near India's

299

southern tip, marked by a great temple) and of the Shiva lingam that Ram is said to have installed there. "The release of union with me," *sājujya mukti;* this is said to be one of five kinds of liberation, in which a soul is eternally linked with the Lord's own form or accoutrements; see *Mānaspīyūṣ* 6.2.26.

5   "Humble suppliants," *pranata;* most commentators assume that Shiva here is referring to himself and reminding Parvati of her delusion that the incarnate Ram could not be transcendent God.

6   "Dolphins, crocodiles," *makara nakra;* these words refer to large aquatic beings associated both with actual species and with mythical, composite creatures. The *makara* is sometimes associated with the river dolphin found in the eastern Ganga basin and serves, in iconography, as the river goddess's vehicle.

7   Many commentators liken the three means by which the army crossed to the several paths or regimens adopted by spiritual aspirants; see *Mānaspīyūṣ* 6.2.37–38.

8   "Hilltops," *sikhara;* commentators note that this may also refer to the tops of trees, which the soldiers break off.

9   This famous couplet offers ten synonyms meaning "ocean," six of which use different words meaning "water" to express "abode of waters." This verbal tour de force suggests Ravan's shock while invoking his most celebrated physical feature. I have tried to find an equal number of synonyms in English.

10   "Held out her sari border," *añcalu ropā;* this is a traditional feminine gesture of entreaty.

11   "Truly," *khalu;* commentators observe that by using this word, Mandodari confirms the derogatory simile invoked by Sita in the *Sundarkāṇḍ* (5.9.4 and the succeeding *dohā*) that enraged Ravan.

12   Mandodari invokes the mythical exploits of Vishnu and his avatars: Madhu and Kaitabh were primordial demons slain by the god; Diti's two sons Hiranyaksha and Hiranyakashipu were slain, respectively, by his boar and man-lion avatars; the demon king Bali was overthrown by the dwarf avatar; and the king called Sahasrabahu ("thousand-arms") was killed by the ax-wielding Parashuram.

13   "Old age," *cauthēpana;* literally, "the fourth stage," according to a traditional division of life into childhood, youth, middle age, and old age.

14 "Guardians of space," *digapālā;* literally, "guardians of the directions." Though traditionally ten in number, here five deities are named: Varun (associated with the waters), Kuber (in the Himalayas), Pavan (the wind), Yama (king of the netherworld), and Kala (time and death).

15 The Gita Press gloss offers the possible alternative reading that it was Mandodari who (further) admonished Ravan, but my reading (favored by the *Mānaspīyūṣ*) seems more apt in the context.

16 "These foolish counselors," *saciva saṭha;* a variant reading of *saba* for the second word, found in some old manuscripts, yields the reading, "All these counselors."

17 "Cultivate his favor," *karahu...prītī;* literally, "act with affection." Commentators gloss this as seeking an alliance with Ram.

18 "The rot that kills bamboo at its root," *benumūla...ghamoī;* although the first compound clearly means "the root of the bamboo" (a plant valued for its firmness, strength, and flexibility), commentators disagree as to the precise meaning of the second word. Some think it refers to a parasitic grass that grows near bamboo, weakening it, whereas others identify it as a fungal disease that attacks the plant from within (see *Mānaspīyūṣ* 6.2.68–69). Most agree that, in the context, Ravan suggests that Prahast has been prompted to speak by his timid mother, Mandodari, and implies that he is a "growth" of a different species than his father; note the characterization of Ravan's words as "harsh and cruel" in the next verse.

19 *Vīṇā (bīnā),* conventionally romanized as "veena," refers to any of several plucked stringed instruments used in classical Indian music.

20 "Indra," *sunāsīra;* as the *Mānaspīyūṣ* notes, this archaic epithet for the king of the gods is used in only one other verse in the epic (1.125.4), when Indra is fearful that Narad's asceticism may overthrow him.

21 What follows—a carefully drawn verbal icon of Ram in repose with his five intimate companions serving him—is presented expressly for devotees to visualize, as *dohā* 11a makes clear. Some commentators identify the "lovely deerskin" as that of the illusory deer (the demon Marich in disguise) that lured Ram away from Sita (*Mānaspīyūṣ* 6.2.76-77).

22 "Vigilant," *vīrāsana;* literally, "in the pose of a hero," an alert posture in which the left foot and ankle rest on the right thigh.

23 "Absorbed," *layalīna;* some manuscripts substitute *lau* ("love," "attachment") for *laya* ("absorption," "immersion") in this compound, with little effect on the meaning of the verse.

24 "Swollen temples," *kumbha;* protuberant domes on either side of the forehead of a mature male elephant that release a fluid called musth when the elephant is aroused.

25 Deadly poison (*garala*) emerged, together with the moon and the nectar of immortality, from the churning of the primordial ocean by the gods and demons.

26 The reference is to the well-known story of Ravan severing nine of his heads as an offering to Shiva, an act that led Brahma to bestow on Ravan the boon of near immortality.

27 "Myriad plant species," *aṣṭādasa bhārā;* literally, "eighteen *bhārā.*" According to the *Mānaspīyūṣ,* the "downy hair" referred to is specifically the line of fine hairs extending upward from the navel, and *bhārā* "designates 123,001,660 species of trees." Similarly, "lower organs" (invoking penis and anus in their bodily function of elimination) are said to correspond to hells filled with urine and feces (*Mānaspīyūṣ* 6.2.102).

28 "His cognition, great Vishnu," *citta mahān.* Literally, the text equates his awareness or cognition with "the great being," but in the context, commentators construe this to refer to Vishnu. The similes offered throughout this stanza have occasioned considerable commentary; see *Mānaspīyūṣ* 6.2.102–104 for a comparison with similar passages in the *Atharvaveda, Bhāgavatapurāṇa,* and *Adhyātmarāmāyaṇa.*

29 Some manuscripts and commentators substitute "poets" (*kabi*) for "everyone" (*saba*); either way, Ravan appears to cite a proverbial misogynistic utterance.

30 "Emboldening," *bhaya mocini;* literally, "liberating from fear." The *Mānaspīyūṣ,* however, favors an alternate reading found in some manuscripts, *bhaya socani,* which yields "pleasing when grasped (though) announcing fear" (6.2.108–109).

31 This *dohā* has generated much commentary. Manuscripts disagree on whether its last word should be *sama* ("similar to"), *sata* ("one hundred"), or *siva* ("Shiva")—thus allowing three different readings concerning the identity of the fool's exalted but ineffectual guru or gurus: "like Brahma" (as I have rendered it), or "like a hundred Brahmas," or "like Brahma and Shiva."

There is debate, too, over which plant Tulsi had in mind, since *beta* can refer to several species of tall grass or bamboo, some of which (to the dismay of commentators) do indeed flower and bear fruit—though the one intended by the poet clearly does not. The *Mānaspīyūṣ* also observes that this aphoristic verse closely parallels one attributed to the great thirteenth-century Persian poet Sa'di of Shiraz (6.2.109–112).

32 "Was sporting," *khelata;* many commentators presume the unnamed prince to have been exercising in a traditional wrestling club, or *akhāṛā,* and to have challenged the monkey intruder.

33 "Did not even flinch," *mana neku na murā;* literally, "his mind did not turn away at all."

34 For an emissary to take a seat before a monarch is itself disrespectful, and storytellers and illustrators sometimes compound the insult by having Angad expand and then coil his tail into a towering seat-cushion that results in his head being higher than Ravan's.

35 These are gestures of self-abasement, signifying that one is like a sacrificial beast and ready to give up one's head in atonement.

36 "At some point, I believe you met?" *kabahū bhaī hī bheṭā;* literally, "a meeting sometime did indeed occur." Commentators construe this as a sarcastic rhetorical question, whereby Angad refers to Ravan's humiliating defeat by Bali in the course of the demon's attempted universal conquest.

37 "Tear your breast," *ura biharu;* traditionally, the heart, rather than the brain, is considered the seat of intelligence.

38 "Has also been seen," *dekhī nayana;* literally, "eyes saw"—but whose eyes? Since Angad has not personally been mistreated by Ravan, commentators offer various interpretations of this half line. Most assume it to refer to Ravan's death sentence for Hanuman (5.24.3), which was changed to bodily mutilation only on Vibhishan's advice. Others cite the story of an emissary sent by Kuber, Ravan's half brother, whom the demon king slew with his sword and then had his guards devour—an atrocity witnessed by either Hanuman or Angad. See *Mānaspīyūṣ* 6.2.137–138.

39 Ravan boasts of one of his celebrated exploits during his universal conquest: lifting Mount Kailash, atop which Shiva and Parvati reside. His simile invokes legendary Lake Manas, with its lotuses and *haṃsa* birds.

40 Here Ravan concedes that the fabrication of the causeway was a

notable feat, but his phrasing implies that practitioners of mere "building crafts" (*silpi karma*) may not be of much use in battle.

41 "Minor errand boys," *laghu dhāvana;* the second word literally means "runner" and is roughly akin to the American English noun "gofer" (from "go for") or the Indian English "peon."

42 Commentators devote considerable attention to justifying Angad's apparent "lies" in this *dohā* and the two preceding *caupāīs,* attributing them to his (noble) mission to weaken Ravan's resolve, or claiming that they are said in sarcastic jest. See *Mānaspīyūṣ* 6.2.142-143.

43 That is, since Ravan is a Brahman.

44 This line may also be translated as, "You are virtuous, monkey, who, for your master's sake."

45 "Ate your own father," *pitu khāe;* Ravan implies that Angad had a role in Bali's assassination.

46 "Demon Bali." This character should not be confused with Angad's father, Bali (Bālī, with long vowels), the monkey king. The stories alluded to in the verses that follow—of Ravan's humiliation at the hands of King Sahasrabahu ("thousand arms") and Angad's father—are told at length in the *Uttarakāṇḍa* of the *Vālmīki Rāmāyaṇa* (7.32-34).

47 In a story to which the *Vālmīki Rāmāyaṇa* devotes a full *sarga* (7.34), Ravan, intent on universal conquest, disturbs Bali at the start of his evening devotions. The monkey king seizes Ravan, tucks him headfirst in his armpit—with Ravan's body and arms "dangling like a serpent hanging from Garuḍa" (7.34.16; Goldman and Sutherland Goldman 2017: 316)—and then proceeds to fly in the cardinal directions to the four oceans to bathe, subjecting his stifled prisoner to much wear and tear. This ultimately leads Ravan to conclude a friendship pact with Bali, to which Angad has already alluded.

48 Ravan once lifted Mount Kailash, atop which Shiva dwells.

49 "Turbulent ocean current," *sāgara khara dhārā;* notably, *dhārā* carries the double meaning of "current" (in water) and "blade" (of a sword or ax).

50 Literally, this half line poses a rhetorical question: "Is he a man, wretched Ten-neck?" The reference is to Ram's confrontation, in *Bālkāṇḍ,* with the martial sage and avatar of Vishnu, Parashuram; see 1.284.

51 "Sustenance," *anna;* literally, "grain," but according to commentators, this refers to the consistent provision of patronage to dependents, which is here distinguished from *dāna,* petty or occasional acts of charity.

52 "Polo," *caugānā;* although this is the common Hindi name for this sport, some commentators identify it as another game played with a wooden bat and balls.

53 Two minor variants occur in manuscripts for this *caupāī.* "Manliness," *manusāī,* is the reading favored by the *Mānaspīyūṣ,* and I have likewise preferred it to the Gita Press's *prabhutāī,* "lordly power," "strength." However, in the second half of the *caupāī* I have used the Gita Press reading of *saba* ("all") in reference to the birds, rather than the repetition of the vocative *saṭha* ("fool") found in the *Mānaspīyūṣ.*

54 It is popularly thought that Brahma inscribes the destiny of individuals on their foreheads before birth and that his handwriting may be seen when a skull becomes visible in a cremation.

55 "My father." Tulsi's alliterative list of names (*Sahasabāhu bali bālī*) would yield (in my transliteration scheme) two that are identically spelled, hence this circumlocution. Angad's statement is, of course, sarcastic, since he has already reminded Ravan of his defeat at the hands of these three heroes.

56 "Tantric," *kaula;* literally, "of high lineage." This term was used to denote initiates in a tradition of "left-handed" Tantric practice, of which pious Vaishnavas disapproved. For discussion, see *Mānaspīyūṣ* 6.2.172–175.

57 Following the practice of some early manuscripts, the *Mānaspīyūṣ* assigns no new number to this pair of *dohās,* instead repeating the number thirty. Hence, its numbering of stanzas diverges at this point from that of Gita Press editions (which I follow), yielding a total stanza count of 120 rather than 121 for *Lāṅkākāṇḍ.* Whereas some commentators attribute the omission of a number to simple scribal error, others consider it to have great significance. For discussion, see *Mānaspīyūṣ* 6.2.177–178.

58 "Bared his teeth," *kaṭakaṭāna;* this onomatopoeic verb refers to the chattering sound monkeys, when aroused, make with their bared teeth. In English, however, the chattering of teeth is mainly associated with cold and weakness, hence this translation as well as (elsewhere) "gnashed their teeth."

59 Ketu and Rahu are demonic beings associated with inauspicious astronomical phenomena; the latter causes eclipses.

60 "Didn't your heart fail," *biharati nahī chātī;* literally, "didn't your breast split open."

61 Angad's terse but extraordinarily audacious oath has generated much commentary. Although most Ramayanis take it as suitably inspired by "Ram's majesty," which the messenger "recalled" (*samujhi*) in the preceding *caupāī,* a few try to finesse it as, "Ram and Sita will go back (after Ram slays you), but I will be defeated." For discussion, see *Mānaspīyūṣ* 6.2.188–191.

62 "Foe of serpents," *uragārī;* this vocative, an epithet of Garuda, signals that Bhushundi the crow is now the narrator. On the four interlocking narrations of the *Mānas,* see the introduction to volume 1 of this translation.

63 "Royal radiance," *śrī;* an epithet of Lakshmi, goddess of fertility and abundance, whose favor is considered essential to a king's continued success.

64 Some manuscripts substitute "spoke to the night-stalker" (*nisācarahi*) for "spoke to Ravan."

65 "A mere line," *laghu rekha.* Mandodari refers to the popular story of a magically charged line drawn in the sand around Ram and Sita's hut by Lakshman with his bow; before leaving Sita to search for Ram, Lakshman forbids Sita to cross this line. When Ravan finds himself unable to trespass it, he must use a ruse to lure Sita to step over it. In popular Hindi idiom, "Lakshman's line" (*lakṣmaṇ rekhā*) refers to a conventional boundary that must not be trespassed and is often invoked in discussions of proper self-control, especially for women. *Mānaspīyūṣ* commentators clearly accept the story (though Tulsi omits it from his own *Aranyakāṇḍ;* see 3.28) and merely speculate on how Mandodari came to know of it (6.2.205).

66 "Right under your nose," *dekhata tohi;* literally, "while you looked on," though this deed was not actually done in Ravan's presence.

67 "Poor fellow," *nīcā.* The placement of this word—meaning "low," "debased," "wretched"—at the end of the line permits several readings. Some commentators take it as a vocative, and have Mandodari assail her husband as "you wretch." Others assume it refers to Ravan's low estimation of Marich's counsel not to provoke Ram; see *Mānaspīyūṣ* 6.2.208–209.

68 "Learned a little about the power of Ram," *jānai bala thorā;*

alternatively, this may be interpreted to mean that he foolishly "supposed Ram's power to be slight." See *Aranyakāṇḍ* 3.1–2 and *Sundarkāṇḍ* 5.27.3. The *Mānaspīyūṣ* speculates that, although Mandodari could not have known the nature of Jayant's offense (a secret known only to Ram and Sita, though revealed by Sita to Hanuman, according to Tulsidas, as evidence of his having truly seen her), the story of Ram's pursuit and punishment of Indra's son was widely known (*Mānaspīyūṣ* 6.2.210).

69 "Stratagem," *bibhedā;* literally, "disunity," "dissention." In the context, this refers to a ruler's tactic of sowing discord in enemy ranks, often through the use of spies and deception.

70 "Knowing this," *asa jiyā jāni;* literally, "inwardly knowing thus." The implication is that the four virtues know that Ravan no longer deserves to be a king and so have left him.

The Battle

1 According to commentators, this bird, called a *ṭiṭṭibha* or *ṭiṭiharī,* sleeps with its feet in the air out of the false belief that it can thus prevent the sky from falling on it.

2 This list of antique weapons includes several types of spears, as well as several others concerning which commentators disagree as to their precise identity and use.

3 "Gnashing their teeth," *kaṭakaṭāī;* see note 58 in the preceding section.

4 This line shifts the meter to *harigītikā chand.*

5 "Anguished," *ātura.* Since this word can be both an adjective and a noun (in the latter usage, sometimes meaning "the diseased," "the sick"), some interpret this line to refer to the three classes of Lankan citizens—women, children, and the infirm—who were not conscripted for the battlefield.

6 With this charming giveaway of the battle's outcome, Shiva as narrator reassures his wife not to be alarmed by this apparent setback for Ram's army.

7 "Animosity," *bayara bhāva;* literally, "the emotion of enmity." In bhakti ideology, any emotional stance that involves concentration on God, including hostility, is considered to yield blessings.

8 In a famous myth, Mandara, the world-axis mountain, was used as a churning rod by the gods and demons to extract the nectar of immortality from the cosmic ocean of milk.

9   "Gaining strength as day waned," *pradoṣa bala pāī;* literally, "gaining the strength of twilight." *Rākṣasas,* whose nature is dominated by the quality of *tamas,* or "darkness," are believed to grow stronger at nightfall.

10 "Dark monsoon clouds and multihued ones of Sharad," *prābiṭa sarada payoda;* the month of Sharad comes at the end of the rainy season, and its more variegated clouds serve as a simile for Ram's simian legions.

11 "Generals," *anipa;* the *Mānaspīyūṣ* treats this word as the name of a third demon, apparently in order to create symmetry with the three substances produced by demonic maya that are mentioned in the next *caupāī.* However, *anipa* means "leader of an army," and Akampan and Atikay are named in other verses as demon generals.

12 "Sharks," *jhaṣa;* both this word and *makara* (the first creature mentioned in this half line) refer to large, carnivorous aquatic creatures, sometimes depicted as crocodiles or fish. For variety, since both appear here, I have used "crocodile" and "shark."

13 In most recensions of the *Vālmīki Rāmāyaṇa,* this character, also known as Malyavan, is identified as Ravan's maternal grand-uncle.

14 Malyavant alludes to well-known mythical exploits of Vishnu, celebrated in the *purāṇas*—the slaying of the demons Madhu and Kaitabh, and of Hiranyaksha ("golden-eyed") and his brother Hiranyakashipu ("gold-clad").

15 "Drew his bow-string to its full extent," *śravana lagi tāne;* literally, "drew it to his ear." This formulaic phrase recurs several times, when a mighty warrior takes aim and prepares to shoot an arrow from his bow.

16 The divine eagle Garuda is the archenemy of snakes and feeds on them.

17 "Male and female goblins," *pisāca pisācī;* Tulsi uses the masculine and feminine forms of a word designating a type of malevolent being, often imagined as an impish fiend.

18 "Nine regions," *nava khaṇḍā;* according to commentators, this refers to traditional subdivisions or "provinces" of the continent of Jambudvipa, an ancient name for the South Asian landmass.

19 "Cremation smoke," *mṛitaka dhūma;* some commentators take this phrase to mean "ashes," and construe the simile as referring to clouds of ash settling on top of glowing embers. Either way, the image is appropriately ominous.

20 "Flame-of-the-forest trees," *kimsuka;* this tree, native to the subcontinent and southeast Asia, produces clusters of bright orange-red blossoms. With its dark foliage, it became a standard poetic trope for the wounded bodies of swarthy heroes.

21 The epithets used for Lakshman in this and succeeding verses, culminating in *dohā* 54—Anant (*ananta* or "endless") and Shesh (*seṣa* or "residual")—are reminders of his identity with the infinite cosmic serpent, known by both of these names, on whom the cosmos and Lord Vishnu rest and who remains when the creation has been dissolved.

22 Some early manuscripts substitute *ananta* for *seṣa* here, a reading preferred by the *Mānaspīyūṣ.* However, it affects neither meter nor meaning.

23 In some myths, at the end of an aeon the universe is incinerated by fire emanating from the mouths of Shesh, the thousand-hooded cosmic cobra.

24 Implicit here is the fact that Hanuman, through his devotion, was able to lift and transport the wounded Lakshman, as the demons could not.

25 "Physician," *baida;* the title of a practitioner of Ayurveda, or traditional medicine.

26 The giver of the order is not identified and may be either Sushen or Ram. Other accounts of this episode stipulate that the herb must be administered before sunrise, or the prince will die (and Bharat, too, warns of this at 6.60.3).

27 "Affirming his own might," *bala bhāṣī;* presumably Hanuman does this to assure his distraught master that he will be able to carry out the mission.

28 The Gita Press and *Mānaspīyūṣ* editions offer significantly different readings of this half *caupāī,* based on old manuscript variants. The latter's preferred text (*ahaṃkāra mamatā mada tyāgū*) would be translated, "Renounce your pride, possessiveness, and arrogance."

29 "Pot," *kamaṇḍala;* the water vessel used by ascetics is often made from a dried and hollowed-out gourd, cut so its upper section forms a handle, or it is made out of brass. In oral *kathā,* I have heard it said that Kalnemi's water pot contains poison or a sleeping potion, and when Hanuman rejects the vessel, the demon adopts the alternate strategy of sending him to an enchanted lake containing a hungry female crocodile.

30   "I will initiate you," *dicchā deū.* A ritual bath normally precedes initiation, usually with a mantra. According to some commentators, it is implied that the promised "knowledge" will enable Hanuman to recognize the correct healing herb in the Himalayas (*Mānaspīyūṣ* 6.2.293).

31   According to the *Mānaspīyūṣ* (6.2.294), the sage is not identified in any text, but the *Ānandarāmāyaṇa* states that he cursed the celestial woman for denying him sexual favors, and that he therefore is disgraced and must remain nameless.

32   "Guru gift," *guradachinā;* a gift, in cash or kind, presented to a preceptor after he has performed a ritual, such as initiation with a mantra.

33   In the understanding of devotees, the demon's dying utterance of Ram's name both effects his own salvation and also constitutes the efficacious mantra he had promised Hanuman.

34   "Crown jewel," *tilaka;* though this often connotes an auspicious forehead mark that shows sectarian affiliation, it can also refer to an eminent person or to an ornament for the head.

35   A possible alternative translation is "By your might, master, and keeping the Lord (Ram) in my heart."

36   This famous lament, and its opening phrase, figures prominently in a critically acclaimed contemporary novel about a Delhi family, one of whose sons becomes a *Mānas* expounder (Bagchi 2018).

37   This extraordinary statement by the paragon of filial piety has occasioned much discussion among commentators. For various interpretations, see *Mānaspīyūṣ* 6.2.309–310.

38   "Blood brother," *sahodara bhrātā;* since this literally means a brother born of the same womb, it technically does not apply to Lakshman, but it suggests Ram's attachment to him as well as his insistence on regarding all three queens as equally his mothers.

39   Once again, this emotional statement is not literally true, since Queen Sumitra gave birth to twins, Lakshman and Shatrughna. Does *eka* ("one" or "sole") imply that Lakshman is her favorite or "primary" son, or the firstborn of the pair? For copious commentary, see *Mānaspīyūṣ* 6.2.315–317.

40   "Heroic mood," *bīra rasa;* "pathos," *karunā;* two of the eight (or nine, in some texts) dominant emotional moods of literature and performance as identified by classical aesthetic theorists.

41   "Drawn," *sukhāī;* literally, "dry," "withered."

42   Tulsi uses epithets to identify two of the notable demon champions: *suraripu* (enemy of the gods) for Devantak (slayer of gods), and *manuja ahārī* (man-eater) for Narantak (man-killer).

43   No verb of speaking occurs here, and some commentators consider the first sentence to represent Kumbhakaran's thoughts, with his actual response to Ravan beginning in the following *caupāī.*

44   "Secret knowledge," *gyāna;* citing varying accounts in older sources, commentators identify this as a prophecy, told to Kumbhakaran by Narad, concerning the downfall of the demons. See *Mānaspīyūṣ* 6.2.328.

45   "Three torments," *tāpatraya;* literally, "three burnings." This is generally said to refer to suffering caused by physical affliction, by the gods or fate, and by ghosts or spirits.

46   "The floss of milkweed," *arka phalani;* the crown flower plant, a relative of milkweed also known as *madār,* produces seedpods that release spheres of downy floss, sometimes used as a substitute for cotton in bedding.

47   The shift from past to present tense in this *caupāī* seems to suggest Parvati's rapt immersion in the battle narrative and Shiva's desire to reassure her at a moment when things do not seem to be going well.

48   Here and in *dohā* 67 Tulsi refers to the enemy soldiers as *pisācā,* a term that often connotes a variety of goblin-like spirit. However, since it offers a rhyme with "iron-tipped arrows" (*nārācā*), he seems to be simply substituting it for more commonly used words like "night-stalker" (*nisicara*).

49   According to ancient myth, mountains originally possessed wings and could fly. Fearing they would cause destruction on earth, Indra severed their wings and rendered them stationary. Mandara is the world-axis mountain used by the gods and demons to churn the milky cosmic ocean.

50   Commentators interpret this *caupāī* to mean that Ram granted Kumbhakaran some form of spiritual liberation, which is affirmed in the *dohā* that concludes this stanza; for extended discussion, see *Mānaspīyūṣ* 6.2.355–358.

51   As is common in the *Mānas,* this quatrain in lyrical *chand* meter offers an extended meditation on the previous *caupāī*—the sight of victorious Ram standing on the battlefield. Since Tulsi presents

this auspicious vision as his own, it seems fitting to render it in present tense.

52 According to the *Mānaspīyūṣ*, Meghnad alludes to a story told in the *Uttarakāṇḍa* of the *Vālmīki Rāmāyaṇa* concerning specific boons granted to him by Brahma, along with the title "victor over Indra" (Indrajit, his common epithet). The reference to a "patron god" or "chosen god" (*iṣṭadeva*) may allude to Brahma or to the goddess Mahakali, whom Meghnad worships in Tantric rites at a place called Nikumbhila; see *Mānaspīyūṣ* 6.2.366.

53 The vocative "king of birds" signals that the narrator here is the crow Bhushundi, addressing Garuda. The *Mānaspīyūṣ* points out that this shift, as a battle with Meghnad commences, alludes to Garuda's doubt about Ram's divinity, which will result from Ram's apparent helplessness in the next stanza. This doubt, revealed by the divine eagle in the final sub-book of the epic (see 7.58), will provoke Bhushundi's narration to him of the Ram story.

54 "Magha" (Maghā) is the name of the tenth of twenty-seven lunar mansions in Indian astrology, and the sun's passage through it is said to produce particularly heavy rains.

55 "Arrow-fences," *sara pañjara;* literally "arrow-cages." The implication is that all escape routes were blocked by the magic arrows.

56 The simile alludes to Indra's mythological battle with the mountains, which once possessed wings (see note 49 in this section).

57 According to the *Mānaspīyūṣ* (6.2.376), several Ramayanas offer differing versions of the terms of this boon, received from Brahma, which restricts the circumstances under which Meghnad can be slain.

58 Here, "night-stalker(s)" may be read as either singular or plural, and many commentators take it to refer to Ravan. Either way, the verb used (*chījnā,* "to decrease," "to waste away") suggests that, once Meghnad is slain, those who remain (including Ravan) will be much reduced in might.

59 This half line also permits the reading "You three, remain with the army," which would imply that these warriors are *not* to go with Lakshman. However, most commentators reason that Ram, concerned for the safety of his brother (who has already been badly

wounded once), would want to send his best warriors to accompany the prince on this mission.

60 See note 21 in this section.

61 To recall the Lord and utter his name at the moment of death is held to ensure salvation and to bring blessing and auspiciousness to one's parents, hence the monkeys' admiration.

62 Here, "Raghu lord" (*raghunātha*) might be interpreted to refer to Lakshman, since the quoted lines that follow praise him with his familiar epithets. However, most commentators feel that Tulsi reserves this epithet for Ram, and that the "renown" to which the gods allude is actually his, since Lakshman invoked him before firing the fatal arrow. ˙

63 Meghnad's hard-won boons and military record, which earned him the title "conqueror of Indra," made him even more dreaded by the gods than his father, and with his death, that of Ravan is assumed to be inevitable.

64 The eight lines that follow are again in the more complex *harigītikā* meter, and from this point on, such lyrical quatrains occur, sometimes in pairs, before nearly every remaining *dohā* in Laṅkākāṇḍ.

65 "Four divisions," *caturaṅginī anī;* traditionally a royal army had four components: elephants, cavalry, chariots, and infantry.

66 "Apocalypse," *pralaya samaya;* the dissolution of the cosmos at the end of an aeon, which is preceded by various cataclysms.

67 That is, he began to doubt that victory would be possible. How such a doubt (*sandeha*) could arise in the mind of this staunch devotee is a great preoccupation of commentators; for various interpretations, see *Mānaspīyūṣ* 6.2.400–401. Notably, it inaugurates Ram's famous discourse on his metaphorical "chariot of dharma," that has likewise generated copious commentary (6.2.402–426).

68 This curious detail is explained by a commentator who notes the bears are covering the bodies so they can come back and eat them later; here, in retaliation for the demons' habit of devouring sages (*Mānaspīyūṣ* 6.2.432).

69 In Vaishnava mythology Vishnu assumes the form of the man-lion to slay the demon king Hiranyakashipu, who is menacing his devotee Prahlad. The demon is protected by a boon from Brahma that necessitates Vishnu's gory method of slaying the demon, by rending his chest and disemboweling him. In some accounts, in

the exultation of triumph, the half-feral god drapes himself with his foe's intestines.

70 "Screeching excitedly," *hūha dai;* literally, "giving forth '*hūha,*'" a sound said to be made by excited simians.

71 "Pulverized," *tila pravāna;* literally, he made them "equivalent to sesame seeds."

72 It is unclear—and there is disagreement among commentators—whether the phrase meaning "incomparable strength" (*atula bala*) refers to Ravan's might (here deployed in vain) or to the unyielding weight (*mahimā*) of Lakshman, whose identity with the cosmic cobra Anant is highlighted in this quatrain. For discussion, see *Mānaspīyūṣ* 6.2.439–440.

73 "You flaunt false piety, like a crafty heron," *baka dhyāna lagāvā;* literally, "you go into heron's meditation." In Indian animal lore, the carnivorous heron affects the calm meditative pose of a yogi—standing on one leg in the water, with eyes half closed—when actually he is watching for small fish to seize and devour.

74 Commentators advance several explanations for Ram's smile, though most take it as acknowledgment of the hypocritical attempt by the lesser deities to conceal their self-interest with supposed concern for Sita's well-being; see *Mānaspīyūṣ* 6.2.455.

75 This alludes to a footprint-shape scar on Vishnu's chest, the remnant of a kick by the choleric sage Bhrigu that the Lord graciously suffered out of respect for the "gods of the earth" (*dharāsura,* the term used for "Brahman" here).

76 "Doomsday," *pralayakāla;* the time of cosmic dissolution, which is initiated by apocalyptic storms.

77 "Rainbows—lovely emblems of Indra," *indradhanu;* literally, "Indra's bow," the standard Hindi word for rainbow.

78 As Tulsi continues his extended simile of likening the battle to the onset of the monsoon, he invokes two different forms of rain: as a shower or curtain of water (*jaladhārā*) and as a heavy downpour of large drops (*bāna bunda bṛṣṭi*). This suggests the image of an approaching storm, first seen from afar as dust-like sheets of rain that then materialize as large drops or even hailstones.

79 "Vampires," *betāla;* a kind of blood-sucking ghost that sometimes reanimates corpses.

80 "Half-immersed corpses," *ardhajala;* literally, "half in water." This refers to a stage in the funeral rite when the body, wrapped in its

shroud and tied to a bamboo stretcher, is immersed in a sacred
river and then left briefly at a slant at the river's edge, with its
lower half in the water, prior to being placed on its pyre. One
commentator notes that this ritual is sometimes performed for
the dying, hence its appropriateness to the image of moaning,
mortally wounded troops.

81 "Fierce battlefield goddesses," *cāmuṇḍā;* this category of
bloodthirsty goddess, like the other supernatural women just
mentioned, is believed to frequent sites of battle.

82 "Saw through," *b̃ācī;* literally, he "read" and understood it.

83 "Hari lifted," *harī hari;* there is untranslatable wordplay here,
because the verb *haranā* means "to snatch away," "to remove."

84 "Lords of the cosmos," *lokapa;* the divine protectors of the cardinal
directions of space—Indra, Agni, Varun, and so forth. Ravan boasts
that they are in his prison (*bandīkhānā*).

85 "Fallen into Ravan's fatal grip," *parehu kaṭhina rāvana ke pāle;*
literally, "fallen under the frost (or hail) of cruel Ravan." Here Tulsi
uses an idiom referring to the devastating effect on crops of a rare
hard freeze or hailstorm in the Indo-Gangetic Plain.

86 "Seized by panic," *māruta grase;* literally, "seized by the Maruts."
The forty-nine Maruts, or stormy winds, are believed capable of
inducing both fear and mental illness.

87 According to commentators, the elephants intend to steady the
earth, lest it overturn.

88 Indra's chariot being divine, its horses cannot be slain but only
knocked down by Ravan's weapons.

89 In the myth of the churning of the cosmic ocean by the gods and
demons to extract the nectar of immortality, the demon Rahu, who
had disguised himself as a god, was decapitated by Vishnu's discus
while attempting to quaff the ambrosial drink. Since some had
already gone into his mouth, his severed head remained alive, and
it constantly seeks to devour the sun and moon (who had alerted
Vishnu to the demon's disguise), causing eclipses. The trunk of
Rahu's body, sometimes said to have joined with a snake, became
Ketu, a lunar node in Indian astrology.

90 "Desire," *māra;* this is also an epithet of Kama, god of lust.

91 "For some time," *daṇḍa eka;* one *daṇḍa* is said to equal twenty-four
minutes—hence the gods' alarm in the following verse.

92 "Little Kalis," *kālikā;* these may be understood either as diminutive

emanations of Kali, the black goddess of destruction, or (according to the *Mānaspīyūṣ*) as yoginis who frequent battlefields in this guise, collecting the blood of slain warriors in skull-cups for their Tantric rites. The commentary adds that the full simile alludes to a rite of worship of a sacred banyan tree, performed by married women on the moonless night of the month of Jyeshtha for the sake of their husbands' longevity. The martial goddesses, the commentator notes, greedy for blood, "crave that the battle may be prolonged" (6.2.487).

93   "To be of no account," *ghāli nahī ... ganai;* here Tulsi employs an expression from the bazaar idiom meaning, literally, "to disregard the counterweight"; used when weighing merchandise on a balance scale.

94   Alternatively, this may be read, "Resolute Hanuman, recalling the Raghu hero."

95   Literally, "I have become one in their estimation." As commentators explain, the gods' temporary relief at his "reduced" state annoys Ravan, who considers himself easily capable of trouncing them again, as he has in the past.

96   Commentators note that whereas ordinary sins can be atoned for by going on a pilgrimage, those committed in a sacred pilgrimage place (*tīrtha*) are ineradicable. For discussion, see *Mānaspīyūṣ* 6.2.499–500.

97   Because attacking an unconscious foe violates the dharma of war, commentators offer several justifications for Jambavan's act— for example, knowing that demons grow more powerful at dusk, he needed to be sure that Ravan was really unconscious so that his own bear troops could retreat to safety (*Mānaspīyūṣ* 6.2.504).

98   In this stanza Tulsidas departs from his usual *caupāī* meter in favor of a shorter, more staccato one with twelve (rather than sixteen) metrical beats in each foot. Commentators identify this as *tomar chand*, or "spear meter," which was apparently considered appropriate to scenes of fierce battle. The poet also uses it in describing Ram's fight with the demon army of Khar and Dushan in the third sub-book (3.20.1–7).

99   The three categories of monstrous creatures cited are all supernatural revenants: the first, translated "ghoul," is a *betāla*, a malevolent spirit that reanimates a corpse in order to prey on

living beings; it is sometimes rendered as "vampire" and resembles the zombie of Caribbean lore and contemporary horror films. A "ghost" (*bhūta*) is a generic, unsatisfied revenant, and a "goblin" (*piśāca*) is a demonic wraith.

100 With this line, the meter reverts to the melodious *harigītikā chand* quatrain.

101 "Could never encompass their glory," *tadapi pār na pāvahī*; literally, "could not reach their further shore."

102 Early manuscripts disagree on the second line of this *dohā;* I agree with the *Mānaspīyūṣ*, that the reading given here seems preferable to that favored by Gita Press editions (*jimi nija bala anurūpa te māchī urai akāsa;* "like a fly trying, by his own strength / to soar into the firmament"). Although both readings convey the same sense of the ludicrousness of the poet's ambition, the words *pauruṣa* (virility, courage) and *masaka* (a gnat or very small fly) give the verse additional impact.

103 Commentators understand this line to refer to vultures gathering above Ravan's chariot. Though he is a villain, he also is a powerful monarch, hence his death is inauspicious.

104 "Radiance," *teja;* "fiery glory," or "effulgence." This is taken to mean that Ravan's soul was granted a beatific state of liberation (*mukti*), which Vaishnava soteriology posits may be of several kinds; for discussion, see *Mānaspīyūṣ* 6.2.530–531.

105 Mukunda is an epithet of Vishnu, sometimes glossed as "granter of liberation." Commentators point out that the poet's use of it three times immediately after Ravan's death (here and in succeeding verses to *dohā* 6.102) highlights both the demon's own spiritual liberation and the freeing of all the beings he had oppressed.

106 This simile depends on the fact that the matted locks of ascetics often become bleached by the sun and acquire a yellowish hue. "Blue mountain" (*nīlagiri*) also designates a coastal range in southeastern India.

107 "Little ruddy birds," *rāyamunī;* a sparrow-size, red-headed bird, also known as the red avadavat or strawberry finch.

The Aftermath

1 "A helpless, unprotected one," *anātha;* literally, "one who has no lord," a term commonly used for an orphan or widow.

2 "Sanak and his brothers," *sanakādi;* literally, "Sanak, and so forth."

This refers to four immortal sages celebrated in the *purāṇas* as mind-born sons of Brahma who wander the cosmos in the form of young boys.

3   "Place and time," *desa kāla;* Hindu ritual is generally contingent on astrological, seasonal, and other contextual factors. The *Mānaspīyūṣ* suggests that Ravan's last rites were performed correctly yet somewhat hastily, owing to the battlefield setting and Ram's other duties (6.2.543–544).

4   "Offered Ravan handfuls of sesame seeds," *dei tilāñjali tāhi;* this offering to the deceased of a palmful of black sesame seeds occurs at the conclusion of a cremation.

5   A *tilak* is an auspicious mark or design, often of vermilion, applied to the forehead. Used in many religious contexts, its application by a courtly *purohit,* or priest, is one of the culminating rites in a royal consecration, akin to the placing of a crown in other cultures.

6   See *Araṇyakāṇḍ* 3.24.1–3, wherein Ram commands Sita to take refuge in their hearth fire while he carries out some obligatory "human pastimes." Here, the epithet "inner witness" (*antara sākhī*) is taken by most commentators to refer to Ram, though some point out that it can also designate Agni, god of fire.

7   "Faithful helper," *negī;* this refers to longtime, trusted servants and close relatives to whom gifts (*neg*) are made at the time of marriage and other festive events.

8   The interpretation of the opening of this quatrain depends on how one construes the final two words of its second line (the fourth line in my translation): does "utterly pure" (*ati nirmalī*) refer to the quality of Shiva's adoration or, going back to the first line, to Sita herself? I favor the former reading; for other interpretations see *Mānaspīyūṣ* 6.2.561–562.

9   In the well-known myth of the churning of the cosmic "milk ocean" by the gods and demons to extract the nectar of immortality, the goddess Lakshmi, also known as Shri ("fortune," "auspiciousness") likewise emerges and is presented to Vishnu as his consort.

10   The following eleven verses of Brahma's *stuti,* or hymn, introduce a new meter called *toṭak chand,* of a structure similar to *caupāī* but with half lines of twelve syllables—of which the third, sixth, ninth, and twelfth are long—that produce a more insistent cadence in recitation. The language is also a more formal register

of Avadhi, with some Sanskrit forms. Much of it consists of a series of lofty titles (such as "ocean of virtues" and "mass of wisdom") periodically capped with the formulaic Sanskrit phrase "I bow to" (*namāmi*).

11 "Divine Hari," *hare;* though this is a vocative form of Hari, one of Vishnu's commonest epithets, commentators also take it to refer to Ram's "removing" of suffering (alluding to the verb *harnā,* "to snatch away").

12 Three words create notable alliteration here: *bibhūṣana* ("great ornament," "crown jewel"), Dushan (the name of a demon killed by Ram in sub-book three that also means "flaws," "sins"), and the name of Ravan's brother who became Ram's ally.

13 "You transcend cause and effect," *kārana kāja param.* Commentators advance several interpretations for this phrase, some construing *kārana* ("cause," "purpose," "reason") to refer to nature (*prakṛti*) or maya, and *kāja* ("work," "task," "objective") to refer to the material world. Both words suggest compulsory activity, which the hymn declares that Ram transcends.

14 "Handsome lover of Shri," *sundara śrīramanā;* alternatively, assuming the adjective *sundara* to refer to Shri (Lakshmi/Sita) rather than Ram, one may translate this phrase as "lover of lovely Shri."

15 "Mere imagination," *dantakathā;* although this term can be translated as "hearsay" or "tradition," the poet appears to use it here to distinguish something conceived by human beings from a truth declared by the eternal, authorless sacred word.

16 This stanza returns to the standard *caupāī* meter.

17 This verse, along with Shiva's aside in the next two, has generated extensive commentary, with several interpretations being offered for the phrases I have rendered as "prior love" (*prathama prema*) and "unshakable insight" (*dṛṛha gyānā*), as well as of the precise beatific state—within various Vaishnava typologies of salvation— that Ram bestowed on his deceased father. Dasarath's chosen path of "dualistic devotion" (*bheda bhagatī*) requires enduring awareness of the difference between devotee and Lord that precludes the nondual experience of "liberation" (*moccha*), yet it is prized by many Vaishnava teachers. For extended discussion, see *Mānaspīyūṣ* 6.2.580–583.

18 Indra's *stuti,* or praise poem, returns to the short, driving *tomar*

chand ("spear meter") that was last used to describe Ravan's illusory deceptions during the climactic battle (6.101.1–8).

19   Ramā is the feminine form of "Ram" and thus signals his consort, Sita. It is also, conventionally, an epithet of goddess Lakshmi; hence "husband of Ramā" (*ramānivāsa;* literally "home" or "resting place of Ramā") may also be understood to mean "the spouse of Lakshmi," Vishnu. Indra's hymn of praise concludes with a lyrical quatrain in *harigītikā chand,* followed by *dohā* 113.

20   This aside by the immortal crow, Bhushundi (who will become a principal narrator of sub-book seven), addressing Vishnu's eagle mount, Garuda, is a reminder of the multiple narrative strands that constitute the *Mānas.* The interjection is not arbitrary, however, for it foreshadows the doubt about Ram's divinity that will bring Garuda to seek wisdom from Bhushundi in the final section of the epic (see 7.58–63).

21   "Born of the gods," *sura ansika;* literally "portions of the gods," or partial incarnations. The monkeys' birth at Brahma's command is described at 1.188.

22   "The triple cities' foe," *tripurāri;* this common epithet of Shiva refers to the myth of his destruction, with a single arrow, of three airborne fortress cities from which demons were harassing the gods.

23   "Your devotee's heart," *jana mana;* the line contains no qualifier for "devotee," but most commentators assume that Shiva refers to himself ("this devotee of yours").

24   Although Tulsi periodically interjects comments in his own voice, the unusual appearance of his poetic "signature" in a praise poem attributed, within the narrative, to Shiva, has been variously explained by commentators; see *Mānaspīyūṣ* 6.2.595.

25   "A full aeon," *kalpa bhari;* variously defined in Hindu texts, a *kalpa* is understood to be an extremely long time span, often said to comprise one "day" of Brahma, the equivalent of 4,320,000,000 human years.

26   The Pushpak (literally, "blooming") was a legendary flying vehicle of immense size. Originally the property of Kuber, god of wealth, it was seized by his half brother Ravan in the course of his cosmic conquests (see 1.179.4).

27   Commentators observe that, in mistaking the bright-colored jewels for fruits and berries, the soldiers display their simian nature.

28 "All those simian species," *nānā jinasa;* as commentators note, this can refer both to the array of simian species in the army and to the haphazard and inappropriate ways in which they have put on human-style dress and ornaments, much to Ram's amusement.

29 "Discerning Ram's intent," *dekhi rāma rukha;* literally, "discerning Ram's countenance." Given the context, I concur with commentators who feel that the monkeys, watching Ram's every expression, discern his resolve that they return home and are pained at their approaching separation from him.

30 Ram refers to the installation and worship, prior to crossing the sea, of a Shiva lingam at the place known as Rameshwaram; see 6.2.2–3.2.

31 Commentators disagree on whether the monkeys participated in the gift giving (perhaps using the wealth that Vibhishan showered on them), though the structure of the *dohā* seems to favor this interpretation; see *Mānaspīyūṣ* 6.2.614.

32 In the *Vālmīki Rāmāyaṇa* (6.113.12–17), Hanuman disguises himself to better determine, per Ram's express instructions, whether Bharat has become enamored of the kingship and will not want to surrender it. Although there is no mention here of Ram harboring such doubt, some commentators interpret the use of the verb "to instruct" (*bujhānā;* "gave instructions to Hanuman") as alluding to this.

33 The Nishad chief, Guha, is Ram's dear friend who ferried the exiles across the Ganga and accompanied them as far as Prayag (see 2.88–111). He apparently assumes that Ram is coming on foot, as he did previously, and will need boats to ferry him and his party across the Ganga to the side nearer to Avadh, on which the Nishad people also dwell.

34 "Fell at the goddess's feet," *carananhi parī.* The word "goddess" does not appear in the text, though the holy river will speak in the next *caupāī.* Some commentators assume that Sita is worshiping an image of Ganga installed on the riverbank. More significantly, Sita here gives thanks for the goddess's fulfillment of the blessing she gave at the time of their journey into exile (see 2.103–104.1).

35 "Marital felicity," *ahivāta;* the auspicious state of a married and unwidowed woman.

36 Verses 7 and 8 are in the lyrical *harigītikā chand* meter.

37 "Dull-witted," *matimanda;* since this may be read as either an adjective or a noun, it is also possible to interpret the line as "Tulsidas says: Sluggish mind…"—addressing his own intellect or that of any listener.

38 "Eternally," *nitya;* I translate this as an adverb, but it may equally be read as an adjective referring to the three gifts: "eternal victory, discernment, and glory." "God" is offered for *bhagavān,* by which Tulsi means Ram.

39 "Support," *adhāra;* this term additionally connotes "foundation," and "basis"; some take it to refer to "means of salvation" from the sins of the Kaliyug.

40 A comparable Sanskrit colophon, reminding readers of the allegory of Lake Manas, with its ghats and stairways, traditionally closes each book of the epic. It is found in some manuscripts and has become standard in printed editions.

GLOSSARY

apsarā an immortal courtesan who performs in the heavenly realms of the gods

AVADH (*avadha;* unconquerable) the kingdom and city of Ayodhya

BHAVANI (*bhavānī,* feminine form of *bhava;* existence, being, rebirth) Parvati, the great goddess, Shiva's consort

GARUDA (*garuṛa*) a gigantic mythical bird, variously associated with the eagle, crane, or vulture species, who serves as the mount of Lord Vishnu

GIRIJA (*girijā;* mountain-born girl) an epithet of Parvati, Shiva's consort

haṃsa mythical bird that lives in the Himalayas, feeds on pearls, and has the ability to separate milk from water; a literary trope for the enlightened soul, it is often depicted by Tulsidas flying above or floating on Lake Manas; sometimes identified with the bar-headed goose that breeds in Central Asia and winters in India, crossing the Himalayas in its annual migration

kinnara a celestial musician sometimes depicted as half horse

KUMBHAKARAN (*kumbhakaraṇa;* pot-ears) Ravan's gigantic elder brother, who sleeps for six months at a time

MALYAVANT (*mālyavant, mālyavān;* crowned with garlands) an elder demon identified as Ravan's maternal grand-uncle or grandfather

MAYA (*maya;* fabricator, artificer) architect and builder for the demons; the father of Ravan's chief queen, Mandodari

maya (*māyā;* fabrication, semblance) the illusory power of the gods, often personified as a goddess

MEGHNAD (*meghanāda;* thunderclap) Ravan's eldest son, also known as Indrajit (*indrajīta,* vanquisher of Indra)

RAMCHANDRA (*rāmacandra;* Ram, the moon) epithet of Ram, highlighting his beauty

SHARNGA (*śārṅga;* horned) the name of Vishnu's bow, which Ram wields in battle

tamāl also known as the Indian bay leaf, an evergreen tree whose aromatic leaves are used in traditional medicine and cooking; its dark trunk and foliage are often compared to Ram's dark complexion

VAIDEHI (*vaidehī;* daughter of Videha) epithet of Sita

323

BIBLIOGRAPHY

Editions and Translations

Kalyāṇ Mānasāṅk. 1938. Edited by Hanuman Prasad Poddar. Commentary by Chimanlal Gosvami and Nanddulare Vajpeyi. Gorakhpur: Gita Press.

Mānaspīyūṣ. 1950. Edited by Anjaninandansharan. 7 vols. Gorakhpur: Gita Press.

Rāmcaritmānas. 1962. Edited by Vishvanath Prasad Mishra. Ramnagar, Varanasi: All-India Kashiraj Trust.

Tulsī granthāvalī, pratham khaṇḍ, vol. 1: *Rāmcaritmānas*. 1973. Edited by Ramchandra Shukla et al. Varanasi: Nāgarīpracāriṇī Sabhā.

Atkins, A. G., trans. 1954. *The Ramayana of Tulsidas*. 2 vols. New Delhi: Birla Academy of Art and Culture.

Bahadur, Satya Prakash, trans. 1978. *Rāmcaritmānas*. Varanasi: Prācya Prakāśan.

Chowdhury, Rohini, trans. 2019. *The Ramcharitmanas*. 3 vols. Gurgaon: Penguin Random House.

Dev, Satya, trans. 2010. *Tulsi Ramayan in English Verse*. New Delhi: Vitasta Publishing.

Dhody, Chandan Lal, trans. 1987. *The Gospel of Love: An English Rendering of Tulasi's Shri Rama Charita Manasa*. New Delhi: Siddharth Publications.

Goswami, Chimanlal, trans. 1949. *Śrīrāmacaritamānasa*. Gorakhpur: Gita Press.

Growse, Frederick Salmon, trans. 1978. *The Rāmāyaṇa of Tulasīdāsa*. New Delhi: Motilal Banarsidass. Original edition, Kanpur: E. Samuel, 1891.

Hill, W. Douglas P., trans. 1952. *The Holy Lake of the Acts of Rāma*. London: Oxford University Press.

Lutgendorf, Philip, trans. 2016. *The Epic of Ram*. Vols. 1 and 2. Cambridge, Mass.: Harvard University Press.

———, trans. 2018. *The Epic of Ram*. Vols. 3 and 4. Cambridge, Mass.: Harvard University Press.

———, trans. 2020. *The Epic of Ram*. Vol. 5. Cambridge, Mass.: Harvard University Press.

Nagar, Shanti Lal, trans. 2014. *Shri Ramcharitmanas*. 3 vols. Delhi: Parimal Publications.

Prasad, R. C., trans. 1988. *Tulasidasa's Shriramacharitamanasa*. Delhi: Motilal Banarsidass.

Other Sources

Bagchi, Amitabha. 2018. *Half the Night is Gone*. Delhi: Juggernaut Books.

Gandhi, Mohandas K. 1968. *An Autobiography, or, The Story of My Experiments with Truth*. Translated by Mahadev Desai. Ahmedabad: Navjivan Publishing House. Original edition, 1927–1929.

Goldman, Robert P., and Sally J. Sutherland Goldman, trans. 1996. *The Rāmāyaṇa of Vālmīki: An Epic of Ancient India, Volume V: Sundarakāṇḍa*. Princeton: Princeton University Press.

Goldman, Robert P., Sally J. Sutherland Goldman, and Barend A. van Nooten, trans. 2009. *The Rāmāyaṇa of Vālmīki: An Epic of Ancient India, Volume VI: Yuddhakāṇḍa*. Princeton: Princeton University Press.

Goldman, Robert P. and Sally J. Sutherland Goldman, trans. 2017. *The Rāmāyaṇa of Vālmīki: An Epic of Ancient India, Volume VII: Uttarakāṇḍa*. Princeton: Princeton University Press.

Grierson, George. 1977. "Tulasīdāsa, the Great Poet of Medieval India." In *Tulasidasa: His Mind and Art*, ed. Nagendra, 1–6. New Delhi: National Publishing House.

Growse, Frederick Salmon, trans. 1978. *The Rāmāyaṇa of Tulasīdāsa*. New Delhi: Motilal Banarsidass. Original edition, Kanpur: E. Samuel, 1891.

Lutgendorf, Philip. 1991. *The Life of a Text: Performing the* Rāmcarit-mānas *of Tulsidas*. Berkeley: University of California Press.

———, trans. 1994. "Sundarkand." *Journal of Vaisnava Studies* 2:4, 91–127.

———, trans. 1995. "*Ramcaritmanas:* From Book Five, the Beautiful Book." In *The Norton Anthology of World Masterpieces,* expanded edition, ed. Maynard Mack. New York: W. W. Norton, 1: 2316–2332.

———, 2000. "Dining Out at Lake Pampa: The Shabari Episode in Multiple Ramayanas." In *Questioning Ramayanas,* ed. Paula Richman, 119–136. New York: Oxford University Press.

———, trans. 2001. "From the Ramcaritmanas of Tulsidas, Book Five: Sundar Kand." *Indian Literature* 45, 3 (203): 143–181.

Macfie, John Mandeville. 1930. *The Ramayan of Tulsidas, or, The Bible of Northern India.* Edinburgh: T. & T. Clark.

McGregor, Stuart. 2003. "The Progress of Hindi, Part 1." In *Literary Cultures in History: Reconstructions from South Asia,* ed. Sheldon Pollock, 912–957. Berkeley: University of California Press.

Orsini, Francesca. 1998. "Tulsī Dās as a Classic." In *Classics of Modern South Asian Literature,* ed. Rupert Snell and I. M. P. Raeside, 119–141. Wiesbaden: Harrassowitz.

Pollock, Sheldon I., trans. 1986. *The Rāmāyaṇa of Vālmīki: An Epic of Ancient India, Volume II: Ayodhyākāṇḍa.* Edited by Robert P. Goldman. Princeton: Princeton University Press.

Stasik, Danuta. 2009. "Perso-Arabic Lexis in the *Rāmcaritmānas* of Tulsīdās." *Cracow Indological Studies* 11: 67–86.

INDEX

ABOUT THE BOOK

Murty Classical Library of India volumes are designed by Rathna Ramanathan and Guglielmo Rossi. Informed by the history of the Indic book and drawing inspiration from polyphonic classical music, the series design is based on the idea of "unity in diversity," celebrating the individuality of each language while bringing them together within a cohesive visual identity.

The Hindi text of this book is set in the Murty Hindi typeface, commissioned by Harvard University Press and designed by John Hudson and Fiona Ross. The proportions and styling of the characters are in keeping with the typographic tradition established by the renowned Nirnaya Sagar Press, with a deliberate reduction of the typically high degree of stroke modulation. The result is a robust, modern design.

The English text is set in Antwerp, designed by Henrik Kubel from A2-TYPE and chosen for its versatility and balance with the Indic typography. The design is a free-spirited amalgamation and interpretation of the archives of type at the Museum Plantin-Moretus in Antwerp.

All the fonts commissioned for the Murty Classical Library of India will be made available, free of charge, for non-commercial use. For more information about the typography and design of the series, please visit *http://www.hup.harvard.edu/mcli.*

Printed on acid-free paper by Maple Press, York, Pennsylvania.